REWORKING CITIZENSHIP

REWORKING CITIZENSHIP

REWORKING CITIZENSHIP

Race, Gender, and Kinship
in South Africa

Brady G'sell

STANFORD UNIVERSITY PRESS

Stanford, California

Stanford University Press
Stanford, California

Printed and bound by CPI Group (UK) Ltd, Croydon, CR0 4YY

Library of Congress Cataloging-in-Publication Data
Names: G'sell, Brady, author.
Title: Reworking citizenship : race, gender, and kinship in South Africa / Brady G'sell.
Description: Stanford, California : Stanford University Press, 2024. | Includes bibliographical references and index.
Identifiers: LCCN 2023048608 (print) | LCCN 2023048609 (ebook) | ISBN 9781503636811 (cloth) | ISBN 9781503639171 (paperback) | ISBN 9781503639188 (ebook)
Subjects: LCSH: Poor women—South Africa—Durban. | Low-income mothers—South Africa—Durban. | Citizenship—South Africa—Durban. | Families—South Africa—Durban. | Kinship—South Africa—Durban. | Point (Durban, South Africa)
Classification: LCC HQ1800.5.Z9 D874 2024 (print) | LCC HQ1800.5.Z9 (ebook) | DDC 305.48/4420968455—dc23/eng/20231030
LC record available at https://lccn.loc.gov/2023048608
LC ebook record available at https://lccn.loc.gov/2023048609

Cover design: Michele Wetherbee
Cover painting: Derrick Nxumalo, *Durbon City*, 1998–2021, acrylic and pen on paper, 1000 x 231 cm. Photographer: Paulo Menezes. Courtesy of KZNSA Gallery.

For our kin

CONTENTS

CONTENTS

ILLUSTRATIONS

ACKNOWLEDGMENTS

THIS IS A BOOK ABOUT how relationships both brief and enduring sustain people in their projects of building a life. A decades-long project, this book is the result of relationships and gifts that I can never fully reciprocate, though I will continue to try.

Both my greatest delights and my greatest debt is to the families who welcomed me into their lives. The following chapters name a few—Asanda, Bronwyn, Cebo, Claudette, Gogo Sopitsho, Maryann, Nokuthula, Thuli, Toussaint, Vijy, Zandi, Zanele, and Zodwa. But there are far more who answered my endless questions, offered me tea, gave me a space to pump breastmilk, and corrected my persistent misunderstandings. Every time I re-read my notes or listen to an interview recording, I gain new perspective on the lessons you tried to teach me. Thank you, friends. I hope that I have done justice to your ideas.

My ability to move withing these Point networks was made possible by the knowledge and work of those who spend their days there. Ntombizandile Krakra Ntakirutimana was an invaluable guide to the landscape of Point mothers and a crucial link to the world of South African women married to foreign men. Much of this book is informed by her critical insights, sharp analysis, and tireless research and translation. For almost a decade Odette Fourie has teased me, laughed with me, confided in me, and together we have watched Ridwaan, Rookaya, Oselyn, Monique, Tyrique, Teagan, and my own son, Max, grow to be tremendous humans shaping the world in their own ways. Nora Saneka has been a steadfast advocate for Point children and inspired me to join her as best I could. Her extensive knowledge of Point history and seemingly endless list of contacts gave shape and depth to the world of Point. The team at the UNISA Bright Site—Bruna Gillham, Barbara MacLean, Simphiwe Mbha Malaza, and Ann Petty—brilliantly combined social justice activism with quality education and gave me entre to their work in the Point and the insights of their students. Val Jenkins, aunty to all Point children, welcomed me into the world of the clinic and introduced me to the highly skilled Judith who showed me an entirely different side to "town." Brenda and Aunty Mandi, through their unflagging work at the Christ Church soup kitchen, made Wednesdays better for a few hundred people. I am grateful also for Rachel Abrams, Yasmin Adams, and Oftense Kepadisa whose own work and activism transforms the lives of Point women.

Much of the negotiations that women engaged in would have been inaccessible to me without isiZulu language training from Mary Gordon, Baba Hlengwa, Sandra Sanneh, the Ngcobo family, Sibu and Khetha Majozi, and Stix Xulu. My erroneous use of the Zulu subjunctive is not an indication of the quality of their teaching.

When I relocated my family to South Africa, I did not expect to gain a new one at Moore Grove. But, Warren and Michelle Chemaly, Sabrina Ensenbach, Joy Shaw, Dominique Laurent, and Samantha and Elton Wyngaard, took us in, made us feel parenting in a new country was possible, and filled our child with oxtail potjiekos. Your fellowship sustained us in so many ways and your continued friendship is a treasure.

In South Africa, the difference between a street intellectual and an academic is only a matter of degree. This book has benefited from relationships with some of the most brilliant and generous scholars of Southern Africa. Thank you to Catherine Burns and Keith Breckenridge who, on one of my first nights back in South Africa after ten years, steered my research in a new direction and introduced me to the Point neighborhood. I am also grateful for the support of John Aerni-Flessner, Hannah Dawson, Bernard Dubbeld, Sarah Emily Duff, Marijke Du Toit, Natasha Erlank, Liz Fouksman, Claudia Gastrow, Casey Golomski, Josh Grace, Shireen Hassim, Mark Hunter, Lauren Jarvis, Liz and Marc Kalina, Matt Keaney, Dan Magaziner, Mvu Ngcoya, Brian Rutledge, T.J. Tallie, Liz Thornberry, Liz Timbs, and

Michael Yarbrough who both on and off the continent have produced brilliant work, talked through ideas with me, read and pushed back against my writing, and generally encouraged me to think more deeply, more precisely, and to stay true to my interlocutors. Chipo Dendere, Meghan Healy-Clancy, Jill Kelly, and Wendy Urban-Mead, allowed me into their feminist support group and held me through some of the darkest times of writing and editing.

I am one of the handful of lucky University of Michigan alumni who have enjoyed a relationship with Stephen Sparks and Nafisa Essop Sheik across two continents. Conversations around their dinner tables, fortified by Nafisa's delicacies and Stephen's banter, have indelibly shaped my thinking about South Africa and my life as a parent. While Aaron, Max, and I wish you were only as far as a trot across the yard, you are always close to our hearts.

One of the numerous benefits of my graduate training in the joint Program in Anthropology and History was exposure to brilliant people in both departments. My scholarship was forged out of conversations with Dan Birchok, Allison Caine, Nick Caverly, Adriana Chira, David William Cohen, Jatin Dua, Liz Edwards, Alysa Handelsman, Aneeth Kaur Hundle, Federico Helfgott, Elizabeth Johnson, Paul Johnson, Alaina Lemon, Josh Morrison, Martin Murray, Davide Orsini, Michael Prentice, Diwas Raja, Chris Sargent, Nik Sweet, Maria Taylor, Anna Whittington, Andrea Wright, and many more. The rigors of scholarship at UM were bolstered by the delights of dinner parties, long walks, or ice-cream-making sessions with Robyn D'Avignon, Max Risch, Ashley Rockenbach, Lori Roddy, Sonia Rupcic, and Ananda Venkata. My lack of culinary ability also led me to attach myself to a treasured group of colleagues whose friendship has spanned many years and locations. Sophie Hunt, Nora Krinitsky, Tapsi Mathur, Kate Silbert, and Matt Woodbury your support has fed me in countless ways.

I was lucky enough to be at the University of Michigan during an especially vibrant era of African studies scholarship. This community was reproduced through the valiant efforts and engagement of Kelly Askew and Derek Peterson. I am grateful for the tremendous influence the African History and Anthropology Workshop had on me and my work through the input of Kristen Connor, Isabelle de Rezende, Kevin Donovan, Gabrielle Hecht, Sara Katz, Doreen Kembabazi, Lamin Manneh, Shana Melnysyn, Pedro Monaville, Emma Park, Jolene Pelton, Tasha Rijke-Epstein, Jon Shaw, Jack Taylor, and Tara Weinberg. Separated by only five hours, my work was also shaped by the intellectual community at the University of Chicago, particularly presentations at the African studies workshop and its attendant conferences. Betsey Brada, Beth Brummel, Jennifer Cole, Brian Horne, Erin Moore, George Meiu, and Emily Osborn have been critically important interlocutors. My doctoral committee has also provided invaluable sustenance and guidance along my intellectual journey. Nancy Rose Hunt was both a consistent cheerleader of and challenger for my integration of anthropology and history. Elisha Renne taught me what it meant to think across the ethnographic longue durée. I am but one in a long lineage of those mentored and inspired by Gillian Feeley-Harnik, and my persistent curiosity about the workings of obligation and kinship bears her indelible imprint. With both humor and analytic persistence Adam Ashforth consistently held me accountable to a goal of writing a book that is actually "about something." I hope I have succeeded.

The bulk of the writing for this book took place during the long and disorienting days of the COVID-19 pandemic while also trying to juggle the demands of teaching, parenting, and being a human worth tolerating. My community of colleague-friends at the University of Iowa and in Iowa City—Margaret Beck, Roslyn Cargill, Maggie Carrel, Hyaeweol Choi, E. Cram, Josie Dunnington, Aniruddha Dutta, Mary Good, Megan Gogerty, Lisa Heineman, Matt Hill, Laura Kastens, Marie Kruger, Katina Lillios, Kristy Nabhan-Warren, Christopher-Rasheem McMillan, Ted Powers, Erica Prussing, Emily Wentzell, Lauren Willberg, Rachel Williams, Tricia Windschitl, and many others—held me, comforted me, inspired me, and encouraged me to think, write, and rest. These humans were a sustaining source of joy at a time when delight was scarce. I also would not have been able to write a book in a pandemic without my writing coach Amy Brown, whose editorial and emotional counsel was invaluable. Dylan Kyung-lim White at Stanford University Press has been a patient and encouraging editor who has made this first book publication process a pleasure. Teresa Mangum and the Obermann Center at the University of Iowa provided the space and support for the kinds of thinking that compel many of us to join the academy. One such space is the Reproductive Justice Working Group, led by Natalie Fixmer-Oraiz and Lina-Maria Murillo who model rigorous, compassionate, justice-oriented scholarship and activism and who are intellectual and interpersonal stars by which I try to steer my own boat. With generous support from the Obermann Center's Book Ends fellowship, my book manuscript underwent a thorough and delightful workshop with Cati Coe, Naomi Greyser, Meena Khandelwal, and Lynn Thomas, whose careful and provocative commentary helped shape the contours of the final product. Though for many the COVID-19 pandemic was a time of constrained mobility, it also reminded us about community that exists beyond and between physical spaces. In conferences, zoom workshops, online writing sessions, this book was informed and enhanced by discussions with Joanna Davidson, Bre Grace, Dinah Hannaford, Pamela Feldman-Savelsberg, Jessaca Leinaweaver, Adeline Masquelier, Melanie Medeiros, Julia Pauli, Daniel Jordan Smith, and Tatia Thelen. While not an official member of their writing group, I have long benefited from the work and support of Elana Buch, Julia Kowalski, and Jess Robbins who have analyzed and modeled how interdependent relationships can and enable people to thrive.

The research for this book was carried out with funding from the National Science Foundation Graduate Research Fellowship Program and Doctoral Dissertation Improvement Grant; the Wenner-Gren Foundation for Anthropological Research; the University of Michigan's Rackham Graduate School, Institute of Research on Women and Gender, Center for the Education of Women, and Department of Afroamerican and African Studies; and a Stanley Summer Research Fellowship from International Programs at the University of Iowa. The writing and analysis was supported by fellowships from University of Michigan's Institute of Research on Women and Gender and the Rackham Graduate School and by an American Academy of University Women (AAUW) American Postdoctoral Research Leave Fellowship. The financial ability to travel, think, and write is an enormous privilege and I am grateful to those funding institutions who continue to support such intellectual work.

Portions of this book appeared in earlier publications. A version of chapter 4 appeared in "Multiple Maternities: Performative Motherhood and Support Seeking in South Africa," published in *Signs: Journal of Women in Culture and Society* 46, no. 1 (2020): 3–29. Portions of chapter 5 appeared in "The 'Maintenance' of Family: Mediating Relationships in the South African Maintenance Court," published in *Africa Today* 62, no. 3 (2016): 3–27.

I am grateful for the ongoing support of Sue G'sell, Richard G'sell, and Cynthia Cannon from whom I learned to love traveling and asking questions; who sent me to South Africa in 1996 and then helped me process all they ways in which I was changed by the experience. Long before I ever read an anthropology book, they taught me about the expansive and flexible nature of kinship and the delight of adding another place (or five) to the dinner table. Relatedly, if kinship (and books) are made through shared food and words, Cyrus O'Brien and Emma Nolan-Thomas are siblings and coauthors for whom I am deeply grateful.

As Gillian once so wisely said, "children leaven the loaf of academic life," and my son's curiosity and exuberance has given rise to a life of joy and connection. My methodological intervention, Max was the reason most Point women were initially willing to talk to me and no doubt is a significant part of why they let me keep coming back. His "I love you" notes slipped under the office door, check-in hugs, and "keep going, I'm proud of you" cake from our local bakery gave me vital encouragement to see this project through. He also offers me daily lessons in compassion and resilience that I work to translate into being a "good enough" mother.

The publication of this book marks twenty-four years of journeying with my primary interlocutor, Aaron Seaman. This document is born of countless kitchen-floor conversations, wine-laced debates, and reading sessions (mostly by him). He has sustained this project and this author through his cooking, editorial insights, ethnographic finesse among Point women, tolerance for solo-parenting, and unflagging belief that this work was important. Our successes are always shared. Bravo!

All royalties from this book will be donated to the Black Sash in support of their ongoing social justice work in South Africa.

ABBREVIATIONS

ANC	African National Congress
ACVV	Afrikaanse Christelike Vroue Vereniging
BIS	Basic Income Support
CSG	Child Support Grant
DOA	Daughters of Africa
DHA	The Department of Home Affairs
DBCWS	Durban Bantu Child Welfare Society
DCWS	Durban Child Welfare Society
DOJCD	Department of Justice and Constitutional Development
ECD	Early Childhood Development
EFT	Electronic Funds Transfer
FEDSAW	Federation of South African Women
GDP	gross domestic product
NP	National Party
RDP	Reconstruction and Development Program
SMG	State Maintenance Grant
SRD grant	Social Relief of Distress grant
TAFTA	The Association for the Aged
UNISA	University of South Africa
UN	United Nations

NOTE ON LANGUAGE

The Durability of Racial Categories

The use and reproduction of racial categories have complicated politics in all places, no less in South Africa. The democratic constitution is a good example of such complexities. The document—and the policies that flow from it—embraces nonracialism through reliance on apartheid-era racial categories. Use of these categories serves as a proxy for redressing the inequalities wrought by race-based discrimination. Of course, as with all proxies, nuance is often lost. Racial categorizations are social constructions that change over time. Even within a short period, people might move between racial categories, well aware of how this changes their position in the racial hierarchy.

In this book, I employ the racial terms used by my interlocutors in 2014: African, white, Indian, and coloured. While many of these do not map neatly onto the people I know—for instance, the children of an Indian man and coloured woman—they are conceptual categories that profoundly shape people's interactions with one another and with the South African state. Noting how or when people located themselves or were located in different racial categories is part of this research project. In the case of the category of coloured, the politics around this term in South Africa differ importantly from those in the United States. When referring to the racial term, I retain the South African spelling (with a "u"). Other scholars use scare quotes or phrases such as "so-called colored" to note the particularly unstable and contested nature of this racial category, a political project that I support. However, I have chosen not to use these markings in order to improve readability. I do capitalize African and Indian since these words are derived from geographic places, though such naming was also contested. I do not capitalize the term *black* because the particular history of the term in South Africa does not, as of this writing, imbue capitalization with antiracist politics as it does in the United States. Further, the term *black* has referred to varying groups of people at different historical periods in South Africa. In light of this, I use the terms "African" or "black African" to refer to those people who identify themselves as culturally belonging to an indigenous ethnic group and whose lineage, language usage, and/or phenotype lead others to assume they would be members of one of those groups.

Naming Relationships

Long-term fieldwork is one of the enormous privileges of anthropology. This book is the product of conversations and relationships that in some cases endured over a decade. In other cases, whole chapters were born from a brief encounter that long-term friends helped me to unpack. As others before me have pointed out, there is no singular term that can account for the relationships with friends, neighbors, research assistants, fellow taxi-passengers, adoptive family, passersby, or the many other people one encounters over two decades of fieldwork. Further, as intimate and long-standing as many of these relationships may be, the inequalities of privilege are not erased. My whiteness, relative wealth, and American-ness gave me access to many spaces and interactions my friends could not enter. It also insulated me from the more painful lived realities of the new South African state. That said, the people I knew had a far greater access to lifeworlds I could not witness. As a young white woman, there were many places and spaces I chose not to go in the inner-city neighborhood of Point both out of concern for my physical safety and as to not place a burden on others to attempt to protect me. I heavily rely on the privileged access and knowledge of others when thinking or writing about such lifeworlds.

Because books have to be written and the writing inevitably flattens the contours of human experience, I have chosen predominantly the word "interlocutor" or "the people I know" to refer to the many categories of people on which I rely. I prefer the latter term, "the people I know," because it invokes an intersubjective experience of exchange and a coproduction of knowledge that is central to how this book was formed.

REWORKING CITIZENSHIP

REWORKING CITIZENSHIP

INTRODUCTION

"DEMOCRACY," NOKUTHULA SNORTED SCATHINGLY.[1] "In 1994, we got our democracy but, up until now . . . the only thing they push down our throats—that they busy showing us—is that we got democracy." It was the eve of South Africa's 2014 general elections, only the fifth in which black African women like Nokuthula had been allowed to participate, and I had asked her how she felt about the upcoming opportunity to cast her vote. Though she prized this long-sought right, Nokuthula was deeply disillusioned with what she saw as the content of her newly minted citizenship:

> We have just been told we are all citizens by being given those green ID books. . . . And now, it's what they have, like, brainwashed us: we have citizenship. So, [*she paused*] a democracy is just a content, an ideology for certain people that it works for them, but it is not working for all of us.

She grabbed her chipped tea mug and sipped from it. We sat at her small table, wedged between the door and the counter that held the hot plate and the paraffin stove where she cooked most of the family's meals. The paraffin stove was a curious item in a flat on the twelfth floor of a high rise whose units once catered to the holiday makers who annually flock to the city of Durban's beautiful beachfront. But the stove's presence here bespoke the very issues Nokuthula was lamenting. Paraffin stoves in South Africa, as in so many other places, are tools of the disconnected—those who by choice or by fortune do not have access to electricity, natural gas, or other energy

1

sources often provided by the state. While those in the rural areas often use paraffin stoves when firewood is scarce, in South Africa the stoves are synonymous with urban shack settlements, places where communities have responded to inadequate housing by seizing land and claiming belonging through their continued occupation. In Nokuthula's building, some units were occupied by squatters who could easily evade the infrequent police visits by escaping down a secondary staircase. Others, like her, were renters, most of whom struggled to pay the monthly electricity and water fees in addition to rent. Thus, between the "load shedding" outages planned by the state electricity utility and the family's unplanned cash shortages, many meals were cooked on the paraffin stove. Nokuthula's ten-year-old daughter walked into the room, waving the paraffin fumes from her nose and sighing at the lidless toilet, visible in the gap where a door once hung. "We pay so much in rent, but . . ." she opened her arms wide to encompass the whole scene, "we live like squatters."

Nokuthula nodded vigorously, taking in her daughter's statement, and continued, "In an economy side, we don't have that democracy which they are talking about . . . [she raised her voice and pounded her chest with her fist]. You find, people they still got anger . . . because now they got democracy but they are still living to an old era which they were living before democracy." She sighed audibly and wrapped her fingers around her tea mug, staring into the dark liquid as if what she sought could be found there. "No," she said, her voice much softer now, "I do not have that democracy, that citizenship," she almost spat the word, "I am a qualified educator and I can barely feed my children."

Relational Citizenship and Political Belonging

Statements such as Nokuthula's are the provocation to which this book responds. Across two decades of research in postapartheid South Africa, I persistently wondered what it meant that the very groups—people racially categorized as black African, Indian, and coloured (mixed race)—who momentously gained a host of rights, social assistance, and representation in the democratic transition, also widely protested that they had been excluded from the new nation. In one sense there are simplistic answers about the political impossibility of radical economic redistribution by 1994 and, relatedly, the enduring discrimination and inequality that continue

to adhere to racial lines. Yet, liberal theories that envision autonomous citizens as bound to states through formalized rights cannot account for my interlocutors' assertions that though they can now vote, or sue an errant father, they are not citizens. This book asks, what does citizenship mean to those who gained widespread formal inclusions yet still experience exclusion? What assumptions about entitlements, obligation, and belonging do they hold? The answers offer new understandings of politics in places like South Africa and beyond.

Across the globe, access to arable land or waged employment is less and less available to larger segments of the population. This has created a high-stakes dilemma for liberal democracies built around the imagined universality of the able-bodied (often, male) worker. If the independence of the wage earner is a central criterion for full citizenship, what does it mean for political belonging that increasing numbers of people cannot, and likely will not ever, find waged work? As this central tenet of the state-citizen covenant erodes, what obligations do states have to support the livelihoods of their citizens? What does citizenship itself mean? I answer these questions through an analysis of how citizenship is profoundly intertwined with economies and kinship. This entanglement is not unique to South Africa, and indeed the insights of this book are broadly applicable to many sites across the globe where national membership is being contested and reconfigured. I center South Africa here because the country's particular history and processes of decolonization render such reconfiguring uniquely visible.

This book forwards a political theory from the street,[2] as generated by women who because of overlapping racism and sexism were barred access to the privileges of citizenship under colonialism, racial segregation, and apartheid.[3] These women also stood the most to gain from democratic liberation. Their paramount concerns—about unemployment that results in hungry children—are borne of both their present needs and a longer history in which full citizenship (historically held by whites) was marked by state support, particularly, of child-rearing. This was also a history in which the expansion of racial capitalism involved the systematic undermining of black African families, even as it relied on and capitalized on their resilience. A central project of colonial, segregationist, and apartheid governments was to create and maintain a racial hierarchy in which whites could obtain and retain political and economic dominance. This was achieved

through a state-directed form of what anthropologist Shellee Colen calls "stratified reproduction," wherein different race groups were given vastly unequal state social protection in alignment with their envisioned place in the racial order (Colen 1995). In response, generations of black, coloured, and Indian women protested the racist state's simultaneously harmful intrusion and exclusion by demanding access to the robust support given to whites.[4] Aware of this history, women like Nokuthula link the state's support of social reproduction with their political status. They contend that political belonging—the affective experience that imbues citizenship status with meaning—is tied to their ability to support themselves and their kin, notably, their children.

Taking seriously women's idea that obtaining long-denied rights does not generate political belonging requires rethinking citizenship as manifested in the benefits conferred to individual subjects. When the women I know decry that their citizenship is "empty" because they cannot support their children, they are arguing for a recognition that citizenship is relational and material, meaning constituted through the layers of relationships in which people are embedded. For Nokuthula, her unemployment was a problem because she struggled to feed her children, pay their school fees, and to buy medicine for her ailing aunt. She was unable to be the mother, sister, niece, or neighbor she desired to be. She did not "have that citizenship" because she was blocked from investing in the relationships that were important to her. Livelihoods can be important in various ways, but, critically, they enable people to regenerate kinship bonds by meeting and negotiating their obligations of care through material distribution and exchange.[5] This is an understanding of citizenship that arises out of notions of relational personhood long recognized as operating throughout the Global South and within poor communities in the Global North (Ferguson 2013; Englund and Nyamnjoh 2004; Rice 2017; Strathern 1988). In this context, participation in these social relationships is what makes people fully, recognizably, human. Definitions of freedom or liberation—evoked across the antiapartheid struggle—do not turn on whether one is dependent on others (e.g., dependence in opposition to independence). Rather, at issue is the control and influence one can exert over how to navigate fundamental interdependence.

Following democratic transition, impoverished black African, coloured

and Indian women formally became citizens but continued to feel excluded because they measured their political belonging by their ability to regenerate their kin relationships—by the security of their social reproduction. They gained juro-political citizenship but lacked what I have termed *relational citizenship*. Inasmuch as the women I know expected and desired the democratic state to secure relational citizenship, in the face of its failure, they did not passively await change. In their words, "when children are hungry, you have to make a plan." Overwhelmingly, these "plans" involved livelihood strategies that braided together state entitlements, informal exchange, and direct solicitation in an effort to secure resources such as food, blankets, cash, or cell phone minutes to support themselves and their children. As they encountered state supports that continued to imagine people as autonomous, rights-bearing citizens—the Child Support Grant (chapter 4), the Maintenance Court (chapter 5), immigration law (chapter 6)—they reworked them. They selected components of these policies, sometimes the underlying logic, sometimes the bureaucratic mechanisms, and pressed them into service to secure their relationships and shore up their sense of belonging. Though these strategies took many forms, what made them cohere as a category was that they were in service to kin obligations (most often mothers supporting their children) and in turn relied on kinship obligations to press their claim.

In order to secure resources, the women I know engaged in what I call *kinshipping*, or the formation and solidification of relationships expressed in a kinship idiom in order to claim support from a broad array of persons and institutions.[6] Kinshipping is a livelihood strategy, a form of what Jim Ferguson calls "distributive labor," or the effort to compel those with resources to share them with those who don't by fostering ties of dependence (2015: 100). In one sense, the targets of these claims could be anyone with greater resources, even marginally so. In many places on the African continent, people operate within a moral economy in which *not* sharing, or "eating for oneself," is seen as not only selfish but asocial and incites accusations of witchcraft (Ashforth 2005; Chabal and Daloz 1999). At the same time, claim-making gains greater traction when grounded in relationships in which the terms of obligation are already known: patron and client or kin being *ur* examples. Kinshipping is a distinct form of hustling in which women specifically used kinship idioms and the obligations embedded within them to make claims of dependence on relatives, former lovers, neighbors, government, and aid agencies for resources. However, these were not claims for women just as singular dependents, these were claims in order to support women's own kin obligations, most often, as mothers. Thus, through their claim-making, they also demanded recognition that they were not autonomous subjects but relational persons who required resources that sustained them as such.

The core argument of this book is that impoverished black African, coloured, and Indian women contest their incomplete inclusion in the nation by using kinshipping to rework their juro-political citizenship to be more relational. In the process they obtain recognition, support for social reproduction, and forge new relations of belonging between men and women, persons and communities, citizens and state. True, these gains are modest, quotidian, and informal. Yet their meaning and import looms large. Centering the political understandings of women like Nokuthula requires thinking about citizenship not as conferred abstractly but worked out in layered relationships through which rights and entitlements, duties and responsibilities are negotiated (Nyamnjoh 2007). Thus, in contrast to scholars who analyze citizenship through a focus on state definitions, here I focus on the lived experiences of citizenship. Drawing kinship theory into an analysis of citizenship, I show how the concept of relational citizenship reimagines rights and obligations not as located in autonomous, individual persons, but as bound up in the web of relationships in which people are embedded. In so doing, I theorize how political belonging is reworked via the everyday interactions through which people "get by."

Citizenship, Kinship, Economy

The interrelationship between citizenship and social reproduction arises out of conversations taking place at multiple scales. For decades, there have been debates over the meaning of citizenship in South Africa, and particularly, what it means to belong to the nation. Everyone from disgruntled grandmothers, to antiapartheid activists, to parliamentarians have participated in such discussions. Academics in South Africa are frequently public scholars, and the same ideas that may circulate in journal articles are also evoked at marches and in newspaper opinion pieces. This is to say that as much as citizenship functions as an analytic category throughout this book, citizenship is also a vernacular term that people put into action in various ways. So too is the notion of social reproduction, which people colloquially discuss as responsibilities to care for kin. While there may be numerous political theories about the obligation of different kinds of states to ensure the social welfare of citizens, for my interlocutors, the link between citizenship and social reproduction under democracy was always clear. Full citizenship in South Africa meant that the state provided, or at least buttressed, secure social reproduction.

This book brings the theoretical linkages between interpersonal relationships and citizenship into historical and ethnographic focus. I employ the work of scholars, particularly those theorizing politics in the Global South, who have argued that citizenship is not solely conferred by the state but is articulated in overlapping collectivities from the microlocal to the supranational (Lister 2003; Nyamnjoh 2018; Ong 1999; Yuval-Davis 1999).[7] These layers determine both belonging and access to resources within the collectivity. None of these "communities" or "groups" are given, natural units, though they are often durable (Anthias and Yuval-Davis 1993; Yuval-Davis 1997). These are ideological and material constructions, whose boundaries, structures, and norms are a result of constant struggles and negotiations (Yuval-Davis and Anthias 1989). I understand citizenship here as "multilayered" or constituted and negotiated vertically and horizontally within these various spheres or layers (Yuval-Davis 1999).

This orientation is especially important in South Africa, where black African, coloured, and Indian women's work to carve out viable lives—for example, raising children, meeting cultural and kin obligations—in the face of state exclusion has been as fundamental a site of politics as more recognized forms of activism such as protests (Healy-Clancy 2012). My interlocutors' linking of citizenship with the ability to feed children aligns with these historic struggles and with the current concerns with "living politics" and "human dignity" that animate poor people's movements today (Chance 2018; Ferguson 2007; Von Schnitzler 2016). They share a demand that the state provide for "basic needs" as a core obligation it holds to particularly its poorest citizens. Informed by my interlocutors, I focus on the tie between social reproduction and citizenship to embed relationality and interdependence into the very notion of citizenship.

I propose a theory of *relational citizenship* to describe my interlocutors' understanding of citizenship as constituted through the relationships in which people are embedded. Their ability to regenerate their interdependent relationships is directly linked to belonging in the national community. This stands in contrast to the autonomous, rights-bearing subject that continues to dominate "Westocentric" political theory despite robust postcolonial and feminist critique (Alexander 1994; Balibar 1990; Hassim 1999; Manicom 2005; Narayan 1997). As many have documented, political policy and claim-making grounded in humanitarianism and human rights within a neoliberal context has had, at best, ambivalent results (Feldman 2007; Malkki 1996; McKay 2012; Redfield 2013; Ticktin 2011; Von Schnitzler 2014). Alternatively, as others have explored, across the African continent, people also use the language of kinship to critique or make demands on the state—often as a father who failed to provide and care for his citizen-progeny (e.g., Schatzberg 2001; see also Van Allen 2009 on claims to nurturing mother leaders and Bose 2017 on notions of the nation as mother in India).[8] However, both of these modes often still retain the understanding of the citizen/recipient as an individuated subject. I show how, in response to austerity policies that constrain provisions to the minimal needs of an individual, the women I know instead ground their citizenship claims in their relationships—often to children—to solicit recognition and resources to sustain those relationships (Brown 1995; Feldman and Ticktin 2010).

For claims grounded in relational citizenship, the obligation to support does not just rest on a dyadic relationship of superior/subordinate but on the dyad as sitting amid a web of relations. Those of my interlocutors who spoke Zulu often described the need to *hlangana*. The isiZulu verb *ukuhlangana*, which conveys belonging, evokes both membership in a group and relations that are "thick" with either blood or obligation or both (Doke et. al. 2008: 710). This belonging is solidified through a reciprocal exchange of care and tribute. In the case of children, it involves the daily caregiving work to *khulisa* or raise a child (*-isa* being the causative suffix added to the verb *ukukhula* meaning to grow or nurture) that can be undertaken by parents, grandparents, or various elders. Resources to support *khulisa*-ing are often funneled through a primary caregiver whose nurturance reinforces the intertwined futures of caregiver and child (Hunter 2015). At the same time, both caregiver and child are embedded in other caregiving relationships (between siblings, child to aging parent or grandparent, cousins, etc.)

whose requirements and assistance shape the contours of what *khulisa*-ing can look like. Thus, women's demands for public support for their mothering ruptures the liberal illusions of autonomous personhood and protests the privatization of social reproduction so characteristic of neoliberal policy (Buch 2018; Muehlebach 2012).

The concept of relational personhood operating here encompasses an idea of self not as preexisting but as "attained in direct proportion as one participates in communal life through the discharge of the various obligations defined by one's stations" (Menkiti 1984: 176). In this conception, personhood is always in process, constituted over the course of one's life through relationships with others (Dossa and Coe 2017; Fortes 1987). Though relational personhood is often described in opposition to the autonomous individualism of the West, it is important to note that in the West as much as in South Africa, independence is, at best, an aspirational discourse put to other ends. Elana Buch potently argues that myths of American independence are upheld through highly unequal, dependent relationships that are artfully disguised from view (2018). In South Africa, Kate Rice shows how in the Xhosa-speaking community where she works, people often deploy discourses of individualism and autonomy to disentangle themselves from one relationship of obligation so they may embed themselves in another (2017). We can understand the concept of relational personhood not as evidence of some kind of cultural alterity or as suggesting a lack of modernity or freedom (as liberal political theory often positions it), but rather as giving name to the myriad ways in which humans across the life course are dependent on one another to sustain bodies and cultivate social worlds. This interdependence is overlooked in theories of liberal individualism that underlie a political and social order in which rights and recognition are tied to individual action that is presumed to be "liberated from the constraints of social roles" as though such a status does, or can ever, exist (Englund 2008; Kowalski 2022: 18).

Relational citizenship instead embraces Kowalski's "politics of interdependence" (2022). Relational citizenship involves the recognition of and support for people's labors to regenerate their interdependent relationships—at the level of the dyad, the family, the community, the state, and beyond. Historically, whites in South Africa achieved relational citizenship through state reserved jobs, robust welfare support, well-funded education, quality health care, and the ability to form marriages that involved cohabitation. People excluded from white privilege found ways to achieve relational intimacy and social reproduction, but they did so in spite of state disruption and deprivation of basic human needs. This meant that they were deeply constrained—by poverty, by restricted movement, by a denial of political rights—when trying to address the competing needs and obligations of their relationships. These competing demands, what Kowalski calls "dilemmas of interdependence," are themselves fundamental to human experience, not something that can be exited, as women's rights discourse often imagines (2022). In his critique of philosophical perspectives that tend to regard human relationships as secondary to human existence, Harri Englund notes, "what gets overlooked is the possibility that the compulsion at the heart of obligation is existential—that it is constitutive of, rather than external to, those who give and receive (2008: 36). That said, what constitutes a dilemma and the capacity to manage and respond to these dilemmas are profoundly shaped by political economies and the distribution of power and privilege along the lines of class, race, gender, age, ability, and such. Interdependent relationships can be supportive or injurious (oftentimes simultaneously). Kin relations, which are often organized by patriarchal logics, are frequently harmful, sometimes lethal, to women. This is tragically evident is the extraordinarily high levels of gender-based violence in South Africa. Thus, understandably, much of the feminist welfare scholarship has diligently sought to reduce women's dependence on kin as a precondition for autonomy.[9] While this has laudable ethical underpinnings, as Kowalski has deftly argued in regard to women's rights discourse around domestic violence, these orientations presume that dependency is inevitably harmful and often envision kinship as static and unchanging, overlooking the dynamic and contingent nature of both (2022). Though dependent relations may sustain harmful social orders, they can also positively transform them (Han 2012; Garcia 2010; Stevenson 2014; Pinto 2011). I take as orientation Deborah Gaitskell's statement that in South Africa, "Family life is and has long been for black women, something to struggle for, rather than against" (1983: 254). Rather than independence, a politics of interdependence seeks means to redistribute vulnerabilities to harm, as well as the accumulation of support, more equitably across kin (Kowalski 2022: 18). To have relational citizenship involves the capacity to participate in the regeneration of interdependent relationships and to have the potential to reorder them.

As a theory from the street, relational citizenship operates as a tool for normatively assessing a political community and as a set of political demands. It is congruent with a unified theory of citizenship, closely associated with English sociologist T. H. Marshall (and espoused in the South African Constitution) that contends that full citizenship has a civil, political, and social component (Lister 2005). Social citizenship to Marshall (and Marshallian theorists) was not simply an issue of juridical rights, or solely tied to income, but, rather, about the right to a minimum level of comprehensive support to achieve "a general reduction of risk and insecurity" and "an equalisation between the more and less fortunate at all levels" (Marshall 1950: 33). As an expansion of these principles, the normative framework of relational citizenship dovetails closely with the capabilities approach within development and political theory (Nussbaum 2000, 2003, 2011; Sen 1990, 1999). In this approach, the central concern is about what people can be or do: in Sen's words "the substantive freedom of people to lead the lives they have reason to value" (1999: 293). As a number of feminists have found, the capaciousness of this approach holds enormous potential for evaluating concerns, such as gender or racial inequity, that cut across multiple domains (e.g., economy, politics, judicial access, etc.) (Agarwal, Humphries, and Robeyns 2006; Hassim 2008; Hochfeld 2022). At the same time, Marshall, Sen, and Nussbaum have all been critiqued for retaining a liberal emphasis on autonomous individuals. Instead, relational citizenship offers an alternative by infusing a politics of interdependence into questions about "leading lives that are valued." It treats relationships as primary to human existence and as sites of creative imagining through which people may build desired futures (Clarke 2018; Kowalski 2022; Livingston 2005; Robbins 2020; TallBear 2019).[10] Thus the question becomes, "to what degree can interdependent relationships be regenerated and reordered so as to redistribute harm, vulnerability, support, and such more equitably?" In short, "what can relations be or do?" For my interlocutors, these abstract ideas mapped onto very concrete demands for support for social reproduction.

I use the concepts of kinshipping and social reproduction to draw attention to the work of bringing relations from kinship to citizenship into being. I build on a rich scholarship that connects social reproduction to issues of gender, political economy, and negotiations of power (e.g., Backer and Cairns 2021; Barca 2020; Bezanson 2006; Bhattacharya 2017; Bhattacharya 2018; Fraser 2016; Hunter 2011; Makhulu 2015; Meehan and Strauss 2015; Mezzadri, Newman, and Stevano 2022; Weeks 2011; Yuval-Davis 1997). Social reproduction is brought about through reproductive labor, what sociologist Evelyn Nakano Glenn defines as "the creation and recreation of people as cultural and social, as well as physical human beings" (Glenn 1992). This labor is often framed as complementing and enabling the productive labor— the creation of goods and services for market exchange—that is demanded, valued, and more remunerated within a capitalist economy. Critical feminist scholars have long argued that the social expectations that women perform unpaid reproductive labor underlie women's oppression and perpetuate intersecting racial, gender, and economic inequality. In South Africa, industrial capitalism took form under colonial and apartheid rule during which a large category of employment for black South Africans—men and women alike—was ensuring the reproduction of white households. While paid and unpaid reproductive labor is overwhelmingly still performed by black African women, this historical inequity holds a new meaning in the relative absence of opportunities for paid productive work. The rightful critique that capitalism thrives off of the surplus labor of workers and the inadequately compensated labor of women who sustain those workers begins to unravel when capitalism no longer demands many workers. This book considers what happens when social reproduction becomes both means and ends.[11] Kinshipping as a concept accounts for labor that is both productive, in the sense of garnering resources, and reproductive in the sense of building and sustaining relationships. It is with this lens that I understand the women in this book to be arguing that while they may have the citizenship intended for the autonomous individual—rights, legal enfranchisement, access to minimal social protection—they do not have the relational citizenship that enables them to achieve full political belonging.

In the face of a state refusal to ensure relational citizenship, my interlocutors engaged in what I call kinshipping. In this book, kinshipping is the means by which people actively forge relationships with others, relationships that afford a flow of resources and sustain the existence of child (and parent). As a concept, kinshipping sits between Modell's (1994) fictive kinship, which implies an ephemerality to nonbiological ties, and Howell's (2003) process of kinning, which involves a permanent transubstantiation of selfhood. Kinshipping names the labor of forging bonds between persons that are at once forceful and contingent. It relies on an understanding that kinship is not simply the result of shared substance, shared space, or even marriage, but requires persistent labor to build and renew social ties and define and meet reciprocal obligations (Carsten 2004; Dossa and Coe 2017; Glenn, Chang, and Forcey 1994; Stack and Burton 1993; Strathern 1992; Weston 1997).[12] In short, it assumes kinship is something that one *does*, not something that one *has* (Ferguson 2015; Franklin and McKinnon 2001). Of course there is no singular way to "do kinship." Via kinshipping, people harness complex ideologies concerning hierarchy; reciprocal rights, duties, and obligations; material support; and sentimental connection to negotiate dependence and obligation (Carsten 2004: 19; McKinnon and Cannell 2013). Dependence here is not as a condition, but "a mode of action," that a person strives to embody (Bayart and Ellis 2000: 218). Through the claim, a person argues that they are worthy of being a dependent and that the relationship already does, or could in the future, entail an obligation for exchange. My attention to kinshipping foregrounds the continuous and careful effort of sustaining a sense of personhood grounded in interdependence.

My use of kinship to refer to relationships that at times are ephemeral is theoretically purposeful and ethnographically driven. When my interlocutors go about making claims, they engage in practices that can also be described as hustling, networking, or judicious opportunism, practices that impoverished people on the margins all over the world engage in (Johnson-Hanks 2005). Women seek support not for themselves as individuals, but for their kinwork—terms that both legitimate their demands and constrain them. Further, their claim-making hails its target in kin terms—using aunty, mama, or sometimes *babamkhulu* for Zulu speakers. In one sense, using kin terms of respect ubiquitously is a shared practice in South Africa (like in many other places), but it is nonetheless deliberate and meaningful. Terms like ma'am, sir, or the Afrikaans *baas* (boss) are also widely accepted and used. For many, the question quickly becomes, "when a woman calls another woman "aunty" does she *really* understand her to be kin?" Like many kinship scholars, I don't take kinship to be a stable category. There is no clear, preexisting boundary between kin and not kin. The boundary and the criteria for kinship are made and remade; they are fluid and processual. This understanding changes the question to be, "what does leveraging the language, meaning, and expectation of kinship *do* in this relationship at this time?" The ethnographic record offers numerous examples of the logic of making strangers into kin of various degrees, the most notable from contexts where kinship was not seen as incommensurable from politics:

> A noteworthy fact of Barotse life is the tendency to expand isolated transactions between strangers into multiplex associations that resemble kin relationships. . . . All these relationships are marked by a public demand for love and affection and generous mutual aid, and people are expected to express these sentiment through material goods and services. (Gluckman 1965: 172–73)

> A kinsman of any degree, is a person in whose welfare one is interested and whom one is under a moral obligation to help in difficulties, if possible. (Fortes 1949: 293)

Analyzing my interlocutors' hustling practices through a kinship lens reveals how women leverage a set of moral obligations to make claims on others and the state to support their maternal labors. Of course, as anyone who has ever been disappointed by kin knows, it is not a given that these moral obligations will be honored (G'sell 2024). Rather, a kinship analysis makes visible the terms under which such claims have traction and the moral economy in which they operate.

Kinshipping gives a name to multiple overlapping processes. In one sense, it creates kinship bonds. Yet, as kinship scholars remind us, kinship is closely intertwined with political economy in ways aren't just structured by, but actively produce and reproduce the economy (Bear et al. 2015; McKinnon and Cannell 2013; Schuster 2015; Stout 2015; Yanagisako 2002). As such, kinshipping functions as a livelihood strategy that enables ties of dependence and claim-making on different categories of people. In today's economic and social uncertainty, the ability to make claims for resources— claims that will be honored—is just as much the stuff of survival and economic innovation as remunerated labor, and often more reliable. Their import has led some researchers to name claims of dependence a system of "informal social protection" (Du Toit and Neves 2009).

This book considers the various ways in which the production of kinship—for example, the making and meeting of obligations—is embedded in and shaped by its particular political economic context. I contend that kinshipping labor can neither be understood as an economic appropriation or instrumentalization of intimate relations nor as the domestication of economic logic (e.g., Constable 2009). Instead, I align with an intellectual lineage, inspired by Mauss, that intimate relationships are always already marked by generosity, obligation, and self-interest that is inherently economic (2000; Parry and Bloch 1989; Zelizer 1995, 2005). However, I take up Caroline Schuster's call to not simply stop at that axiom but to consider "how and for whom social reciprocity takes hold and the uneven ways the social units of debt are created" (or not created) (2015: 17). Notably, claims to kinship are not always successful or desirable, as many women regularly found (on the "new middle class," see also Barchiesi 2011; James 2014; Niehaus 2012; Offe and Standing 2011; Southall 2016). Such claims can be disputed or denied, and oftentimes people go to great lengths to refute or evade requests by indirect means that cannot be attributed to them directly. As such, this book reveals how moral relations of care, generosity, dependence, and obligation are intertwined with the tactical concerns of livelihood strategies under conditions of economic and social insecurity.

Kinshipping practices cover a broad terrain. Kinshipping might involve leveraging the governmental Child Support to request support from other sources. It might involve giving a child the father's surname—*isibongo* in Zulu—to firmly locate the child in that lineage and enable claim-making on the father's family even when the father was absent. It might include chronicling one's stellar caregiving on the body of a child through cleanliness, well-ironed clothes, warm hats, and full cheeks. Or, it might involve making connections with others, via a child. For example, few Point women would say they had friends, yet they did talk about having people:

Z: Do you have someone who helps you if you need something?
M: Yes, there is someone. She is my ears.
B: How so?
M: She calls me when she knows a place that needs workers; she helps me with things like that.

B: How do you know her?

M: Her child is smaller so I pass clothes to her when my child is finished.

Acts of redistribution help solidify different kinds of social relationships such as those between kin, those between lovers, those between neighbors, and those between patrons and clients, practices that have long been documented by scholars (Barnes 1986; Bayart 1993; Bratton and van de Walle 1997; Ekwensi 1987; James 2014; Smith 2003; Tibandebage and MacIntosh 2005; Vansina 1990; Weinreb 2001). These exist within a political economy where power and prestige are acquired through "wealth in people," or dependents (Barnes 1986; Guyer 1993; Guyer and Belinga 1995; Kopytoff and Miers 1977; Miers and Kopytoff 1977; Vansina 1990; Smith 2004). In addition to redistributing resources, exchange practices forge these "ties of dependence" through the obligations of reciprocity they entail (Swidler and Watkins 2007: 150; Polanyi 2001). Such ties enable people to weather social and economic insecurity by preserving the potential for future support (Shipton 2007).

Finally, in the absence of robust state support, kinshipping generates recognition and shores up political belonging. I use belonging as Feldman-Savelsberg does to encompass "relatedness based on 1) social location 2) emotional attachment through self-identifications and 3) institutional, legal, and regulatory definitions that simultaneously grant recognition to and maintain boundaries between socially defined places and groups" (2016: 8). Alongside the multilayered definition of citizenship already given, this reveals how belonging is assembled and reassembled through a collection of immutable (gender, race, nationality) and mutable (class, language) characteristics; caregiving actions (caring for elderly kin or sending nieces and nephews to school) (Thelen and Coe 2019). Kinshipping is a means of negotiating these multiple spheres of belonging. Via kinshipping, women forge webs of relations—within households, between lovers, between neighbors, across communities, and between states and citizens—that are the very structure by which economic resources are distributed and social reproduction is enabled. It is a process through which women imbue their juro-political citizenship with relationality.

In this book, I draw kinship theory into an analysis of citizenship in order to show how citizenship is fashioned in layered relationships through which rights and entitlements, duties and responsibilities are negotiated. In so doing, I bring together historic contributions of Africanist anthropology to kinship theory and stateless political systems with theories of the state under late capitalism (e.g., Fortes 1969; Holston 2009; Hutchinson 1996; Mbembe 2019). The anthropology of kinship arose from scholarship on stateless societies. While these scholars ethnographically showed how kinship organized politics, their theory of kinship maintained a Eurocentric distinction between the domestic and the politico-legal as differently functioning domains. This separation was retained in later theories that viewed the absence of kinship in political processes as the mark of a modern social order (for a genealogy on the maintenance of this separation see Thelen and Alber 2017). This has been frequently critiqued, most widely by feminists. Nevertheless, a presumed opposition between kinship and the (modern) state has endured, notably in citizenship studies. It reverberates in contemporary scholarship that attempts to bridge the divide through examinations of patronage, nepotism, corruption, or ethnopolitics. Yet, such scholarship reproduces the notion that kinship logics represent political malfunctioning. Instead, I align with scholars who view kin-based critiques of power as potentially transformative (see contributors in Englund and Nyamnjoh 2004). In these formulations, critiques of the state, for example, as bad kin, do not posit a solution as less kinship, but kinship appropriately done (Englund 2008). They seek to order their dependent relationship with the state away from patriarchal oppression and toward "paternal" care and positive obligation. Relational citizenship advances a theory of belonging that is not defined by patronage between people and politicians but rather as articulated through webs of relational obligations. I thus join my foremothers in challenging a persistent presumption that kin relations are antithetical to the political processes of modern states by ethnographically demonstrating how women use kinship logics to turn entitlements into substance and rework citizenship.

Making Relationships, Making Meaning

Through an analysis of South Africa, this book addresses widespread redefinitions of national belonging happening in response to increasing inequality. Wage labor regimes are declining globally, and liberal democracies premised on full employment to tether citizens to the nation are scrambling to respond. In the Global South, new forms of government assistance attempt to shore up livelihoods shattered by a dramatically shifting economy. Though such interventions are critical for their recipients and for the new forms of governmentality they portend, they are often designed to supplement wages and are thus inadequate. The reality is that a diversity of livelihood strategies is now necessary to sustain social reproduction and bolster belonging. Strategies overwhelmingly involve claims of dependence, on people, communities, and states, grounded in ideologies of kinship. Relationships such as these are reshaping economies and political belonging across the globe.

I consider these global phenomena from the perspective of those raising their children in the heterogeneous, inner-city Point neighborhood of Durban, South Africa's third-largest city. A social worker in 1963 described the neighborhood in terms just as applicable in 2014:

> A densely populated residential area. It is centrally situated and has easy access to religious, recreational, social and shopping facilities. The area, however, is unsavoury, noted for prostitution and idle persons under the influence of liquor. Many of the buildings in this area are in a poor state of repair, and are overcrowded. As such, the successful rearing of children in such a place requires diligent care.[13]

A multiracial and variably classed neighborhood, the Point is a microcosm for issues affecting the country more broadly. In the span of a generation, the social reproduction of South African household has moved from reliance on a predominantly male worker *earning a living* through paid employment to dependence on men and women *making a living* through a variety of livelihood strategies (Hunter 2010; Webster and von Holdt 2005).[14] Indeed, the population of the Point is a present-day reproduction of what Marx called the lumpenproletariat: "vagabonds, discharged soldiers, discharged jailbirds . . . swindlers . . . pickpockets, tricksters, gamblers . . . brothel keepers . . . ragpickers . . . knife grinders, tinkers, beggars . . . those who fall out of the production based class categories and instead live on the crumbs of society" (Marx 1898). Much of this "living on the crumbs" was part of the diligent work of raising children there. Point residents are experts in the multifarious "arts of survival" practiced by those at the margins of the formal economy (Du Toit and Neves 2014). The often kin-based relationships of dependence and exchange that are the lifeblood of impoverished people in many places, are, in Point, brokered across differences of race, nationality, and class. It is a context where relatedness or shared understanding cannot be assumed. Thus the negotiations of belonging and claim-making are starkly evident to an observing researcher interested in how it is that caregivers get by.

This book arises out of two decades of engagement with South Africa and a decade of language training in isiZulu and involvement with Point residents. My work to build connections and trust in Point took place over research trips of one to three months in 2011, 2012, 2019, and 2022 and a year of resident fieldwork in 2013–14.

In order to examine how South African women previously excluded from citizenship evaluate and respond to life under democracy, I began with ethnographic methods of participant observation and interviews with neighborhood women. I learned from this research that Point women located their complaints about their current conditions of their lives— poverty, nonsupporting men, and hungry children—within broader critiques about how, despite the state's liberatory rhetoric, their lives had not substantively improved since apartheid. At play was clearly more than a present-day material crisis of social reproduction (Bezuidenhout and Fakier 2006; Fakier and Cock 2009; Webster and von Holdt 2005).[15] Women were angry because their poverty too closely resembled life under apartheid and did not match their definitions of what it meant to be a citizen of democratic South Africa. To comprehend these dynamics, I delved into the history of how these expectations were formed. Moving between historical research and contemporary ethnography, my research shows how Point women use strategies learned over generations to rework state entitlements and to protest a century of exclusion from relational citizenship.

My historical research draws on secondary sources covering the period from the early days of the colony through the creation of the welfare state and into the apartheid era in order to situate the link between social reproduction and citizenship as part of a longer trajectory of state-making. I focused my primary source analysis on the 1960s to 1990s because this period had important salience for my ethnographic interlocutors and my topical focus. For my interlocutors, many of whom were born in the late 1970s and early 1980s, the late 1950s and early 1960s was often discussed in their families as an important historical comparative touchpoint. It was a time of robust state-making—akin in many ways to the decades following democracy—in which the apartheid government attempted to realize its vision of society through new policy, much of which focused on reshaping families. It was also a time of intense activism against an increasingly elaborated racial repression. Amid this political backdrop, the early decades were a time of relative economic abundance and high employment until the shift in the 1970s to labor surplus and unemployment. The Point, as a settling place for poor whites, black African migrant workers, immigrants, single mothers, and street children, was a microcosm for these changes. My research drew on a robust archival record left by welfare organizations, city planners, and state legislators to catalog how welfare policy was outlined and what logics were used to target different groups of people. To understand how that policy was implemented and experienced, I reviewed and annotated 235 welfare case files of white, coloured and some black African mothers living in Point from 1960 to 1996 and conducted oral history interviews with older mothers and former social workers. I compared how state and other aid organization supported and managed the social reproduction of differently raced families. Support was closely tied to families' place within the apartheid racial hierarchy and whether fathers were working, even after the 1970s low-skilled labor market decline. However, reading the welfare files against the grain, I discovered how black African and coloured women found ways to negotiate access to state support, strategies that often were retooled by their progeny in the present day.

This history informs the experience of my ethnographic interlocutors. Many of the coloured and white women I interviewed in 2013 were the daughters and sometimes granddaughters of those mothers profiled in the welfare case files. Others, particularly black African women, had grown up in regular contact with social workers and children's homes in other towns. I conducted participant observation in two low-income buildings (fifty-four households), moving between private rooms and common hallways, observing socializing, child disciplining, and negotiations about how to allocate resources. I followed twenty-three key informants as they went about their day using kinshipping to make claims on various people and institutions for support. I learned the "scripts" they used in these claims, noting how they defined support, articulated who was obligated to provide it, and legitimized their claim to it (Carr 2011). In over two hundred interviews in English and isiZulu I asked participants to reflect on these claim-making practices, what they understood themselves to be doing, and why. Their responses emphasized their desire for recognition and support of their relational personhood on multiple scales.

A Brief History of State-Making and Social Reproduction

Nokuthula and the other black African, coloured, and Indian women whose experiences of motherhood form the core of this book, came of age in the last years of apartheid as the laws around spatial segregation, job reservation for whites, and differentiated state support were overturned in spurts. Though children are often desired and delighted in, it is not a given that all South African women would become mothers or would identify as mothers at all stages of their life. Rather, as a primary act of kinshipping, the women I knew had chosen to become and/or remain mothers by the time I met them. They were raising their children in the second decade of a still nascent democracy, and their experiences reflect the liberatory promises that have, and have not been, realized. They were living in the inner-city Point neighborhood, which, decades before, was legally only open to whites or closely surveilled black African male laborers. Their children attended a multiracial school whose infrastructure—sports fields, electricity, plumbing—bespoke its legacy as a formerly white institution. They also had access to monthly child support grants from the state, that, while small, were crucial amid widespread unemployment. Not least of all, they could now vote and could expect that at least some of their leaders would look like them.

Yet, the symbolic import of their newfound political rights was colored by profound disappointment and anger about what they saw as apartheid-era continuities. Outside of the rapid success of a small but highly visible black African middle and upper class, class differences still adhered to racial lines, and income inequality is some of the highest in the world (*The Economist* 2021). Like the majority of South Africans, these women were poor and unemployed (Budlender 2005). To them the all-too-familiar gnawing hunger reflected the new state's failure to grant those previously excluded, full relational citizenship.

Across the last 150 years in South Africa, citizenship status has been marked by state investment in social reproduction. Both the colonial and apartheid governments sought to create and maintain a racial hierarchy grounded in white supremacy. This was no small task in a country with a black African majority, pervasive white poverty, and an economy whose diversity spanned from subsistence agriculture to urban industry. Following the turn of the century invention of "the social," successive regimes targeted families as core sites for this national project of social engineering (Donzelot 1979; Ferguson 2015). However, this was not the equalizing, redistributive project of welfare systems in northern nation-states, but a settler colonial endeavor. Instead, racial hierarchy was built and sustained through inequitable state investment in the very elements families needed to ensure social reproduction (Seekings and Nattrass 2005; Wolpe 1972). White families were uplifted through reserved jobs and education, inflated wages, and generous social benefits. Coloured (mixed race) and Indian families were allowed fewer and less generous wages and benefits while black Africans were either wholly excluded or, in the case of wages or pensions, received a fraction of what was given to whites (e.g., in 1921, the cash value of white earnings was twelve times that of black African workers [Wilson 1972: 66]). Not only were these supports inequitable, they were interdependent. Above-market wages for the small white population were made possible by paying the black African wages far below subsistence (Wylie 2001). White ascendence relied on black African oppression.

This program of racial ranking had profoundly gendered effects. While the duty of social reproduction—caring for the sick and the infirm; raising the children; ensuring food, clothing, and education—is the responsibility of all, the actual labor is overwhelmingly performed by women. Across various regimes, the South African state reinforced this gendered division of labor and leveraged it for the task of racial ordering—state-directed stratified reproduction. Legislators argued that white men (and occasionally coloured men) required "family wages" sufficient to support both the worker and his family. In the event that white families lacked an income earner, the state took on the role of provider through unemployment insurance, pensions, and, critically for children, the State Maintenance Grant (SMG). Coloured and Indian families received some support, but at levels far below that of whites. Black African families were not only excluded from family wages and frequently from state grants, they were excluded under the pretense that "the extended African family" residing in rural reserves provided sufficient support (Iliffe 1987; Kaseke 2002; Posel 2005). In other words, by state design, black women were the welfare system for the black African population for over a century.

Given this history, it is not surprising that women previously excluded from citizenship imagined that democratic transition would bring a redistributionist revolution wherein the wealth and privilege that had long been reserved for whites would become the purview of all. There was good reason for them to expect this. For a century, women's activism, particularly that of women excluded from white privilege, had centered on demands for a comprehensive and inclusive welfare state as an essential component of political liberation (Armstrong 2020; Du Toit 2014; Hassim 2006, 2014; Healy-Clancy 2012, 2017; Sandwell 2022). As a result of this activism, the new Constitution not only guaranteed traditional civil and political rights of nondiscrimination, it also provided for a minimum standard of life in the form of rights to housing, health care, food, water, and social security. The ANC promised to bring about "a better life for all" through investment in jobs, education, and housing. In other words, the democratic state explicitly recognized its obligation to ensure the social reproduction of all citizens.[16] However, much of these redistributive promises hinged on the expectation that the economy, unshackled from its apartheid-era bonds, would grow, creating new jobs and prosperity that could be shared.

In an unfortunate historic confluence, liberation did not beget widespread job growth, and the "homegrown" structural adjustment program South Africa undertook to stimulate the economy led to a net shedding of jobs and policies of deregulation and privatization that ran quite counter to the ANC's roots in the communist labor movement (Bond 2005: 23; Seekings and Nattrass 2005). Thus, the government is now left as the direct provider of "basic needs" for a large portion of the population who cannot and likely will not ever have a job (Ferguson 2015). In almost every interview I conducted, the final question women had for me was, "Can you help me find a job? I really need a job."

The Work-Citizenship Nexus

Because of the country's particular history, waged labor holds tremendous political significance in South Africa. Prior to 1994, what little political rights black African, coloured, and Indian people (predominantly men) were afforded were tied to people's status as workers in an economy hungry for their labor (Nattrass and Seekings 2010). Within what has been termed the "work-citizenship nexus," social citizenship in South Africa has long been linked to employment and production (Barchiesi 2011).

Participation in work is thought to both signify and bring about the essential capacities necessary to shoulder the responsibilities (and earn the privileges) of liberal citizenship. It is through work that people habituate themselves into rational self-determination, self-deliberation, individualism, and morality—not to mention commodified consumption habits and thrift (Barchiesi 2011). For much of the last century, recruitment of black Africans into waged labor was both essential for the settler economy and was framed as a moral imperative to discipline a population viewed as lazy and irrational into proper modern subjects (Bozzoli 1991; Cooper 1996; Wylie 2001). At the same time, the "dignity for work" for whites, in the form of high wages, supervisory positions, and decent conditions, was maintained by constraining black Africans to deeply undignified, read exploitative, conditions. So it was that as racial capitalism became more entrenched across South Africa, much of the struggles against colonial and apartheid oppression were struggles against the precarity, abuse, and exploitation of work (Cooper 1996; Isaacman 1995).

Organized labor and particularly black African trade unions had a decisive role in bringing about the fall of apartheid and shepherding in the democratic transition. Work was central to the vision of "dignity, freedom, economic achievement, and social stability in a deracialized future" (Barchiesi 2016: 150). Having shaken off the indignities, violations, and inequities of the past, new jobs under democratic rule were to enable South African citizens to work their way out of poverty and to build a self-sufficient nation. Engagement in fair labor was not just the entitlement of democracy, it was also the primary vehicle of social inclusion, and a tool to transform ungovernable antiapartheid activists into constructive citizens. Thus, even in the new social order of democratic South Africa, the privileges of full citizenship—social recognition, rights, and, importantly, social reproduction—were, once more, to be earned through participation in wage labor (Barchiesi 2011).

In South Africa today, the waged worker remains the ideal political subject around whom juro-political citizenship is fashioned. This is despite the fact that since the 1970s, the economy has had a labor surplus and unemployment, particularly among unskilled and semiskilled workers, has only expanded since transition. In 2014 when I conducted the bulk of the fieldwork for this book, the national expanded unemployment rate was 35 percent and in KwaZulu-Natal, the province in which Durban is located, it was 39.5 percent (STATSSA 2015).[17] Women faced disproportionately high levels of formal unemployment, and that is only exacerbated by racism. In the same year, the unemployment rate for black African women was the highest of all groups, 46 percent as compared to coloured women, 39 percent, Indian women, 34 percent, and white women, 22 percent (STATSSA 2015). Though the government widely acknowledges the widespread problem of unemployment and its contributions to poverty, no grant currently exists to assist able-bodied adults between the ages of eighteen and sixty. Rather than extending social protection, the state retains a "discourse of work reverence" that encourages unemployed people to embrace entrepreneurship and develop microenterprises rather than to "wait" for the state to provide jobs (Hochfeld 2022: 11). This has led many to conclude that effectively, "post-apartheid social citizenship excludes the unemployed" (Hochfeld 2022: 12; Seekings and Nattrass 2005).

This rise of economic insecurity has brought about profound relational insecurity. With the loss of reliable wages, many black Africans have not been able to formalize marriages through the exchange of *ilobolo* or bridewealth.[18] Though marriage rates fluctuate year to year, formal marriage rates have declined overall in South Africa since the 1960s, most dramatically among the black African population (Budlender and Lund 2011; Posel, Rudwick, and Casale 2011).[19] At the same time, childbearing remains critically important both for the delight that children are thought to bring and to the social value of parenthood, so fertility has not differed much by marital status (Moultrie and Timæus 2001).[20] Thus many women prefer extramarital childbearing and single motherhood (common if stigmatized practices) over the melancholy of childlessness (Sennott et. al. 2016). While some couples have substituted cohabitation for marriage, many, particularly black African women, avoid cohabitation because it is stigmatized and because they are unwilling to perform domestic labor for a (likely unemployed) man without the elevation in status that marriage brings (Posel and Rudwick 2014; Walker 2013).[21] Overwhelmingly, women today are like Nokuthula, attempting to raise children on their own without husbands, jobs, or the political inclusion and recognition the state reserves for laborers. It is not surprising that they view democracy as an "ideology" and little more.

Relational Citizenship Has Not Been Granted[22]

South Africa's continued emphasis on employment and self-sufficiency deviates from the standard neoliberal narrative in important ways, not least of which is the state's sizeable investment in social protection. Prior to the COVID-19 lockdown, 44.3 percent of South African households received at least one government grant with 20 percent of households depending on grants as their main source of income (STATSSA 2020).[23] Just as the global economy was contracting state involvement, South Africa sought to "deracialize" and expand state social protections by removing race as a criteria for eligibility, and grant amounts were equalized across recipients. Despite these efforts of inclusion, the social protection measures— government grants, water allowances, RDP houses—retain legacies of the apartheid and colonial past, designed to supplement the full employment South Africa long enjoyed. As such, state welfare policy continues to rest on the assumption that unemployment, and the poverty that flows from it, is a temporary condition. Government grants—the largest domain in which the government upholds the obligation to support livelihoods—are only available to categories of the population not expected to work: children, people with disabilities, and pensioners. Others, those expected to participate in productive labor, are subjected to what Hein Marais calls the "fetish of coping," wherein discourses of self-reliance legitimate a move to privatize social reproduction and liberate the state from an obligation to support (2011). Therefore, entitlement to citizenship under these terms is contingent on participating in paid labor or being excused from the expectation to do so.

My interlocutors were part of the large population of South Africans unemployed and excluded from eligibility for state support. They were too young to collect a pension and too able-bodied to collect disability grants.

Many did collect the Child Support Grant (CSG) for their children, the largest of South Africa's social protection programs, reaching 60 percent of children (Hall 2021). The CSG has, rightfully, attracted international attention for its radical formulation and its important effects. It is radical because it is noncontributory, meaning recipients need not have paid into some collective fund, and it is also nonconditional. Aside from having a household income below a given threshold, recipients do not need to do anything to receive the grant—no meetings with a school worker, no job-seeking requirements, and so on. Relatedly, there are no bureaucratic constraints on how grant monies are spent such as on food versus other items, a flexibility that has inflamed antigrant discourse. The CSGs are direct transfers of money into caregiver's bank accounts. Finally, in one of its more innovative components, the grants are not structured around euro centric ideas of family and care. Any caregiver of the child—father, mother, auntie, grandmother, or nonkin—can claim the grant on the child's behalf. This has important implications for gender, care, and feminist policy making. Male caregivers can and do receive grants, though the numbers are small (Vorster and De Waal 2008). The dearth of men receiving a CSG is often used to argue that able-bodied men are the most excluded from state support because there is no grant that targets them. However, this is an overstatement. Though the CSG is often referred to as a "women's grant," women as individuals are no more viable dependents of the state than men. The fact that overwhelmingly mothers and grandmothers collect the grant for their biological kin is a result of the gendered structure of care obligations and not, as has historically been the case, an eligibility requirement (Hochfeld 2022). Men who do not receive the CSG are not left out because they are men, they are ineligible because they choose not to engage in caregiving. As feminist scholars of welfare have shown, the basis of welfare entitlements is a crucial aspect of the "politics of needs articulation" that is foundational to political recognition (Fraser 1989).[24] On the one hand, it is problematic that the CSG does not contain a recognition of the needs of caregivers themselves. At the same time, the eligibility structure recognizes that caregiving for children can be undertaken by anyone, regardless of gender, and thus creates opportunities for more egalitarian policy making in the future (Hassim 2003; Hochfeld 2022).

As the largest (in terms of reach) of the government grants, the CSG has had important economic and social effects. It is widely acknowledged that whatever inroads the South African state has made in reducing poverty, these overwhelmingly have come from the successes of the CSG (Grinspun 2016; Woolard et al. 2015; World Bank 2014). The grant has consistently been shown to improve child nutrition, health, and schooling outcomes by enabling caregivers to buy food and school necessities (Agüero, Carter, and Woolard 2009; Department of Social Development, South Africa Social Security Agency, and United Nations Children's Fund 2012; Grinspun 2016; Woolard and Leibbrandt 2010). Longer term, there is evidence that grant receipt is associated with a reduction in risky behavior among adolescents and increased household resilience to emergencies (Grinspun 2016). In a political climate still highly critical of dependence on state support, many note that access to a grant did not diminish but enhanced caregiver work-seeking efforts and enabled investments in potential "micro-enterprises" (Department of Social Development, South Africa Social Security Agency, and United Nations Children's Fund, 2012). At a microlevel, CSG receipt continues to have positive effects, if more tempered. Many women, my interlocutors included, expressed that access to small but predictable infusions of cash enhanced their autonomy in the household and in the community and offered them more choices in terms of decision-making and the ability to negotiate with others (Patel, Knijn, and van Wel 2015). Knowledge that the grant was available also reduced the daily stress for women trying to manage economic precarity and gave them a form of collateral for borrowing from others or asking for credit at nearby shops (Granlund and Hochfeld 2020). Overwhelmingly, the CSG had the largest impact on households in rural areas with lower income opportunities and lower expenses as compared to the urban areas, where I conducted my research.

While the CSG is undeniably valuable and has been effective at ameliorating the harshest effects of poverty, it is materially inadequate to enable women to transform their lives (Hochfeld 2022). By design, the grant amounts are low, indeed below the food poverty line, in order to fiscally enable widespread dispersal and to not discourage job-seeking (Van der Berg, Patel, and Bridgman 2022). The reality is that the grants cannot fill the gap for the 30 percent of children (5.9 million) who live in households where no adults are working (Hall 2021).[25] Especially in urban areas, the grant monies are so small, they cover only a fraction of a child's needs. Increases in CSG amounts have barely kept pace with food inflation, meaning that between 2010 and 2019 the inflation-adjusted value of the grant has either declined or stagnated (Webb and Vally 2020). During my fieldwork in 2013–15 the CSG increased from R300 to R320 (roughly $30 to $32), which was equivalent to the cost of a month's worth of either diapers or milk and bread for a household of four, but not both. While these grants are often shared within the household, they are insufficient to sustain the individual child recipients, let alone their kin (Neves and Du Toit 2012). Most Point women said of the grant, "It comes, and it is finished in one day."

If grants like the CSG do not materially enable relational citizenship, what then of their symbolic impact? In the virtual absence of jobs, access to essential resources and meaningful recognition of need from other individuals and institutions is increasingly important. Now, as it was in the past, the most prominent actor to make claims on is the state, and grants are the most formalized distributive mechanism. While, recently, scholarship has praised the radical structure of the CSG as heralding a new politics of distribution in which people can claim resources from the state on the basis of ideas of universal citizenship not tied to their status as workers, these politics remain aspirational (Ferguson 2015; Li 2017). Akin to what informants of other scholars have revealed, my informants viewed grants as provisional gifts, not entitlements. Unlike jobs, grants were unsuitable for investments in futurity (Dawson and Fouksman 2020a; Dubbeld 2013). On the one hand, as I argue in chapter 2, the grants need to be understood as the most recent instantiation of a long history of state support of social reproduction; on the other, the political recognition they engender and family ties they enable are thin at best.

In the case of the CSG, the legitimate recipient of state support—the child—is a legal subject that cannot represent itself. Children require a caregiver to hold their rights and interests in trust (Ruddick 2008). Children bear the right to state support in part because they are not subject to the moral requirement to work. Adult caregivers are only the mediators. This reflects a key change from the State Maintenance Grant that existed from 1923 to 1996, which contained a payment for the applicant mother in addition to a payment for each qualifying child. This change was not arrived at lightly, and indeed the policy process to transform the SMG into the CSG was an early testing ground for putting the constitutional guarantee of socioeconomic rights into practice. Unexpectedly and regrettably, in debates about how to allocate very limited welfare resources, "the aim of racial equity came to compete with that of poverty reduction"—creating an unwinnable situation for impoverished black and coloured women (Hassim 2003: 519). In 1995, the SMG consisted of a parent allowance of R410 (roughly $200 in 2023 terms) and a child allowance of R127 (roughly $60) for each child. It was estimated that extending the SMG equally to the eligible women and children in all race groups would cost over R12 billion, the equivalent to the total social assistance budget in 1995/96 (Lund 2008). Members of the Lund Committee for Child and Family Support, appointed to make research-grounded recommendations about the new welfare policy, feared that such a large budgetary ask risked a total refusal from the government and the loss of any budget for family-related social security.[26] Thus, after careful consideration, the Lund Committee made the difficult decision to recommend replacing the SMG with a new grant (the CSG) that achieved a far broader national reach in part through reducing grant amounts and providing payments only for the child.[27] The Lund Committee gambled that if they could develop a well-conceptualized, if underfunded, grant that stayed within the budgetary constraints given to them in 1996, with time, activists could push for reforms to expand it. In many ways their gamble paid off. Over the last two decades, the eligibility age and grant amounts have expanded such that the grant now reaches over two-thirds of the country's children and its budget is over 1 percent of GDP ("Child Support Grant" 2023).[28] However, the compromise in the CSG's design also has negative effects that drew heavy criticism in 1996 and now.[29]

Currently, poor women (and men for that matter) cannot access state resources or recognition except through a child. It is only by framing themselves not as a universal citizen, but as a citizen-caregiver for a rights-bearing child, that women can claim state support. However, this recognition is limited as women can only make claims for the child, not directly for themselves. I concur with Tessa Hochfeld who, drawing on Nancy Fraser's work on welfare and social justice, argues that the small amount of the CSG and the lack of comprehensive welfare support around it functions as a form of political misrecognition of women's needs and social worth (Fraser 1996). Hochfeld writes, "The primary message at present appears to be that receiving a CSG ought to be enough to manage your life, and that the state has absolved its responsibilities to you" (2022: 140). This renders women's own needs invisible and transfers the burden of pulling poor households out of poverty onto women who are exhorted to be "self-sufficient." Thus, even in the current context of expanded social assistance, black African and coloured women are left to make up the difference for inadequate state support, as they have for a century.

For the women I know, the impossibility of social reproduction under democracy is a continuity of historic oppression that overshadows other forms of inclusion. Newly minted citizens like Nokuthula have newfound rights and privileges as a citizen but are left without jobs and without state support, trying to raise a family with empty hands. They are, in her words, "still living to an old era which they were living before democracy." To them, they have been left out of the promises of democratic liberation.

Hustling to Get By

Without the support of reliable work or robust state support, my interlocutors, like many excluded from the formal economy, used a host of livelihood strategies to meet their daily needs. In vernacular terms, Point women drew a sharp contrast between a highly desired "proper job" and the unreliable, insecure, and oftentimes harmful practices of *ukuphanda*, or hustling to scratch out a living.[30] Though the precise origins of the term *the hustle* are unclear, the term's meaning in South Africa resembles its usage in African American vernacular. South Africans were exposed to this dialect through radio, music, movies, and, after the 1970s, television, which was ubiquitous by 2014. In South Africa, the concept evokes an identity of resourcefulness (Peterson 2003), a "survival strategy" (Stack 1974), a form of creative opportunism (Venkatesh 2002; Thieme 2013), and a form of deceit through either manipulation or charm in the pursuit of pecuniary gain (Wacquant 1997). Zulu speakers often used the word *ukuphanda* to describe activities such as begging, stealing, or, more vaguely, making things happen. In both cases, to hustle or ukuphanda evokes a moral ambiguity of survival by any means. In this book, I use the umbrella term *livelihood strategies* to encompass the varied processes—the relationships cultivated, the tasks performed, the emotions managed—by which people garnered resources to support social reproduction.

I focus on kinshipping as the primary livelihood strategy through which Point women rework modes of political inclusion that effectively exclude them. Women used components of state supports—for example, the Child Support Grant (chapter 4), the Maintenance Court (chapter 5), immigration law (chapter 6)—to seek anything from cash to cell phone minutes from relatives, former lovers, neighbors, government, or aid agencies. They took up individuated state entitlements and infused them with kinship obligations to broaden their reach and claim support. Yet, these were not claims for women as singular subjects, but claims to support women as kin with dependents, namely, children. Thus, through their claim-making, they demanded collective recognition that they were not just autonomous subjects but also relational persons who required resources that sustained them as such. In other words, they reworked their citizenship.

Outline of Chapters

Moving chronologically and thematically, each chapter of this book highlights a different example of how Point women use kinshipping to rework modes of political inclusion to obtain recognition, support for themselves and their children, and a modicum of the relational citizenship they seek.

Chapter 1, "'In Point, it is the same as if you are alone': Kinshipping in a Kinless Space," introduces readers to the inner-city neighborhood of the Point. Through a description of the particularities of the field site—its long history of multiracial mixing notably between poor whites and black African migrant workers, livelihoods built on hustling, urban segregationist policy, and welfare intervention—I also underscore key historical changes affecting South Africa as a whole. The centrality of kinshipping to this study arises out of the unique social dynamics of the Point wherein residents are highly dependent on one another for survival yet lack connection or mutual trust, living as if they were alone. In order to survive, residents broker relationships in a social context where relatedness cannot be taken for granted and neighbors are suspicious. This kinshipping in a kinless space renders the labors of doing kinship uniquely visible and shapes the methods of this study. I end by describing the contours of ethnography in a context of pervasive mistrust and outlining the robust archival record that was left by city planners, state legislators, and social service agencies who intervened in the lives of Point families.

Chapter 2, "'You Are Mothers of the Nation'—Citizenship and Social Reproduction," shows how present-day disappointment in the juro-political citizenship that came about in 1994 has roots in definitions of citizenship and national belonging outlined in the colonial era. I trace the longer history of how citizenship became tied to state-supported livelihoods through the state use of welfare policy—particularly child support policy—to uplift white families and sustain white heteropatriarchy. The inequitable investment in families' social reproduction maintained a racial hierarchy wherein white women became mothers of the nation and black African women became the de facto social safety net to black men whose belonging was predicated on their status as workers. In light of this history, the democratic government's Child Support Grant is not a radical departure as much as a recent instantiation of the long-standing use of child support policy as a technology of South African statecraft—now attempting to redress previous inequities. However, without jobs or comprehensive grants that people can live on, women of color feel the impossibility of social reproduction under democracy as a *continuity* of historic reliance on their uncompensated labor to offset inadequate state support.

Chapter 3, "'She is not conscious of her maternal role': Kinshipping in the Welfare Office," highlights the welfare cases of three impoverished mothers living in Point in the 1960s. This period offers important insights for my study because it was a crucial time of nation-building for the apartheid era in which ideas of citizenship and belonging were being outlined, akin to what is taking place in the present day. Further, for many of my interlocutors in the 2010s, the 1960s were an important historical touchpoint in familial memory. The argument makes use of archives of welfare case notes, court testimony, and oral history interviews from residents and former social workers to show how mothers made kinshipping claims on the state as a kind of patron. This chapter demonstrates how a white, coloured (mixed race), and black African mother each negotiated their entitlement to aid by invoking state obligation to support "mothers" as universal moral subjects. I argue that coloured and black African women used encounters with the apartheid welfare state to rework their political belonging under racist rule.

Chapter 4, "'We are mothers, we are hustlers': Kinshipping in the Community," compares earlier generations' livelihood strategies to those of Point women in 2014 who now hold juro-political citizenship and are equally eligible for the state aid for which their mothers fought. Yet they are still poor. Waged work remains the ideal means to livelihood and political inclusion; however, with pervasive unemployment and insufficient state support, Point women continue to find themselves excluded from relational citizenship. I show how Point women merge notions of state obligations to poor children embedded in the Child Support Grant with kinship logics to make claims on neighbors, lovers, or organizations for resources. In what they call hustling, or *ukuphanda*, Point women enact different performances of motherhood to audiences that often hold divergent definitions of deservingness. I argue that through this kinshipping in their community, Point women obtain important recognition of their caregiving labor—labor that had long been overlooked—yet the recognition is tenuous because it depends on their ability to adequately perform motherhood to each public.

Chapter 5, "'Me and him we only have a child together nothing more': Kinshipping in the Maintenance Court," describes women's complex relationship to the Maintenance Court, widely praised as a venue of political inclusion where women could claim their newfound rights and combat the gendered and economic injustices wrought by irresponsible men. However, like the Child Support Grant, the court largely relies on women's uncompensated labors to discipline men into paying and ensure the needs of children are met in the likely event that men again stop paying. I show how this produces differing outcomes that demand a more nuanced understanding of what counts as success in the court. Some women in the court experienced deep disappointment and alienation from their former lovers and from the state that purported to back them. Others, however, leveraged kinshipping to use court process to meet their goals of relational citizenship, even if their financial position changed little. For women less dependent on the monetary success of a case, the ability to appeal to the authority of the state to enforce obligations or enact retribution was an important symbolic affirmation that enhanced their feeling of inclusion in the new nation.

Chapter 6, "'We are able to stay together as a family': Kinshipping with Foreign Spouses," considers Point women's kinshipping efforts in the domain of marriage. For black Africans, marriage remains closely tied to wage labor through bridewealth expectations. Due to the secure social reproduction it suggests, and the recognition it generates, marriage is the archetypical means of achieving relational citizenship. Nevertheless, marriage to an unemployed man in the 2010s was neither feasible nor desirable. Instead, a small number of black African Point women braved rampant xenophobia to marry employed immigrants from the rest of the African continent. Like the strategies detailed across the book, the effects on Point women's sense of belonging were uneven. At one level, marriage to a foreigner and, for these women, conversion to Islam, marked them as outsiders no longer readily recognizable as members of the black South African community. On another level, through kinshipping they negotiated marriages that met critical cultural expectations of bridewealth exchange, appeasing elders and ancestors and allowing them to achieve the revered status of *umakoti*, or bride. I argue that through marriage to a foreigner, these Point women gained the ideal form of relational citizenship in their own country, but at a high cost.

In the conclusion, I consider the broader implications for the theory of relational citizenship in a world of declining wage labor and increasing economic and political inequality. I argue that, as we have seen across the book, a notion of citizenship as coproduced by state entitlements and people's everyday relational work, returns kinship once more to the center of thinking about political belonging. Relational citizenship as an analytic enables anthropologists, genders studies scholars, political scientists, and sociologists to bridge a long-standing divide between domestic and political modes of sociality persistently viewed as conceptually, temporally, spatially, and scalarly distinct. Analyzing the state and kinship together, I propose, allows scholars and laypersons alike to see how present-day forms of marginalization are produced and mitigated. Further, this offers inroads for imagining mechanisms of inclusion grounded in secure relationships from the family to the community, to the nation.

1 "IN POINT, IT IS THE SAME AS IF YOU ARE ALONE"

Kinshipping in a Kinless Space

ZANELE WAS EFFICIENTLY BATHING HERSELF in a bucket in the center of the small room. Her practiced motions spoke of a childhood spent in rural Zululand without running water, only now, her skills were being put to use in the inner-city Point neighborhood in Durban. Though her room lacked the tap that others in the building had, Zanele was fortunate. Her longtime boyfriend, notably named Lucky, father to her younger daughter, worked for the building's owner, and the three of them lived in the room for less than half of the usual R2000 in rent (approximately $200). With this luck, Zanele was able to sidestep the neighborhood's expensive (by working-class standards) rents and still enjoy its benefits such as its central location, its public primary school and hospital, and its robust hustling economy. Surprised, I asked Zanele why amid this relative privilege she was so eager to leave the Point. Zanele was bathing in preparation for another day of searching for a "proper job," a job with reliable income that would allow her to move away from the press of humanity in the Point and invest in a more permanent existence. "If I die, they will move my body out of here and another person will move in," she said, speaking of the tenuous connection she felt to her home of the last decade. She did not want that life for herself, or for her children. "They must know where they belong and that their mother made this place for them." An orphan herself, Zanele felt acutely the need to provide her children with a sense of belonging, of long-term security, and rootedness. At the same time, Zanele had run away to the city to escape her rural adoptive household because of abuse and neglect—actions she saw as kinship gone wrong. She sought to build a new family that upheld obligations of care and provided her security to raise her own children. She was doing so in the context of the Point in which a disparate mosaic of persons lived cheek to cheek with one another, simultaneously isolated and mistrustful and entangled in webs of relationships on which they were highly dependent for support.

Before she could catch a *kombi,* or minibus taxi, to start her job search, Zanele needed cash. Lucky's wages were their primary income and because they reliably arrived every week, Zanele put them to additional use. Zanele was a favored moneylender in the building because she was seen to be fair and consistent, qualities the other tenants attributed to her rural upbringing. This was in contrast to the other lenders in the building such as the drug dealer or the building manager whose known swindling was taken as evidence that they had been tainted by city ways. It was the first of the month, when government grants were paid out, so collection would be fairly simple. Making the rounds together, Zanele and I came across Maryann, a coloured woman who in an effort to clean her room, had emptied its entire contents into the passage. Maryann refused to leave her belongings unguarded, knowing that the building manager's "boys" would try to steal them, and instead sent me to the shop with her grant card and her eighteen-month-old son to collect her government Child Support Grants. The lines at the store were long and jammed with carts overflowing with bags of rice and vegetables as shoppers waited to collect their grants and make their monthly purchases. In our line alone, the cashier distributed over R10,000 in cash (approximately $1,000) while I waited, a tangible reminder that the majority of South Africans rely on at least one government grant. As such, few people in this mixed-race neighborhood batted an eye at me, a young white woman with a coloured boy on my hip, collecting a grant. Maryann's R900 (approximately $90, or $30 for each child) was meager, and she could do little more than repay Zanele, buy a few kilos of potatoes and onions, and purchase diapers. But it was dependable and together with what Maryann's boyfriend brought in and what she could scrape together, they could pay rent and eat for the month.

Back in the passage, Zanele wrote out a receipt for Maryann on a scrap of paper and, cash in hand, left us to head downstairs to pay a Xhosa granny, Gogo Sopitsho, to watch Zanele's young daughter for the day. Maryann carefully stored the receipt—which she had convinced Zanele not to date—in the top drawer of her cupboard where she kept her others. Maryann had a precise system for negotiating household finances with her boyfriend, Damien. She used receipts—from Zanele, the shop, or the landlord—to show where known income such as the grants or the money he gave her had been spent. This meant she could use other monies she might bring in such as gifts from an old friend she hadn't seen in years or the odd payment from her elder daughters' father, on things like clothes for her girls or betting on a horse race. If the receipts had no date, Maryann could show them to Damien more than once and effectively launder the money she brought in, money he would otherwise want to control. "I can't be asking him and asking him, Brady," she once explained to me, adopting a high whiny tone that was nothing like her usual forceful, throaty voice. "Please babe can you give me . . . No! We are women and we need our own things. . . . You have to have separate money." Today, Maryann had a plan for her money.

She was on her way to a new prayer group that Auntie Manu, an Indian lady who lived downstairs, had told her about. The prayer group was run by a wealthy white woman who wanted to uplift mothers and generously gave away groceries, blankets, and school supplies. Maryann figured if she could stock their cupboards with the prayer group donations, she could save her other money for a new refrigerator. "How will you explain that?" I asked, incredulously. "Oh, I will tell him I got it from one of the churches," Maryann said breezily, acknowledging the history she had of receiving large donations from various Christian church groups. The refrigerator itself was far more important than its source. For the past eight months, she had used a stove and a refrigerator that a "sister" from the children's home where she had grown up had left with Maryann while she went to try to make her fortunes elsewhere. This was a windfall for Maryann who could then buy meat more cheaply in bulk and could spark relationships with others who needed refrigeration. Auntie Manu was one such person. Until the sister had returned to reclaim her appliances, Maryann had stored insulin for Auntie

Manu's husband, an exchange that had led to this most recent prayer group invitation.

Much to Maryann's visible annoyance, she was not the only one whom Auntie Manu had invited. As we walked, we encountered other women from the building headed toward the prayer group meeting. Maryann seemed particularly rankled that Claudette was there. She and Claudette had grown up together in the state home reserved for coloured children and were rivals even then. Auntie Manu was especially fond of Medina, one of Claudette's children who more closely resembled Medina's Indian father than her dark-skinned, coloured mother. Auntie Manu walked ahead holding the young girl's hand, and Claudette and another woman, Ann, followed behind, carrying the babies. No doubt Claudette had invited Ann, an older coloured woman whose elder children were grown and who was raising her grandchildren on her government pension. Claudette had been close friends with one of Ann's daughters before she had died, and Claudette made sure to give Ann any extra food she had or to invite her to any potentially profitable events. Though both had lived in many buildings across the neighborhood, they chose to move together, often living, as they did this year, across the hall from each other. This arrangement was quite helpful to Claudette who had seven children, three of whom were not yet in school. It was challenging to run errands with so many small ones in tow so Claudette would often leave them in her room. If anyone came by and raised their eyebrows at unattended children, or threatened to call "the welfare," Ann vouched that she was watching them.

Ann's generosity had its limits, though. Nisha, a Congolese woman, also lived across the hall with her two small children. She was struggling to build her hair-braiding business, but the building manager—also a hair stylist—would not allow Nisha's clients in the building and was constantly admonishing Nisha if she left her children alone to go out to see a client. Ann and Claudette were happy to have Nisha practice new hair styles on them, but they would not watch her children if she left. It was not surprising, then, that Nisha was not at the prayer group meeting. Also absent was Asanda, granddaughter to Gogo Sopitsho, the Xhosa child-minding granny. Likely she was out job hunting with Zanele, but she, too, might not have been invited, excluded, as she often was, from activities that demanded English fluency.

FIGURE 1.1   Women trade laundry-watching duties in a Point alleyway. Photo by Brady G'sell.

The above offers a glimpse into the events of one bustling morning in Point in 2014 and a group of women who make up one set of the various relational networks that crosscut the neighborhood's dense and diverse population. These networks were assembled out of blood relations, long friendships, new acquaintances, proximity, racial affinity, and a shared dependency on others for support in the arduous task of raising children in poverty. They relied on one another for money, childcare, food, key information, and so much more. That day, those twenty who attended the prayer group meeting went home and filled their cupboards with bags of groceries, set for another month. Next month would come soon enough.

Though a portion of the neigborhood's population are long-term residents, the Point is a place of outsiders. Many of the residents I knew had come to the neighborhood with similar aspirations. They came seeking a better life in one form or another—better schooling, more employment opportunities, "proper" housing, a dream of an elusive middle-class life. Some moved in an attempt to manage the kinship obligations that they chafed against. The smaller flats and limited visitation policies of the inner-city buildings meant that family could not descend unannounced or en masse to make demands that were difficult to refuse. Others came from poorer areas with the vision of obtaining a job and sending remittances home. When they were confronted with the realities of scarce employment, they often cut family ties out of shame. Still others, like Zanele, were running from a toxic home life riddled with the abuse and neglect that often goes hand and hand with poverty. Regardless of the motivation, those seeking independence were frequently disappointed. Much to their dismay, many of them found that they didn't escape obligations, but merely shifted them. As one resident put it, town was a place where you, "left behind one family to make another."

Far from the freedom that many envisioned, life in town for poor women necessitated building complex webs of obligation and accountability in order to get by. As across the country, people survived based on claims on a small pool of wage-earners and those with cash infusions such as government grants or the occasional windfall. Those like Auntie Manu were fortunate because a member of the household (her husband) received a sizeable disability grant from the government. Women such as Auntie Manu prided themselves on being what one woman termed "neighborhood mothers," redistributing scarce resources in relationships of care and exchange. "Everyone here [in Point] is doing the same thing—trying to get food on the table," Auntie Manu noted. "If you are hungry and need help, I will help, I won't chase you."

However, the needs of the community far exceeded the capacity of the "neighborhood mothers," and they had to make distinctions. Auntie Manu followed up, "you can't be always giving, giving, giving. You must draw a big red line. By the month end, everything gets wiped out." Because so few people in the neighborhood had extended kin and because of the population's heterogeneity, the terms of exchange and redistribution could not be assumed and were not always clearly defined, especially for newcomers.

This ambiguity led to a profound sense of isolation for many. As one woman put it, "The challenge of staying here is the neighbors. It is the same as if you are alone because even if you are short of anything you are on your own."

Making a life in Point involved kinshipping in a kinless place. Point women had to broker relationships of debt and dependency across divides of race, language, and nationality. As these relationships were formed, the terms, norms, and obligations they entailed had to be negotiated. While kinshipping occurs in many other places, often such negotiations are tacit and based on shared taken-for-granted expectations. In the Point, shared expectations could not be assumed, and the kinshipping processes were starkly visible and observable. My observations of how these processes unfolded and changed over months and years form the heart of my ethnographic data.

In this way and many others, the analysis in these pages is enabled by the very specific realities of the Point neighborhood. While a unique urban space in South Africa, it also encapsulates in one small neighborhood, the unemployment, xenophobia, poverty, and familial reorganization experienced in urban areas across the country. I contended that the promises and challenges of life in Point are emblematic of those of democratic South Africa more broadly and, indeed, a harbinger of the future. Freedom in the form of economic security was anticipated and sought by Point residents and by the South African majority. But, when well-paying jobs failed to materialize, people were left to manage ongoing material deprivation and inequality through livelihood strategies grounded in deep layers of interdependence. In the case of Point, this interdependence was worked out with persons who were not readily recognizable—to Point inhabitants and the anthropologists who trail along beside them—as kin. Yet through, often gendered, practices of kinshipping, Point women hailed these unfamiliar others to perform kin support of women's own maternal labors.

Thus the Point offers an illustrative entry point for understanding the interrelationship of kinship, citizenship, and economy at play in South Africa and many other places. Only twenty blocks long and five blocks wide, the dense urban space of the neighborhood requires consideration from various vantage points to grasp the impact of its geography and history on those striving to raise children there.

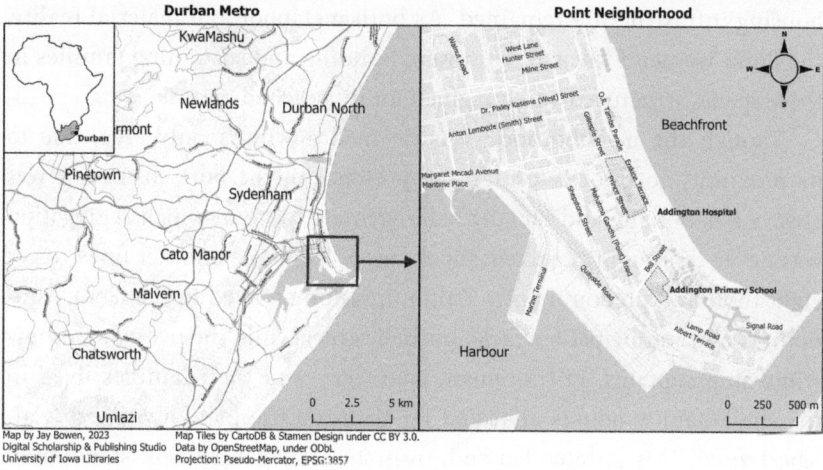

FIGURE 1.2   The Point in geographic context. Map by Jay Bowen, 2021.

What Is the Point?

The Port

The peninsula of the Point embraces Durban's harbor, which is the largest port in sub-Saharan Africa. Until its recent relocation, South Africa's first rail line extended into the Point, and both the port and the railway have economically and socially shaped the neighborhood into a space of racial, national, and class-based heterogeneity that was unusual for much of South Africa. Since the nineteenth century, the port and the railway (both run by the parastatal South African Railways and Harbors) has been a large source of jobs and, later, subsidized housing. Until as late as the 1980s, the port demanded large numbers of laborers to handle break-bulk cargo, or cargo that is neither containerized nor bulk packaged and thus needs to be loaded and unloaded piece by piece (Callebert 2017). Overwhelmingly, black African migrant laborers provided the hands and the backs that did this work while other race groups acted as lift operators, truck drivers, coal shovelers, switchboard operators, or the various other occupations required to make the port run. Between 1912 and the 1970s, the southwest portion of the Point was dominated by housing for stevedores, shore men, and rail workers (Callebert 2017). Predominantly, this was housing for single, laboring men to occupy for short (e.g., a few months or years) work stints. When containerization reshaped the labor needs of shipping industry, this housing infrastructure remained. As both metaphor and material reality, the Point women I knew in 2014 were building and sustaining families in these spaces structured and imagined for unattached men.

Though the neighborhood was deemed a white's only area, due to its proximity to the city center, the presence of the port ensured it was always a nationally and racially heterogenous space in which segregation was never thoroughly enacted. Blocks away from one another upwards of eight thousand predominantly Zulu migrant men lived in the labor compounds and municipal barracks on Bell Street while the overwhelmingly white ship captains, rail foreman, engineers, and their families lived in the single-family houses allocated for them on Camperdown Road (Callebert 2017). This unintended and, from an early government standpoint, unwanted, racial integration reflected the ongoing tensions between state projects of racial separation and businesses who relied on large numbers of poorly paid black African laborers alongside workers of other race groups. Such tensions played out around the politics of housing, and the Point was an exemplar. Starting in the 1930s, large numbers of black African men migrated to Durban seeking paid employment.[1] Not only were more men migrating, they were migrating for much longer time periods and needed to be housed. In the case of *togt*, or casual day laborers, who dominated the Point's shipping industry, laborers were expected to present themselves to be considered for a job by 6:30 a.m., and if they worked overtime (as many were required to do) they stayed until 11:00 p.m., making residence in any places other than the Point a challenge (Callebert 2017; Maylam 1995). Durban's municipal government had an ongoing dispute with both the national government and the business community as to who was to bear the cost of housing for Africans. The national government's investments were woefully insufficient, and in 1949, for example, the Native Administration Department manager estimated that 30,000 of the 90,000 African males registered to work in Durban were without formal accommodation, a number that didn't account for the thousands of unregistered women and children who carved out lives for themselves in the cracks between municipal legislation (Maylam 1988). This huge population of unhoused people slept predominantly in back rooms, parks, or in shack settlements, which, despite their lack of sanitation, offered relative freedom from the regulation of townships or hostels. Point was one of many areas deemed a "black belt," which multiple generations of municipal officials viewed as hotbeds of crime, vice, and disease. These were highly unregulated spaces in which a great deal of informal trade—most notably beer brewing—and racial intermixing took place in areas quite close to the (white) city center, causing enormous anxiety for municipal administrators who undertook recurring attempts at slum clearance and police crackdowns (Maasdorp and Humphreys 1975; Maylam 1983).

In addition to the South Africans, sailors and soldiers from China, the Philippines, Norway, Greece, Portugal, Italy, and many other countries came for extended shore leaves, bringing their languages, cultural preferences, and their wages with them. Unlike Cape Town or Johannesburg, Durban has never been known as a cosmopolitan city, however, the peninsula of the Point has a long-established leisure industry that catered to an unusually diverse crowd. This diversity gave the neighborhood a reputation of licentiousness, a place where boundaries of all kinds could be traversed. In some cases, this operated as a form of titillation, such as with the notorious nightclub Smugglers Inn or "Smuggies," which attracted white middle-class voyeurs in the 1960s and 1970s looking for an opportunity to drink and dance with drag queens, strippers, tattooed ladies, seamen, and even coloured people. In other cases, such transgressions were used to authorize the forced removal of a mixed community in the name of slum clearance.

Along with jobs, the port brought money and resources into the neighborhood. Though dock work was dangerous, grueling, and unpredictable, Callebert found that his African informants had long careers of twenty or thirty years on the Durban docks because of the relative economic opportunities the work brought (2017). Dock workers were not only laborers, they were also consumers, and a host of petty traders, canteen cooks, barbers, legal and illegal liquor distributors, prostitutes, and washerwomen made a living by servicing this large labor force. Point residents created a large secondary trade industry with cargo that was damaged and could be recycled or directly pilfered and resold both in the Point and in Durban's townships (Callebert 2017). In 2014, my interlocutors also obtained a variety of goods—everything from new televisions to children's snorkels in bulk—from similarly "damaged" containers to resell throughout the neighborhood.

Like many other ports, the intermingling of many different kinds of people, goods, and economies gave the area a sense of lawlessness. At one

level, the neighborhood has one of the most complicated property ownership schemes in the country, making for a great deal of uncertainty as
to what entity was responsible for managing which part of the street and
enforcing which laws. The western strip along the harbor belongs to the national government but is leased by shipping companies or managed by the
parastatal South African Railways and Harbors. The beachfront land on
which Addington Hospital sits belongs to the province of KwaZulu-Natal,
but not the nurses' quarters adjacent to the hospital, which is municipal
property. Much to its present-day chagrin, Durban Municipality owns
pockets of subeconomic housing that dot the neighborhood, and since early
2000s, the Municipality has been embroiled in frequent court battles over
who is responsible for derelict buildings (Broughton 2012; Fourie 2012). The
southernmost tip of the peninsula is owned by a Malaysian development
conglomerate attempting to create a luxury residential and commercial
site. In an effort to attract investors and residents, the section from Bell
Street south, installed its own water, electricity, and police—an independence of great import as the national and municipal infrastructure provision declines.

The heterodox nature of Point governance also exists at another level.
The neighborhood has long been associated with crime and deviance either
from the numerous drinking establishments and robust vice economy or
from the circulation of contraband brought by ships (Leggett 2001). People
have long taken advantage of the ambiguity wrought by heterogeneity, such
as the case of one of my interlocutors, an elderly Greek gentleman who led
a gang of young men from Spain, Italy, and Greece in the 1960s. Lacking a
shared tongue, they developed their own language, unintelligible to those
they sought to rob, who were left with confusion and empty pockets. While
the aging whites of Durban argue that the crime of Point's past was tame
compared to what is perpetrated by the overwhelmingly black African
population of today, my research found that the Point's unsavory reputation has been remarkably durable across this racial demographic shift. In
one example, a Children's Court case from 1963 described a white mother/
daughter/aunt team who collaborated to steal from beachgoers and local
shops and resell the goods for profit.[2] From the residents in the 1950s to my
interlocutors in 2014, crime, safety, and the neighborhood's negative influence on their children have been abiding concerns.

A climate of suspicion was further produced by the widespread transience of the neighborhood's population. In earlier decades, shore leaves could last multiple weeks, but the present-day populations of sailors and soldiers were constantly circulating. As an urban place where money could be made, the Point was often the first site of entry for people coming to the city from the countryside or other countries. Part of the "better life" these people sought was to put these earnings toward lives elsewhere (as in the case of the African migrant workers) or to earn enough to move away from the neighborhood's crime and cramped quarters, especially if they had children. Thus, those who could, quickly left the neighborhood. For those who couldn't, leaving often remained their ultimate goal and precluded close ties to neighbor's. Even for those who lived for twenty years in the Point, it was rarely described as a community to which they belonged as much as a stopover on the way to a different life.

The Beachfront

In contrast to the workaday grittiness of the Port, the Point's second face, the beachfront, presented an image of carefree leisure. A line of art-deco-style high-rises painted in bright pastels abutted the white sand dotted with palm trees and colorful kiosks selling everything from "traditional" Zulu beadwork to inner tubes. Though this southern end of Durban's beachfront was never the destination for the well-heeled, it has consistently attracted droves of less prosperous visitors looking to holiday next to the vivid blue waters of the ever-warm Indian Ocean. Durban is a primary destination for South African's seeking relief from the summer heat during the Christmas and New Year's holidays. As such, over the years various businesses have sprung up to entertain and amaze Durban's holiday makers. Whites in their sixties or older often reminisce about the trampoline park, the kiddie pools, the Mermaid Lido with its "homosexualist" organ grinder, Mini-town, the Snake Park, the Surf and Rescue Club, and Little Top.[3] Prior to the 1980s when the beaches were racially integrated, many of these diversions trafficked in the consumption of exotified racial difference such as the Indian snake charmers, the Zulu gumboot dancing competitions, or the flamboyantly dressed rickshaw drivers that are iconic Durban figures.

The beachfront's daytime amusements had after-dark counterparts in the bars, restaurants, and nightclubs that line the neighborhood's streets.

FIGURE 1.3   An aerial view of Point. Durban's iconic beachfront is on the left and the harbor is on the right. Photo by Hugh Bland.

It was also the place where extralegal indulgences could be bought, such as drugs, hard liquor, or sex. Whether it be the delight of a flea circus or the companionship of a sex worker, the Point was a well-known locale for the gratification of various pleasures. For the neighborhood residents, this had a number of important effects. The pleasure economy was a large source of revenue. A number of my interlocutors had at some point worked as waitresses in a neighborhood bar or nightclub. Sales of trinkets or panhandling on the beachfront was a reliable and quick source of cash, as was engaging in transactional companionship or sex. The constant presence of holiday makers also enabled other forms of income generation, such as the reselling of pilfered cameras or ready marks for counterfeit schemes. This economy additionally offered many temptations such that a day's earnings could quickly be spent on readily available consumables. The neighborhood's atmosphere of carefree hedonism contributed to a devil-may-care attitude that many inhabitants shared. What residents termed a "fast life," was reinforced by a political economy in which future planning was often thwarted.

The Street

The vision of the neighborhood from the street offers an important third perspective. Residents living in Point referred to it as living "in town" in contrast to either the townships (also known as locations) created under apartheid for the Indian, coloured, and African racial groups or the suburbs that ring the downtown and that remain overwhelmingly white. Point is a short distance from the city center, making the city's commercial and financial services as well as the employment opportunities a short bus ride away. The small middle and working class that lived in Point were civil servants, bank clerks, or office cleaners looking to save on transportation costs by living closer to downtown.

Partly due to its proximity to Durban's commercial hub and partly due to its historical status as one of the first places of white settlement in the city, the neighborhood was very well resourced. In addition to the natural asset of the sea, on the east end stood both the large state-run Addington Hospital, and, next door, the Durban Children's Hospital, which grew to international prominence midcentury for its exceptional care (Burns 2011).[4] Bearing the same name was the neighborhood's primary school, whose historic Afrikaans and English-language curriculum was expanded in recent years to include a madrassa that served the growing immigrant population from other African nations. Point residents had the unusual privilege of quality medical care and primary education within walking distance. In contrast, rural or township residents had to arrive at the hospital before 6:00 a.m. to attempt to access same-day services. Similarly, many sent their children to informal boarding houses where twenty or more children live in a neighborhood flat, cared for by a housemother, in order to access Addington School. Furthermore, residents enjoyed the presence of three large supermarkets within the neighborhood such that they could comparison shop as they walked their children to school.

Despite the presence of a small middle class and a few clusters of holiday flats, long-term residents in the Point have historically been poor. The neighborhood's reputation and industrial sector prevented the gentrification that many city planners imagined for such a centrally located neighborhood.[5] Until the 1980s, various undesirable elements of urban infrastructure were located in the Point's southern tip, such as the sewage plant, a small jail, and a "Zulu hospital" for injured migrant workers. This made for inexpensive yet

FIGURE 1.4 (a, top) Pedestrians and kombi taxis rush by. Photo by Cedric Nunn. (b, bottom) Students from Addington Primary School walk home along a busy Point street. Photo by Cedric Nunn.

accessible land for the city's construction of various subeconomic schemes that sought to transform poor whites into respectable citizens through the technology of family housing and welfare intervention. The most notable is Elwyn Court, a monolithic block of 140 flats that spans a full city block. Built in the 1940s to house poor white families who paid heavily subsidized rent, the building was municipally run until 2001, when the individual flats were sold off to their owners at a nominal cost. When influx control ended in the 1980s and more black African and coloured people began moving to the neighborhood, those white families who could afford it, either sold their flats or rented them out and moved to the suburbs. Those who remain are the poorest renters or owners. Growing debt and the poor management of the building has plagued the municipal government. Horror stories of residents trapped on the seventh floor because of elevators that have not worked in a decade crop up every few years in the local papers (see Rond-ganger 2015).[6] In the more successful housing schemes, begun after 1999, the municipality refurbished old holiday flats and charged well-vetted occupants close to market rent, making them accessible only to those with jobs. Serving a different population, The Association for the Aged (TAFTA) runs three large buildings for low-income senior care. In a poignant display of spatial and temporal confluence, the TAFTA buildings overlook the former site of the municipal beerhall built to fund and effect the management of black African migrant men.

Alongside this relatively stable population was a much larger transient population—sometimes including people who had been there for years—that circulated through the neighborhood. Known as a place where fast cash could be made, the neighborhood attracted persons associated with social deviance who were constant targets of the city's cleanup efforts. The bulk of work opportunities were contingent jobs subject to daily or sometimes hourly changes in demand. From the 1950s to the 1970s, much of the neighborhood was made up of short-term boardinghouses or "hotels" to house a mobile workforce. Durban's temperate climate also enabled workers to sleep out on the beachfront or on the verandas of dockside sheds (Callebert 2017). In 2014, former boardinghouses had become bachelor flats that could be rented by the week or month or the lodges and "shelters" that served those who could not pay in advance.

The presence of so many whites, and notably white children, living in poverty and purportedly "improper" circumstances prompted some of Durban's early elite women to target the Point as a site for improving child welfare (Burns 2011). Between the 1920s and the 1930s, their activism created the Durban Child and Family Welfare Society, whose first initiative was to create crèches, or daycares, for white children in the neighborhood. Later they formed the Child Family and Community Care Centre of Durban, which employed social workers throughout the neighborhood to work directly with poor white families. However, the black African, coloured, and Indian population of the neighborhood was often denied access to these resources.

Though the welfare landscape has changed substantially, the neighborhood has a robust, though disaggregated, network of private aid institutions. Churches throughout the neighborhood run a weekly feeding scheme, and other organizations distribute food and occasionally toiletries on the beachfront. The Point is a manageable target for individuals or institutions looking to serve South Africa's poor and/or save wayward souls because of its accessibility, contra the townships, and its population of poor people who include enough white faces to calm the nerves of some skittish white liberals. Some started informal prayer groups that also distribute goods; others set up a more established outreach and counseling center in Addington School. For a handful of years, the University of South Africa ran an experience learning program for fourth-year social work students in the Point who supported many formal and informal organizations. Importantly, the large concentration of poverty relief efforts is yet another resource the neighborhood offers.

The majority of people living in Point sought to eventually leave the neighborhood, yet many found it challenging to do so because living there was quite expensive. Because the available work was so unreliable and so low paying, unless they already had a family home elsewhere—as in the case of migrant workers—it was challenging for people to save enough cash to move away.[7] Very few people owned their home in Point, and even those who did had to pay monthly levies and utility costs. For those who rented, rent for a single room—or even a month at the shelter—was consistently ten times what a similar space would be in one of the townships. There was no greenspace so food was purchased instead of grown, and children could not simply play in the yard or the street but had to be watched by a neighbor who inevitably demanded remuneration for her services. Often residents became trapped in cycles of debt in which they were constantly owing back rent or interest to loan sharks who funded last month's costs, leading one resident to say, "In Point, everything is money."

The Vibe

Photos do not easily capture a final essential perspective on the neighborhood, namely, its social atmosphere, or what South Africans call "the vibe." Little, if anything, is shared across all Point residents, other than geographic space, but during my fieldwork, there were ideas about the neighborhood and how it operated that were collectively understood by many I encountered.

A unique feature of the neighborhood that shaped social life there was the high concentration of multistory apartment buildings, the density of which was seen in only a handful of other places in South Africa. Thus, what residents termed "flat life"—referencing an apartment—occurred in small rooms or apartments and their adjacent hallways, in contrast to the stand-alone houses surrounded by a yard that have long been the norm. Occupants and their children did not have access to an outdoor extension of domestic space, a condition that many found unnatural and confining. They were also subject to the nuisances of sharing intimate space with non-family. "We are up in each other's shit," one woman joked when describing a fight taking place on her floor because one sick neighbor had blocked the communal toilet. Neighbors' proximity also invited and supported a great deal of surveillance. Building managers, neighbors, or their guests could all view what packages were brought home from the shops, what furniture was visible through always-open front doors, hear arguments or cries of passion, and smell what was for dinner or whose rubbish had been left out. This public visibility of intimate domestic life led many to say, "In town, you can never be free," indicating a feeling of claustrophobia in which every decision was subject to public scrutiny.

The old Blenheim Hotel, one of two buildings on which my research focused, offers a good example of these dynamics. Built in the 1920s as a boardinghouse to house white and foreign (often not-white) workers or sailors, it was never a space designed for family-making. The rooms are small, roughly 100 square feet (9.29 square meters), and only three out of

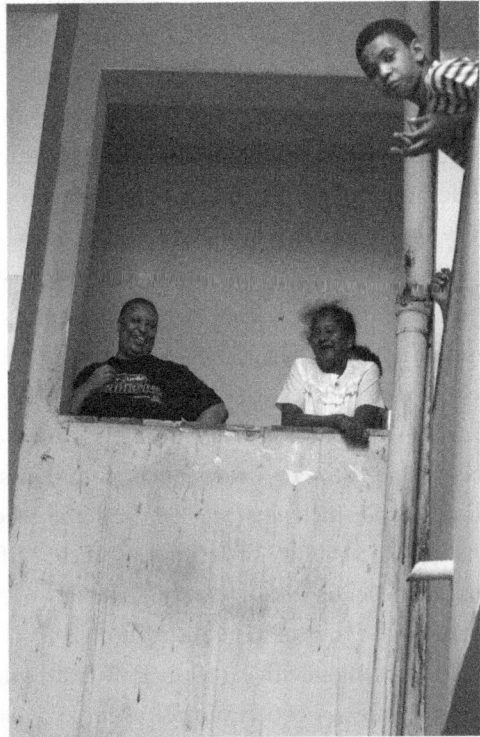

FIGURE 1.5A AND B Breezeways often serve as gathering spaces for playing and chatting. Photos by Brady G'sell.

thirty-five have an attached toilet or bath. The others share one communal toilet and shower per floor. Though there was a dining room and kitchen on the ground floor where boardinghouse residents used to eat, it now serves as a storage room, mostly for the items of those evicted waiting to be sold, donated, or for their owners to pay the arrears. Most residents cooked on hotplates in their rooms. Because the rooms are so small, most socializing took place in the shared passageways, which, like many South African buildings, are open to the sky and to other floors. I stood for hours with residents as they hung over the ledges, smoking, gossiping, shouting at rowdy children, and peered at what packages or persons were brought in.

The identities of the other persons with whom people shared space were important. Longtime white residents attributed a rise in the crime and degradation of the Point to the arrival of black South Africans following the repeal of the Group Areas Act in the late 1980s. Black South Africans, in turn blamed the influx of "foreigners" from the African continent after South Africa opened its borders in 1994. Yet race is only one category of difference in Point's diversity.

As one woman noted, "Everyone comes from all over." Indeed, a single hallway could contain white Afrikaans families who had lived in the neighborhood for years, black immigrants from Tanzania and Congo, coloured South Africans born in a Durban township, black South Africans from deep Zululand, aging white Greek immigrants who had come in the 1960s, and third-generation Durban Indians. For some, this fostered a valuable cross-cultural education, such as one Zulu woman married to a Burundian immigrant who said, "In town, it is easy to meet different people and learn different languages. If the children were to stay at the farm and only be amongst people there, their mind won't open up and won't be wise. They will be suspicious. To learn another language is to understand." For others, diversity produced a great deal of turbulence. Because there were few shared norms of greeting or of sharing, people frequently offended or aggravated one another. Whether items exchanged were gifts or loans was a question of constant debate as well as the terms of reciprocation or compensation.

As part of this diversity of origins, a sense of rootlessness pervaded Point's occupants. Most people came to the city on their own, seeking a better life and new opportunities. Even if they had children in Point, their larger kin networks often remained elsewhere and thus unknown and inaccessible to other Point residents. Furthermore, the inability to amass wealth often strained relationships with kin living outside of the neighborhood. Nama, a Zulu woman, summed up a common misperception, "When you live in town, life is fast so they think since you staying in town they assume you have money, all those things."[8] People often broke off ties with rural family when they tired of the constant requests for money that they could not meet.

The high cost of neighborhood resources also precluded relationships within Point. People were constantly "shifting," as they called it, running from debts or seeking a less expensive place to live. One interlocutor, Zandi, encapsulated it well, "In flats, people are coming and moving. You don't know who your neighbors are. Someone can do something and just disappear." She compared it to an idealized vision of a township community saying, "In location, if they run away you can find them because they will come back. Their family is there. . . . In the flat [in Point] you only bring your bag. [In the township] Even if they lie, you've still got their family." By contrasting "family" to "a bag," Zandi highlighted not only a difference in social personhood but also the lack of social accountability and durable connections that characterized relationships in Point. This sense of disconnection between residents manifested in pervasive mistrust.

This lack of trust was based on profound social and epistemological concerns. Without extended kin or long-term connections to ground them, people felt they could not dependably *know* their neighbors. They worried that their neighbors may not be what they seem or may have questionable intentions. While I observed that my interlocutors had some relationships that were closer than others, all resisted the suggestion that they had friends. When asked who their friends were, a common response was "I do not have friends; I do not believe in friends at all . . . because I know what they're capable of."[9] The implied danger was betrayal either through gossip or action, which many had previously experienced.[10] They were vexed that it was so challenging to "know someone's heart" to determine their trustworthiness. While this is a concern in South Africa more broadly and certainly beyond, the Point's climate of deception enhanced their anxieties (Ashforth 2005). Most people supported or supplemented their livelihood through forms of panhandling that involved various degrees of duplicitousness. One might beg on the street, which often involved highlighting characteristics that attracted more resources (e.g., a physical disability or care of children) that may or may not correspond to that person's daily life. Others sold *amagwinya* (cakes) cooked in their kitchen or goods pilfered from the docks. Zulu speakers would describe these through the morally ambiguous term *ukuphanda*. Likewise, English speakers switched between the more passive terms "coping" and "getting by" or the active verb "to hustle" to similarly thread an ethical needle. While those with whom I spoke set apart their own actions, and often those of their closest confidants, as morally vindicated, anyone else's behavior was highly questionable.

Ubiquitous chicanery produced a deep sense of insecurity in Point residents. They were concerned that children would be snatched by nameless criminals who could disappear or that they would be unknowingly sold drug-laced food that would turn them into addicts. However, the most pervasive fear was that their neighbors would lie to them or about them—or, perhaps even more worrying, that their neighbors would tell the truth about them to someone else. Their vulnerability was heightened by the fact that people in the neighborhood were tremendously dependent on one another for survival. Neighbors loaned money or cooking oil when you were short. They told you when people were distributing food on the beachfront or where one could get donated clothes. They also bore witness to your daily activities and were privy to extensive information about one's intimate life, which they could choose to share with others. There was little space for the management of one's image in Point, and because of the density, the repercussions for malicious talk were high.

Research in a Context of Mistrust

This book is informed by over two decades of engagement with South Africa, over a decade of which was spent in the Point. The bulk of data I use here were collected during a three-month visit in 2011, a year of fieldwork in 2013–14, and follow-up visits in 2015, 2019, and 2022. In May 2011, I traveled to Durban to conduct preliminary research on women's livelihood strategies. The phenomenon of unemployed women who were raising children with little help from the children's fathers was widespread, but I sought a field site where the specificities of place shaped the particular contours of this pervasive social condition. I also sought to account for the experiences of people in multiple race groups, whose lives were impacted quite divergently by apartheid and the putative deracialization under democracy. Catherine Burns, a longtime mentor and then history professor in the University of KwaZulu-Natal was researching the history of the historic Durban Children's Hospital in Point and introduced me to the neighborhood. At her suggestion, I began looking into the history of the Point neighborhood as a very different sort of social space. It was neither an insular township on the edges of the city, nor was it a suburb. It could not be understood as a cosmopolitan haven of racial mixing such as Cato Manor in Durban or Alexandria in Johannesburg. It was segregated yet heterogenous, interdependent yet discordant, and poor yet rich in resources. The neighborhood offered unique perspective on South Africa's history, and one that has attracted little historiographic attention.[11] Further, I believe, it is a harbinger of South Africa's future.

Ethnographic Encounters

For my longest stretch of fieldwork, I moved to Durban in 2013 with my husband and six-month-old baby in tow. I had a twenty-block neighborhood to focus on and a network of contacts, but this was very different from achieving access to and legitimacy with the residents whose experiences I sought to learn. Furthermore, the very real insecurities of the neighborhood meant it was not prudent for any outsider—let alone a young-looking, white American woman—to traverse the streets without a clear destination. So as to not contribute to the outrageous rent inflation taking place in the Point and to distance myself and my family somewhat from the neighborhood arguments into which I would inevitably be drawn, I lived a short distance away, arriving each morning by minibus taxi after all the children had been dropped at school.

Initially, I established myself with volunteer activities at sites across the neighborhood that put me in contact with Point parents, most often mothers. In one storefront ministry, I helped peel potatoes and dish plates for the twice-daily feeding scheme, organized clothing and toiletry donations, and occasionally taught computer skills. Those women who lingered and helped with the cleanup—aware they would receive additional resources—took our quieter time together to interrogate me about what brought me to Point and why. Was I a missionary? A social worker? A spy? Realizing that these were the intelligible categories for someone with my presentation, I identified myself as a student wishing to learn enough to write a book that explained to Americans "how those raising children in South Africa coped." This became my introductory line when I went to churches to attend the women's ministry meetings or outreach events, on home visits where I acted as an isiZulu translator for the community aid worker from a development agency run out of Addington Primary School, or when I sat for hours at the Maintenance Court amusing bored toddlers and keeping anxious women company as they waited for their case to be heard.

My recognizability in the neighborhood also derived from my friendship with important gatekeepers who had developed the trust of residents. Val Jenkins, or "Jenks," had retired after thirty years of service in the HIV ward of the Durban Children's Hospital and, later, Addington Hospital. A taciturn coloured woman with a quick wit, Jenks was a walking kinship map. She knew every mother, granny, sibling, and cousin who came to the hospital, whether they took their meds, and how often the children went to school. I accompanied her on her days volunteering in the inner-city drop-in clinic, holding babies and chatting with parents before and after their appointments.

Nora Saneka, the principal of the formerly white Clare Ellis Brown pre-primary school in Point, had worked in the neighborhood for decades and was a longtime activist for the neighborhood residents, especially the children. At her invitation, I volunteered at the school, assisting with events like sports day or after-care activities. She introduced me to parents, former pupils, former teachers and numerous historic and present-day neighborhood stakeholders. A seemingly endless font of passion and vision, Nora was working to establish an Early Childhood Development (ECD) Forum of childcare centers to help improve the care these underresourced, understaffed, and often illegal centers provided. The Forum brought members together to share resources and knowledge (how to make toys out of recycled materials or to talk to parents about nutrition) and to advocate for municipal policies to enhance ECD. I assisted with a project to map the landscape of childcare centers in Point, developing a questionnaire about their staffing, hours, fee scale, and demographics of the families they served. Data from the questionnaire help support a successful advocacy effort to obtain municipal support of subsidized breakfasts in the centers. Those data also appear in this book.

From 2011 to 2016, the University of South Africa (UNISA) Department of Social Work ran a service-learning center in Point. The vision of the center was to integrate social science research and community engagement with the practical training of fourth-year social work students. Supervised by Barbara McLean, the students undertook internships at sites or with groups throughout the neighborhood (e.g., at the refugee center or with the cardboard collectors). As part of their internships, students were expected to develop, implement, and assess an outreach project that met the needs of that community. During my time there, I offered guidance on qualitative research methods and accompanied students to their sites. Through the students' work, I attained a much broader understanding of the various communities within the Point and their very specific circumstances.

Numerous Point women have also been invaluable advisors and guides to my work in the neighborhood. One of the most long-standing has been Ntombizandile Krakra, or Zandi, a graduate of the UNISA social work program. A student-researcher herself, Zandi was a keen observer and a tenacious investigator who, with two children at home, had spent six months integrating herself into the world of Point's cardboard collectors, understanding their rhythms, the internal dynamics of the group, and the challenges they faced. Zandi's initial role was to introduce me to women in the neighborhood, and through her I met many mothers scattered in buildings throughout Point, the most notable being a growing group of South African women married to foreigner men who I would never have encountered otherwise. Over time, Zandi became a respected assistant and eventual collaborator. She provided isiZulu or isiXhosa translation when my skills were insufficient, translated and contextualized slang terms specific to Point, acted as a sounding board for me to check my understandings and interpretations, and revised my interview questions to better reflect the conceptual categories of Point residents. After I returned to the United States, Zandi continued to conduct interviews, as we had done together, focusing on South African/foreigner couples and their specific circumstances. She also transcribed her interview recordings, and we continue to talk regularly to discuss the transcripts, my writing, her social work job, and the ongoing questions we have about the complexities of Point life.

In addition to Zandi, two other Point women helped me access and understand the multilayered social groups of the neighborhood. Zama, a woman in her thirties whose children lived in the rural areas with her mother, often accessed the resources of different aid groups by acting as a volunteer—setting up, helping to cook, serving food, organizing donations, and the like. She was trusted both by the aid groups and by the women who visited them, and her willingness to allow me to accompany her granted me legitimacy across the neighborhood, for which I am deeply grateful. Ofentse, also in her thirties, had lived in Point since her teens and had deep ties to the dense network of street children. Both brilliant and ambitious, like Zama, Ofentse had leveraged her keen analytic eye and high level of organization for jobs at neighborhood nonprofits and with other researchers who came to the neighborhood. In addition to assisting me with interviews—a skill in which she was well versed—Ofentse also boldly tackled archival research both in the comfort of the municipal archive and amidst the rubbish of an abandoned municipal building.

All of the contacts I made—both brief and enduring—were essential to my ability to conduct research in this complex, heterogenous neighborhood, pervaded by deep levels of mistrust. Everyone from the fellow passenger sitting next to me in the kombi taxi to the panhandlers outside the hospital to my closest interlocutors taught me something about the workings of the Point. Across my visits, I conducted over 220 semistructured interviews. Depending on the interlocutor, these moved between English and isiZulu (in which I am conversant) in addition to Swahili, isiXhosa, and Setswana, which Zandi or Ofentse spoke. I asked questions about household composition and needs, sources of support, where women sought resources and why, and neighborhood relationships. These questions also prompted larger conversations about gendered and generational obligations of kin, desires for their own and their children's futures, and assessments of the state of South Africa's democracy.

Interviews, while important, were only part of my methodology. Through ethnography and particularly participant observation, I was able to track how women engaged in kinshipping to garner enough resources to meet the needs of daily life. I identified a subgroup of twenty-four women as key informants, and I spent extended time with them throughout the day, both observing them in their care work at home and following them as they traversed the neighborhood, building networks of support. I observed how they negotiated with neighbors, social workers, or church employees, what kinds of claims they made, how they defined obligation or dependency, and how they worked to construct their relationship to the source. By following women throughout their networks and by triangulating that observational data with interviews, I was able to discern how support claims affected larger systems of kinship, gender relations, racial tensions, and, finally, national belonging.

Participant observation offers a particularly potent methodology for accessing data that cannot or would not be metanarrated: the rhythms of a woman's day, the ways she responds to a neighbor's request, how a room is organized and children are dressed. These quotidian minutiae are the meat of social scientific analysis. They are also the data that Point women most carefully guarded. As a young white woman asking questions about the raising of children, I was frequently interpreted to be a social worker or an aid worker. For those women who didn't outright avoid me based on my assumed identity, it was an understood practice that I would ask a series of questions about their lives and their household and they would offer well-rehearsed answers in exchange for immediate or future resources. Indeed, this is the format to which many of my first interviews conformed. To those who seemed most open, I would ask if I could come and visit them, which occasionally led to some very awkward cups of tea and clear cues that I was not welcome to linger.

One day in 2014, I had a visit scheduled with a woman, Bronwyn, who had been eyeing me cautiously for several weeks. I had visited her neighbor—with whom I later learned she had turbulent relations—as part of a home visit with the community aid worker, but I had never received more than a polite greeting from her. It was a terrible day for a visit. My baby, then eight months old, had not slept well the night before and we had no child care. I was exhausted and my postpartum back pain had flared up, making standing—the only thing that kept the baby from fussing—a challenge. With no means to contact Bronwyn, I took my son along, expecting the interaction to be short and that we would swiftly return home after another guarded tea-drinking session. Oftentimes in South Africa, children, and especially babies, are greeted with delight and showered with affection. I knew such a reaction was possible, but Bronwyn, after an initial lukewarm cuddle, quickly passed the baby back and turned to prepping the tea. The baby began to fuss and I wincingly stood to rock him. I fumbled through polite conversation, distracted by the baby, fatigue, pain, and Bronwyn's piercing gaze. She interrupted me with an abrupt, "feed the baby and give him to me." Startled, I sat down and complied. "Did you have a cesar?" Bronwyn asked pointedly, using the colloquial term for a cesarean section. "No," I replied, but Bronwyn spoke over me. "I did with my second and my back was not right for years. It still pains when the weather changes," she said, taking the baby. As she rocked, she grilled me about my diet, my sleeping, my sex life. Hours later, when the baby woke up, she sent me home with brusque instructions about what I needed to do differently. She also invited me back.

In relaying this event, I am not suggesting Bronwyn and I shared some universal experience of femininity or motherhood. At the most basic level, I had given birth in a well-funded hospital in the United States and had already seen a host of specialists about my back pain. I also had a husband with a flexible schedule who took on most of the physical labor of childcare in those early years. Bronwyn had a cesarean section in a government hospital during medication shortages and did not get the full dose of painkillers. Her husband could not take time away from his invaluable hourly job, nor did his vision of paternal responsibility include childcare. She was left to care for an infant and toddler on her own. I highlight this interaction because it marks a shift in authority that was important to my building trust in the Point. I was experiencing difficulties about which Bronwyn had more knowledge and expertise. She chose to counsel me and to embrace the relative position of power that enabled. This shift did not undo the fact that I was a white, well-resourced, American in a situation that valorized all of these attributes. However, it did recast me *as also* an inexperienced first-time mother, another identity that was intelligible to Point women, and one many found acceptable for continued engagement with me.

As such, much of my initial participant observation involved collective teasing about my incompetence and foolishness: I was useless in the kitchen, I was a walking target for neighborhood crime, and I clearly did not know what and what not to worry about with child-rearing (of great concern to them was warm clothes, lesser was what nonfood item went in babies' mouths). Many days were spent in cramped rooms, smashing the cockroaches who wandered past, leaning on the balcony railing, or sitting on the small stoop next to the street. When mocking me waned, the women would complain about the building manager, other neighbors who were safely out of earshot, men, or the politics of distribution of the various resource sites. This was often a time for me to ask clarifying questions about what I had seen when I had accompanied one woman or another to the feeding scheme, a prayer meeting, or the school aid center. Undoubtedly such questions initiated another round of taunting, but the playful banter over how to describe an event also revealed the terrain of concerns that women identified as important.

Overwhelmingly, my data are about the experiences of women. This is not the result of selection bias or a preconceived definition of caregiving responsibility but a reflection of the gendered division of care labor in my field site. My research began with questions about who was providing care for children under conditions of poverty, the resources and relationships the caregiver(s) drew on, and the terms of the exchanges in which they participated. Men figure in my data to the extent that they appear in these negotiations. In my years spent in Point, I knew two single fathers, both of whom, according to mutual friends, were terrified about the disciplinary potential of "the welfare" where they thought I worked. I never moved beyond a greeting relationship with them. Excellent scholarship has been done in the past two decades about how masculinity and particularly black masculinity is being reworked in the context of virtually nonexistent marriage and waged work (Dawson 2023; Decoteau 2013; Jewkes et al. 2012; Hunter 2004; Langa 2020; Morrell 2001; Ratele, Shefer, and Clowes 2012). Cognizant that masculinities and femininities are always reciprocally coproducing each other, my research provides another perspective about how impoverished women are raising children under conditions of racialized and gendered discrimination.

Long term, my goal is that my research will positively impact the lives of my interlocutors. In the short term, I also offered more immediate, if consistently insufficient, reciprocation for the tremendous access that my interlocutors granted me. I provided a great deal of childcare so women could run errands unconcerned that they would be disciplined by the police or "the welfare" for leaving their children unattended. I acted as a guard for laundry hung outsides on the line, for rooms that could not be locked, for a pile of foraged blankets. I hauled water for laundry or baths, held babies, washed dishes, and helped compose testimonies that might win praise from prayer group leaders. However, I believe the greatest contribution of my presence was diversion. For as much labor as Point women were constantly performing, many found their days to be quite tedious. Teasing me, teaching me, arguing with me offered a small, low-stakes distraction. Further, their irksome, daily labors were exactly what most fascinated me. I was an enthusiastic audience to their pride in a well-performed hustle and celebrated with them the windfalls of a new set of blankets from a donor. I was a researcher, utterly unexceptional in an academic landscape, overjoyed at the willingness of Point women to allow me in to their lives. At the same time, I was a white and, particularly, an American woman, desiring to listen to them, in a context where Point women had long been either intervened upon or disdainfully ignored by people who looked like me. They demanded that I be a conduit to convey their ideas to an audience far beyond the neighborhood, and they chose their words carefully and adamantly checked and rechecked that I was accurately capturing their experiences and opinions. At their request, I have retained many of their names and have indicated when I use pseudonyms.

The Past Is Present

To say that my ethnographic subjects were also historical actors is not to name something unique to Point residents, however, historicity featured in their lives in two quite specific ways. First, South Africa's sociopolitical context produced a certain orientation to the past. The recency of the democratic transition provided an important colloquial periodization that people used to evaluate the present. Most of my interlocutors were thirty years old or older, meaning that either they remembered well the apartheid period or they had parents who experienced most of the arc of apartheid rule. There was a before and after transition and people were very clear with what *should* have marked the difference. People articulated their dissatisfaction with conditions in the present via a nostalgic recalling of previous security and by grieving over a future that never came to pass.

There were also important historical continuities that people envisioned across the two regimes. As is seen throughout this book the specter of "the welfare" haunts the postapartheid moment. Many of my interlocutors had personal experience with social workers and children's homes under apartheid rule, but even in the late 1980s and early 1990s, state removals of children or the intense disciplinary work of state social workers was much less frequent than the previous two decades. Following transition, the children's homes were filled with AIDS orphans, and child protection social workers were stretched thin dealing with a much larger target population. And yet the threat of "the welfare" who would come and remove children loomed large in the imagination of Point women.

Second, and more specific to the Point, historical knowledge was both quite prized and highly elusive. Because so few people saw themselves as fully belonging in Point and kin were almost always elsewhere, the neighborhood was a space where people could write their own histories. This produced a great deal of freedom and anxiety. Historical grounding is what gave a person moral legitimacy. Thus, people were often engaged in the projects of unearthing others' histories while also obscuring their own.

Because the Point was a space of so much state intervention, there are a number of records that attest to the management of the infrastructure and population in the town clerk files in Durban's municipal archive. These mostly focus on the municipal beerhall and migrant labor barracks, Elwyn Court and other subeconomic schemes for whites, issues of vagrancy and crime on the beachfront, and shipping concerns in the railway and port. The Killie Campbell Africana Library in Durban housed the archives of early women's groups who worked in the Point, transcripts of interviews with dockworkers, and Durban newspapers. In Pretoria, I also accessed the public records of the central government to examine the management of the SMG in Durban. I traveled to Johannesburg to examine the Transnet archives for the parastatal South African Railways and Harbours.

By reading these textual sources against the grain, I could glimpse fragments of the lives of people who lived in Point, but the fuller contours of their daily challenges remained shrouded. However, under apartheid, any form of governmental aid to a child (maintenance grant, grocery voucher, housing subsidy) had to be confirmed by the Children's Court. These court records contain not only testimony by the social workers and clients, and reports by the social worker, they often included case file notes, letters to and from clients, and interviews with clients' networks. I was able to access 150 case files of families living in Point seeking governmental or private support between 1960 and 1978. To find sources for the later years, I sought other repositories. When clients had children younger than thirteen years, their case was handled by Durban Child Welfare Society. The agency provided me unlimited access to their library and archives, but a fire in 2002 and the merging of the segregated agencies of the apartheid era meant a great deal of material was lost. In one of the fortuitous moments historians dream about, through my contacts in the welfare system, I was able to gain temporary access to an abandoned government building where Durban's Department of Social Welfare files from 1978 to 1997 were lying in bureaucratic limbo. Donning masks and coveralls, Ofentse and I spent weeks combing through the thousands of files amid ashes from squatters' fires and rat droppings. In the interest of efficiency, we prioritized only the files for the white race group on the topics of maintenance grants and aid to families. While we likely could have found Point residents among the other race groups, I was cognizant that for our health and safety, it was not advisable that we remain in that building very long. In total, we photographed over 243 case files.

I coupled this written data with oral histories of current and former Point residents, some of whose families feature in the case files, and social workers who worked in the area. When possible, I would bring segments of a case file to interviews with social workers in an effort to seek the background thinking to a files' creation. I understand these interviews to be social texts as much as my archival sources. Their content and production are shaped by the social, cultural, economic, and political context. As with any text, I read them through a contextual lens and in critical comparison with my other available sources.

———

When I returned to the Point in 2019 and again in 2022, the neighborhood was at once quite different and utterly the same. A family court had been built there that allowed more women to press maintenance court or domestic violence cases without incurring transport costs. Some of the derelict buildings had been renovated, at least on their exteriors, and now sported private security guards who prevented people from squatting in the otherwise empty rooms. Blenheim, too, had been remodeled and was now reserved for housing university students. The residents I knew had scattered across the neighborhood to new rooms, in search of increasingly scarce low-cost rents. Some Point women had found jobs, especially as the babies went into school full time. Others had lost jobs or long-term boyfriends with jobs and had reconnected with estranged parents who were now pensioners. I had joyful reunions with shy toddlers who had grown into strapping teens and shared many mugs of tea with tired mothers whose worry lines were etched a little deeper. The COVID-19 pandemic lockdowns and the 2021 Durban riots had brought a new edge to old problems of relational and economic insecurity. In 2022, Point women were concerned about their eldest children who were on the cusp of graduation. Would their public schooling have been enough? Could they help support their younger siblings? They closed our visits with a new version of an old question, "Please, can you find my child a job?"

2 "YOU ARE MOTHERS OF THE NATION"

Citizenship and Social Reproduction

SOUTH AFRICA IS LIKE MANY postcolonies in that citizenship operates simultaneously as an abstract concept and an intimate, lived reality. This is due, in part, to the recency of democratic transition in 1994 and the lived memory of resistance against apartheid. Up through the early 2000s, it was not uncommon to find that in the homes of black Africans, be they small shacks or multiroomed houses, there would hang a framed photo of Nelson Mandela and the bill of rights. As smoothly as they made tea, those previously disenfranchised could discuss the new guarantees of both primary rights—freedom of expression, property ownership, movement, labor relations, and a fair trial—and secondary rights to access health care, food, water, social security, and education. Even amid these celebrations, they were also well aware of the capaciousness of citizenship as a concept and how it could be leveraged "promiscuously" toward various agendas with altogether different ends (Manicom 2005, 31). It was everyday knowledge as to how claiming citizenship could be powerfully used to contest marginalization and disenfranchisement and how citizenship also operated as a technology of subjugation to make unruly populations governable (Cruickshank 1999).[1] So it was that Point women such as Nokuthula could complain to me that citizenship was "every day being pushed down our throats" in

the democratic era and that it was incomplete and lacking. While these ambiguities in the meaning of citizenship and its political implications make
for disjointed scholarly conversations, the agendas and desires of Point
women were clear. Complete inclusion in the nation entailed secure social
reproduction that, in the absence of jobs, would be ensured by the state.

Though the democratic transition and the last twenty years of nation-
building in South Africa have reinvigorated conversations about citizenship, these present-day discussions are informed by ideas in circulation
since early colonial attempts to carve up the population into categories of
belonging. The making of political subjects was a long process that situated
people differently in regard to their class, race, or gender in addition to
other key social markers. Claims to citizenship might appear at one level
to be universal, yet the universality of language disguises highly differentiated histories of oppression and exploitation. For example, black African
women experienced very different forms of oppression on the basis of, if
they lived in town or the rural homelands, if they were part of the mission-
educated elite or working class, were married or unmarried, or a host of
other identity categories that shaped the modalities of power to which they
were subject. Here I trace the longer history of how citizenship became tied
to state-supported social reproduction in the form of labor and welfare provisions. Across the colonial and segregationist eras, there were widespread
debates over what form state support should take, often centering on state
obligations to the black African, more impoverished, majority. Rarely, if
ever, was state support tied to necessity. Instead, there was a shared understanding that the reach of state support delineated the boundaries of inclusion in the nation. In many cases, arguments about inclusion and support
hinged on arguments about who, exactly, were "mothers of the nation."[2]
This involved defining what counted as valued (support-worthy) mothering
as well as the contours of the nation itself. Categories such as race, class,
gender, geography (urban/rural), and religion became key markers for outlining who deserved support and the boundaries for national belonging.
Across the decades, successive white states developed a welfare system designed to preserve, not ameliorate, race and class inequalities. This system
upheld white children as the future of the nation and prompted decades
of activism by women who were excluded (and their white allies) who demanded the state had an obligation to support them. These measures left a

legacy of "racialized, sexual, and gendered 'unbelonging'" both in policies and in the political imaginations of people like Nokuthula (Manicom 2005, 28). These legacies impact the lives of Rosemary, Magdalena, and Rose in the 1960s and the Point women I met in 2014, as discussed in later chapters.

Carving Out Colonial Citizens and Tribal Subjects

The legal status of black African, coloured, and Indian South Africans across the past century and a half bears a direct (if complicated) lineage from the British efforts to establish a segregationist settler-colonial system in Natal during the second half of the nineteenth century.[3] The colony of Natal, which encompassed the present-day city of Durban, from its inception in 1843 developed modes of governance that were distinct from the other southern African colonies (e.g., the Cape Colony or the Orange Free State).[4] These pernicious innovations in racial rule would have lasting effects on South African statecraft. Like most British colonies, Natal putatively embraced the principle that all Crown subjects were bearers of undifferentiated rights. However, a (relative) scarcity of funds and white settlers prompted Natal's administrators to eschew the more costly assimilationist policies practiced in other colonies in favor of systems of segregation that carved up belonging according to race (Essop Sheik 2014).[5] Ideas of racial identity were not entirely static or immutable, grounded as they were in European mores of sex and gender, and were not strictly tied to phenotype (Tallie 2019). Thus racial categories could be traversed based on gender, religion, and educational status. For example, Indian traders who paid their way from Gujarat were called "Arabs" due to their dress and the Islamic adherence of their most prominent members (Vahed 1997). These higher-class, educated, property-owning Indians were considered British subjects, whereas their indentured "coolie" counterparts were not. When white settlers became threatened by the economic success of both this trading class and the growing numbers of formerly indentured, now "free" Indians who took up trades in the cities, nonindentured Indians were legally subordinated, deprived of the vote, and their immigration was curbed (Swanson 1983).[6] In the case of Africans, colonial policy paired geographic segregation—relegating them to territorially and administratively bounded native reserves—with institutional segregation that made residents of these locations subject to a separate code of law. Through this system, white settlers, and those few persons deemed assimilable, remained British citizens under colonial law whereas black Africans inexorably became tribal subjects governed by the Natal Native Code, a settler reworking of traditional tribal law.[7] The net effect of this twofold segregation was that Africans in Natal functionally became foreigners in their own land without access to land claims (Simons 1968, 21; Tallie 2019).

This early colonial marking of black Africans as tribal subjects—in contrast to British citizens—gave them a fragmentary status of belonging in the colonial body politic that would reverberate into the 1970s. This disjointed inclusion and exclusion was an early answer to an enduring settler question about how to incorporate black Africans as workers into an economy hungry for their labor, without conferring them the full rights of citizens. It would shape decades of settler state understandings about the relationship of African labor to African social reproduction and state obligations to support Africans not engaged in wage labor. In the early decades of the colony, the native reserves still supported small-scale farming and pastoralism, enabling Africans to retain relative self-sufficiency. Most black Africans were unwilling to subject themselves to the degrading conditions of waged work for Europeans except in cases where it furthered their goals of social mobility (Atkins 1993). Frustrated by Africans' resistance to conscription into wage labor, the Natal government imposed an annual hut tax that had the threefold effect of eroding the subsistence economy of the African homestead, compelling African men to sell their labor to the colony, and funding colonial bureaucracies (Guy 2014).[8]

However much colonial policy sought to pull Africans into the waged labor pool, African labor was viewed as categorically different from that of other race groups. Colonial officials saw Africans as "target" workers who labored for wages to meet a particular financial goal, such as the payment of *ilobolo* to solidify a marriage, not to meet the necessities of everyday life (Goodfellow 1939; Ochonu 2013). Instead, it was assumed that the African extended family—often idealized as steeped in a culture of communal support—provided the labor and resources for social reproduction. This logic held that care for the ill, the infirm, or those unable to work was the responsibility of the African family, not the state (Atkins 1993). Even as decades of taxation, the rise of consumer goods, and settler land dispossession eroded the economic autonomy of African homesteads, the target worker label and their status as tribal subjects rendered black Africans ineligible for the meager state poverty relief that existed at the time.

There were profoundly gendered effects to the colonial state consigning responsibility for poor relief for black Africans to the imagined African family. Colonial officials and tribal leaders both recognized the crucial role that black African women played in ensuring the viability of the African homestead. The Native Code, pointedly described by Jeff Guy as an "accommodation of patriarchs," effectively solidified male control over the labor and bodies of black African women (2018). In an infamous move that would endure to the democratic era (and for rural women, beyond), the Code deemed African women perpetual legal minors subject to the legal authority of their male husbands or relatives, and native administrators, respectively, and unable to take legal action in their own name (Guy 2018). Colonial officials argued that this organization of power was simply a reflection of already-existing tribal customs. However, there was very little precedent for this in precolonial practices (Guy 2018; Krige 1950). In one sense, this codified the obligation of patriarchs to support women and the children born to them—regardless of the woman's marital status.[9] This support obligation was less of an issue of familial duty as much as an effort to retain male authority while the rural subsistence economy still functioned. The Code outlined which patriarch received the benefit of adding to their household women and children who would likely produce more than they consumed and who would enhance the prestige of the lineage. At the same time, the Code normalized assumptions that black African women's reproductive labor was an asset to be possessed and traded among men and left black women little legal or social avenues to shape the conditions under which they did or did not raise children.[10] This authoritative indifference to the desires or burdens of African women grew increasingly pernicious as the self-sufficiency of African homestead life declined and support for unattached women and their children became scarce.

Who Are Mothers of the Nation?—The Making of the Welfare State

While the legal status of differently raced South Africans was outlined in the nineteenth century, the contours of labor regulation and the obligations of state to support children, particularly, were developed in the early decades following the creation of the Union of South Africa in 1910. These

elements that underpinned the economic dimensions of citizenship laid
the foundation for the welfare state (Seekings 2016). In various parts of the
globe, there was a changing relationship between the state and the family
(Davin 1997). In South Africa, provoked in part by a spike in infant mortality, this manifested in increasing state intervention into how mothers
raised their children (Clark 1999; Duff 2015, 2016). In a pointed invocation
of South Africa's place within the British Empire, the chief justice of the
Union declared that there was "no portion of the British Empire" in which
"the child is such a valuable asset as South Africa" and urged that collective
action was needed to protect these "trustees of civilization" so that "civilized children, white or black, [will not be] flung into the sea of barbarism
and ignorance" (quoted in Walton 2021, 66). Statements such as these were
emblematic of a turn in which parenting, particularly motherhood, became
a national—and civilizational—duty and one in which the state and private
welfare societies had a vested interest.

The 1913 Children's Protection Act put children of all races under the
protection of the state and gave the state authority to intervene in their
care through the removal of needy, neglected, and ill-treated children from
their families to state-subsidized institutions (Bhorat 1995). Though the act
was written without a mention of race, its administration largely centered
on white children (Du Toit 2018). Indeed, the relationship between race
and definitions of problematic motherhood in this period were somewhat
ambiguous, however, the maternal ideal was incontrovertibly the white
middle-class mother (Gaitskell 1983).[11] Various private child welfare societies sought to inculcate urban working-class whites, Africans, Indians, and
coloureds into an ideology of good mothercraft founded on this ideal (Badassy 2011; Duff 2016).

Mothercraft training among white women in the early twentieth century was a direct response to fears about white racial degradation and civilizational decline engendered by the growing number of poor whites in
the city (Muirhead 2012).[12] In the province of Natal, the presence of poor,
mostly Afrikaner, whites in the expanding urban slums inflamed tensions
between British whites and white Afrikaners, which were already raw from
the South African (Anglo-Boer) war of 1899 to 1902 that had consumed the
province (Badassy 2011). During this period, discourses about "race" degeneration pointed to perceived differences *between* the white ethic groups

as much as they invoked concerns about phenotypical categories of race (Klausen 1997). White Afrikaner women were far more strictly surveilled socially and politically in Natal because they were perceived by leadership as the "most disloyal" to the new British-dominated government (quoted in Badassy 2011). Such white ethnic tensions never fully abated, especially in Natal, which considered itself deeply tied to Britain. Echoes of these divides are visible in the treatment of Magdalena in the 1960s, as the next chapter covers. It was only in the mid-1920s that discourses of "race preservation" shifted from concerns about intrawhite differences to colorist distinctions, largely driven by the need to foster British and Afrikaner cohesion in order to ensure white supremacy in the face of growing African populations and militancy (Dubow 1995; Klausen 1997; Marks and Trapido 1987).

Concerns about white poverty were less of an issue of absolute economics—many impoverished whites were still better off than the majority of people in other race groups—as they were about relative racial distinction. Poor whites were problematic because they engaged in practices that did not conform to middle-class European norms of respectability, such as: consuming alcohol to excess; irregular religious observance; an ambivalence to labor; untidiness of person and household; illegitimacy; prostitution; theft; and, most egregious, socializing with persons of other race groups (Klausen 1997). With this habitus, poor whites were seen as acting in a manner associated with black Africans. This troubled the conflation of whiteness with higher levels of civilization on which much of the racial hierarchy was premised. Indeed, as one contemporary writer put it, the definition of a poor white was "someone of European extraction who cannot support himself according to a European standard of civilization [sic], who cannot keep clear the line of demarcation between black and white" (quoted in Muirhead 2012). Importantly, too, under the eugenic logic of the day, the degradation of poor whites was inheritable, and the medical community called on national leaders to intervene into white motherhood "for the good of the nation" to halt white racial devolution (Klausen 1997; Lange 2003). Without racial distinction, fears of *swartgevaar*, or the perceived threat of black Africans to white dominance, loomed large.[13]

The mass influx of both poor black Africans and poor whites into the cities—driven by industrialization and rural impoverishment—heightened segregationist anxieties and ignited public debates about what institutions were responsible for ensuring proper motherhood (Klausen 1997; Lange 2003). A widespread shortage of housing in the cities meant that newcomers were often living in multiracial groups wherever accommodation could be found. In Durban, this often involved people of all races sleeping in the crowded alleyways of Point or erecting makeshift shelters in gardens or beachside dunes. Alongside very material concerns about waste removal and infectious disease transmission, urban slums induced an ideological "sanitation syndrome" among white urban planners, a moral panic that racial intermixing would cause widespread social illness and white racial degradation (Swanson 1977).[14] In addition to undermining assumed racial purity, there was also the nightmare that a political union that crossed racial lines could upend the white ruling class (Breckenridge 2007; Freund 1988). The nascent welfare intervention overwhelmingly targeted the white children who were seen to be threatened by this racial intermixing. White mothers were trained in better disciplinary measures so their daughters would not end up like one white Point teenager, Bertha Clarisse, who had a mixed-race child with Jetoo, an Indian domestic laborer who worked for her family (Badassy 2011).

While in most other places in the Union, mothercraft overwhelmingly focused on training white mothers, in Natal there were important exceptions. On the one hand there were organizations like the Helping Hand for Native Girls and the Mothercraft League who directly targeted black African women (Badassy 2011; Burns 1995). The Mothercraft League described themselves as "a league of South African women of all colours, who wish to serve Christ by the promotion of Christian training in the home and Christian social services for Natives in towns" (Cobley 1997, 85). Yet, their primary concerns were policing the conduct of coloured and black African women whose care was thought to have a "damaging influence" on white children's health and welfare (Chisholm 1990; Stoler 2001). The general secretary of Natal's Mothercraft League wrote a letter expressing concern that the "native girls" who "fall into sin" on their arrival in town pose "a serious menace to the whole community and especially to the little children in the charge of such girls" (quoted in Badassy 2011). At the same time, black African women activists in Durban were also able to seize on this widespread concern about mothercraft to successfully convince the municipal government to provide a medical clinic for black African women and children.

Isabel Sililo, one founder of the Durban Bantu Women's Society in 1930 (Bantu referring to the black Africans), argued that Durban was shamefully behind "practically all other large centres and even mission stations" because it lacked such a "Child Welfare and Maternity Clinic' where black African women could receive "advice about child rearing" (quoted in Du Toit 2014).[15] The clinic was built in the city center, just west of the Point.

The presence of black Africans in the city was seen as posing another key threat to white domination because unskilled white farmers could not compete with them for jobs. This made livelihoods that would lift poor whites out of destitution hard to achieve. Additionally, there was a growing number of mission-educated black Africans, like Isabel Sililo and her husband, in town who had converted to Christianity and achieved some economic success. These *amakholwa* (believers), as they came to be called, embodied ideals of European middle-class respectability far more than their poor white counterparts, though their elite status was deeply relative as low wages, exclusionary property laws, and color-bar legislation made their economic position quite tenuous (Seekings 2007). Caught between the promise of incorporation into white society and their ties to an otherwise reviled black culture, *amakholwa* forged their own unique identity and used imperial technologies—for example, petitions, letters, books, and newspapers—to resist subjugation and claim a place in the nation (Healy-Clancy 2012; Mokoena 2011). The violent class and racial conflicts that erupted in the early 1920s also inflamed white anxieties and hardened the idea that protecting white prosperity required constraining black African physical and economic mobility. In response, white leadership proposed a twofold segregationist solution to (1) uplift poor whites through welfare-based social rehabilitation and job protection and (2) to further curtail and reverse black African class mobility by slashing black wages and restricting black residence in towns. Welfare policy was central to this project.

Civilized Labor; Civilized Life

In the decades when the foundation for South Africa's welfare state were being laid, poverty was widespread and cross-racial. However, since these early days, state aid has rarely if ever been based on economic need. During white minority rule, white leadership used earlier colonial discourses to divide the population into civilized and uncivilized persons, categories linked to the deservingness for state support. The state was only obligated to support the livelihoods and welfare of civilized citizens. These categories of civilized and uncivilized—widely used in various settler colonies—only partially mapped on to race in South Africa, the taxonomies of which were constantly in flux. It was an ambiguous discourse that was subject to different interpretations and often crosscut by geography, religion, and the vagaries of white supremacist politics. For example, in a government circular in 1924, Prime Minister Hertzog defined civilized as "persons, whose standard of living conforms to the standard of living generally recognized as tolerable from the usual European standpoint" (Prime Minister's Circular no. 5, 1924, quoted in Seekings 2007, 382). At times this category included coloured persons and was likely used to appeal to both white and coloured voters, which Hertzog heavily courted (Seekings 2007). In contrast, uncivilized labor referred to "the labour rendered by persons whose aim is restricted to the bare requirements of the necessities of life as understood among barbarous and undeveloped peoples" (Seekings 2007). Largely, uncivilized labor referred to black Africans, harkening back to the colonial definition of Africans as "target" workers. However, better-paid, urban black Africans, especially those who had converted to Christianity, at times could argue that because they were "detribalized," and had adopted a "European standard of life," they were deserving of support (Du Toit 2018). Key here is the idea that "people accustomed to modern lifestyles and consumption patterns" deserved greater social protection to uphold their standard of living—and the moral status it was thought to reflect—and to preserve a clear distinction between the civilized and uncivilized (Van der Berg 1997, 485). Conversely, black African poverty was both diminished and naturalized—Africans were only seen to require the bare necessities of life and nothing more—thereby minimizing state obligation to them.

Making civilized citizens and uncivilized others was a deeply intertwined process. Welfare and labor policies designed to secure a civilized standard of living for white (and occasionally coloured) people did so through the systematic disadvantaging and exclusion of those black Africans deemed uncivilized. It also, once again, relied on the uncompensated labor of black African women in the rural areas. Job reservation and wage-setting legislation sought to substitute black African labor with white workers paid at inflated wages that enabled civilized lifestyles that included large houses with gardens and the employment of black African domestic labor (Report of the Economic and Wage Commission, 1925, quoted in Seekings 2007). Definitions of a civilized standard of living were often tied to the metropole, and, notably, white South African artisans earned significantly *higher* wages than their counterparts in Britain between 1910 and 1930 (Seekings 2016). This was made economically possible by deflating wage levels of black African workers to below poverty levels (at times one fifth that of white workers) (Seekings 2016). Deplorably low wages for black Africans were justified using the logic that as uncivilized laborers, they simply required less. Further, in contrast to white workers, black African wages were not intended to support a family. Even amid worsening poverty and malnutrition in the homelands, white leadership maintained that "broadly speaking, there is no starvation because each man will share his food with others," making state support of black African social reproduction unnecessary (Legassick 1974; Wolpe 1972).[16]

Excluding black Africans from state social protection required furthering the segregationist project begun in the nineteenth century. For the next sixty years, until the 1986 repeal of the influx control laws that regulated black African residence in cities, the lives of black South Africans were profoundly shaped by the terms under which they could legally enter or reside in urban areas and the social and economic benefits that came with it. The 1923 Native Urban Areas Act put into law the "Stallard Principle" that municipal enfranchisement could be denied to urban black Africans if their right to residence in municipalities was withdrawn. This meant that black Africans were only permitted to enter the cities "to minister to the needs of the white man and should depart therefrom [to return to the 'Reserves'] when he ceases so to minister" (Transvaal Provincial Administration [TPA] 1922).[17] African men's access to cities became regulated by passes linked their employment status, and black residence in cities was segregated to designated locations, often on the outskirts of the city, and with poor housing stock and little infrastructure. The 1913 Land Act had stripped black African men of any right to property that might have enabled their claim to the "ordinary economic rights under common law" and the landed forms of political legitimacy it conferred (Chanock 2001, 361). In Durban this meant that black Africans frequently rented from Indians, who could still own property, an arrangement that often inflamed interracial tensions.[18]

African exclusion was further hardened when the 1927 Native Administration Act made the "Natal Approach" of tribal law—meaning the use of the Native Code—the basis for the oversight of all black Africans, nationwide. The effect was, in the words of one legal scholar, to "place Africans beyond the 'rule of law' in the constitutional sense . . . from which the establishment of separate courts, and the acceptance, Union wide, of separate private law followed" (Chanock 2001, 281).

Black African Urbanization

The city of Durban was a national leader in addressing the colonial quandary of how to manage black African migration to cities in ways that ensured a readily available supply of cheap African labor but did not threaten whites' desired standard of living. The port and the railway, large employers that were central to Durban and South Africa's economy, were key sites where these demands were negotiated. As early as 1901, Point's workers' strikes disrupted the shipping industry, winning wage increases and terrifying white capital (La Hausse 1992, 1997). Efforts to regulate the thousands of black African laborers who kept Point industries running served to elaborate the urban forms of South Africa's racial capitalism. Much of this regulation hinged on attempts to constrain black African family life (and by extension black women) to the countryside, and retain black male labor in a disciplined but impermanent form. Durban's answer was the infamous Durban system, which prohibited black African's production and consumption of alcohol outside of municipally owned beerhalls—one of the first of which was built in Point—and to pay for the regulation of African life with beerhall profits (La Hausse 1984). Though the Durban system was implemented across South Africa, Durban was the only city in South Africa with a self-supporting Native Revenue Account.

Beer and beer brewing were the grounds around which a host of actors debated normative definitions of the black African family, black motherhood, and the position and behavior of black women in an urban environment (Minkley 1996). In brief, a fermented sorghum beer, also called *utshwala*, has long been a key part of black African sociality (Mager 2010). Brewed by women, it is consumed at ritual events and informal social gatherings and is used in exchanges of labor and resources to solidify relationships (Crush and Ambler 1992; La Hausse 1988). In the face of an increasingly impoverished countryside and limited access to urban employment, black African women, frequently single or "unattached" mothers, found ways to ensure social reproduction and regenerate kin ties by providing beer and beer-drinking spaces to migrant laboring men in the city. The success of this economy ran counter to the colonial agenda in numerous ways. At one level, the services that brewers provided, grounded in leisure and pleasure beyond the confines of work, undermined attempts to discipline and control black male labor (Sadler 2002). In 1908 there was a flourishing shebeen (informal bar in a home) in the Point run by thirteen women and twenty men that was known to have riotous music, dancing, and occasional brawls—activities that undoubtedly resulted in missed work time (La Hausse 1984).[19] At another level, the presence of financially independent black African women in the city rankled groups from rural African patriarchs who worried about losing control over "runaway" women to white urban managers who sought to manage "fears of prostitution and miscegenation, fears of the assertion of an independent black female desire and fears of 'moral decay'" (Minkley 1996, 138). Notably, among increasingly stringent laws, women's brewing was never effectively halted and continued to be an important strategy by which black African women carved out viable lives for themselves (Mager 2010; Minkley 1996).

Municipal beerhalls themselves became sites for resistance to the harm the Durban system posed to black family life, most pointedly in the riots of 1929 and 1959.[20] Women brewers, African Christian elite, and union leaders argued in different ways that beerhalls siphoned men's meager wages away from women and families—a 1928 study estimated that African men spent a week's wages every month on municipal beer—and that the system undermined women's abilities to participate in (and profit from) traditional practices that knit together African social worlds (La Hausse 1984; Minkley 1996; Sadler 2002).[21] Further, although proceeds from the beerhalls funded Durban's Native Revenue Account, almost none of that money went to support impoverished African families.

Growing levels of poverty following World War I, and the Great Depression impelled a push for the state to take a more active role in protecting child well-being (Muirhead 2012; Posel 2005). Care for impoverished children had for decades been the purview of voluntary child welfare societies dominated by white women (Muirhead 2012). Though the majority of these societies targeted poor whites, by the late 1920s, there was a broadening of concern, explicitly framed around the universal rights of children "irrespective of race, class, politics, or creed" (quoted in Du Toit 2014). The legislation that created the Department of Social Welfare and Pensions in 1937 and a new Children's Act in the same year made no explicit mention of race, leaving it ambiguous (at least on paper) as to how social protection and particularly maintenance grants should be allocated.[22] This was a welfare state that accepted core responsibilities for providing health care, education, old age pensions, and livelihood support for the "social community" in its ambit. Yet the simultaneous creation of a state welfare infrastructure and a barrage of segregationist legislation left it up for debate as to what institutions were obligated to address poverty, for whom, and how.

The relative ambiguity of the new legislation offered a window for a variety of actors to help define the "social community" for which the welfare state was responsible, and women of all race groups were prominent participants. Stallardists argued that black Africans should be viewed as "temporary sojourners" in the city "whose entitlements to civic goods and services were directly determined by the terms and extent of their labour" (Posel 2005). Senior bureaucrats of the departments of Native Affairs and Social Welfare argued that rural African children should be excluded from provisions of the Children's Protection Act of 1937 because it undermined Native law. They contended that state support would cause the "head of Kraal" (meaning the male head of household) to shirk his "natural duty" to support minor children (quoted in Du Toit 2018). Rather, they suggested that the state should first "repatriate" impoverished African children living in the city to "relatives living in rural areas" and only secondly offer minimal support so as not to encourage black African women to "flock" to cities (quoted in Du Toit 2018). In contrast, a small group of liberal whites contended that some black Africans were permanent urban residents to whom the state held a notably paternalistic obligation of trusteeship to assist because they had experienced tribal breakdown (Posel 2005; Du Toit 2014, 2018). Yet, in a perverse racist twist on a need-based argument for support, officials in the Native Affairs Department gave a very different rationale for exclusion, namely, that poverty among black African families was so pervasive that the country simply could not afford to give child grants to all who needed them (Du Toit 2018).

Members of the urban, mission-educated African *amakholwa* were also vocal participants in these debates. In Durban, much of the discussion centered on how to handle a growing number of homeless African children in the Point and the city center. In the face of discourse that framed the problem of these "juvenile delinquents" as the fault of a lack of parental control and supervision from the African community, black African women lay the blame and the responsibility for African youth homelessness squarely at the feet of white leadership. The Durban Bantu Women's Society issued a memorandum, covered extensively by the newspaper the *Natal Mercury*, arguing that disruption to the African family structure was a result of the inability of the municipality to provide for "normal family life for Natives." This was evidenced by a severe lack of housing for black African families and the exorbitant rents the municipality charged for them coupled with "the low wages paid to the Natives," which forced both wives and husbands to find extra employment. The society called for the inclusion of Africans into state social welfare policy on the basis that it was the "duty of government" to provide for children's education, support "indigent Natives who are too old or infirm to work," and provide the unemployed "relief works, *as it does for the other sections of the community*" [emphasis added] (quoted in Du Toit 2014.) In her activism, Sililo argued that "Bantu boys and girls belong to South Africa and can claim no other country" and were "therefore future citizens that will help to build or mar the progressive future" and should be supported as such (quoted in Du Toit 2014). Though they didn't explicitly use the language of "mothers of the nation," African women's welfare societies "articulated explicitly African nationalist ideas" that were grounded in a desire to "uplift the African race" (Du Toit 2018, 979; Healy-Clancy 2012). For both black and white women, mothering was not solely about social reproduction but was tied to a larger obligation to uphold their respective races and, ultimately, to claim their place in the nation.

Alongside their claims that the government was responsible for ameliorating the issue of African youth homelessness, members of the Durban Bantu Women's Society and the Daughters of Africa (DOA) formed the Durban Bantu Child Welfare Society (DBCWS) to more directly assist urban African families struggling with poverty. Their work had important effects at both the local and national level. Locally, they were able to leverage the nonracial wording of the 1913 Children's Act (and its 1921 amendment) to extract from the state, child maintenance grants (also called mothers pensions) for African women. When the (comparatively small) increase in grants to African women prompted the Department of Social Welfare to restrict African access to grants, the women of the DBCWS and DOA fervently protested the exclusion. Isabel Sililo, founding member of both organizations, called out the deep contradictions of a national policy that supposedly sought to "rehabilitate the family" by helping "the mother to keep her children together" but denied maintenance support to the African families most in need (Sililo in 1939 DBCWS annual report quoted in Du Toit 2018). With support from the South African National Council of Child Welfare, Johannesburg's Joint Council of Europeans and Africans, and the South African Institute of Race Relations, Isabel Sililo and the women of the DBCWS and DOA prompted the Department of Social Welfare to reinstate cash grants for African children, with the caveat that they must be "urban" (Du Toit 2018). In 1940, for the first time, urban Africans were formally included in the racially tiered child-maintenance grant system, marking a critical victory for welfare reformers seeking racial inclusion.

The success of extracting state support for black urban families, while critical, also reinscribed the legislative distinction between rural Africans as tribal subjects and urban Africans as civil subjects and aspiring citizens.[23] Urban African's claims to inclusion were grounded in membership in the category of "civilised" persons—"whether the families had become detribalised and whether they had adopted European standards of living" (quoted in Du Toit 2018, 981).[24] Proving this status required documenting geographic status: "where children were born . . . chiefly allegiance . . . pass law exemptions," religious and cultural adherence: whether "parents married according to Civic, Christian or Native rites . . . details of lobola payments," and norms of middle-class respectability such as father's profession and housing status (quoted in Du Toit 2018:981). Food also became a key marker of status. For example, some urban Africans argued that taking tea without sugar or eating mielie meal—a staple of the black African diet—without relish was "living below an acceptable level of consumption" (Wylie 2001, 109). Debates over who could claim the status of "civilized" and the benefits it might confer were bound up with larger contestations over respectability politics particularly around black African womanhood (Higginbotham 1994; Thomas 2006). As Thomas aptly notes, "racial respectability refers to

people's desires and efforts to claim positive recognition in contexts powerfully structured by racism" (Thomas 2006, 98). Appearances mattered,
but their meaning was fluid. Some women, overwhelmingly led by the
amakholwa elite, encouraged an embrace of a Victorian-inflected version
of motherhood closely associated with middle-class whiteness. Performing
this form of motherhood was seen as an integral part of their Christian
conversion and progress toward a modern condition (Gaitskell 1983; Hall
1979). Mission schools, church groups, and purity leagues trained women in
proper childcare practices, housework, and sexual modesty (Marks 1991).[25]
However, this domestic ideology was also fraught with contradictions for
black African women. Housework training was as much about capacitating
future housewives as it was about creating skilled domestic servants for
white houses. Further, as activists and, at times, social workers noted, life
under racial rule made many Victorian ideals impossible to meet. Black Africans' low wages meant that "most African women could not afford to be
full-time housewives and mothers, no matter how solid their marriage or
devout their faith" (Gaitskell 1983, 252). Temperance laws made navigating
this contradiction all the more complicated for Christian women because
beer brewing was one of the most lucrative types of work black African
women could perform, and it combined well with childcare and housework. For many black African women activists, claims to the right to live in
families unbroken by migrant labor and to care full-time for their children
became a foundation for struggle against a state that made such things impossible—a theme we see reverberating in women's concerns in 2014.

Also during this period, white middle-class Afrikaans men and women
were constructing a notion of Afrikaner nationalist culture that explicitly
positioned Afrikaans women as mothers of the nation, or *volksmoeders*
(Du Toit 1996).[26] The *volksmoeder* discourse responded to anxieties about
changing gender roles and the moral perils of modernity as well as the dual
fear that poor, Afrikaans-speaking whites would produce an inferior stock
of children and could forget their race-consciousness and consort with
those of other races (Du Toit 2003). Female Afrikaner nationalists espoused
that women in their mothering held a moral duty to their *volk* (people in
the nationalist sense). "Mothers, you see what lies on our shoulders. The
future not only of our children, but also of our country, people and church"
(quoted in Du Toit 2003, 164). For it was mothers who had the responsi-

bility to "teach children their first prayers in the mother tongue" and instill "love for church, language and religion" (quoted in Du Toit 2003, 164). While not universal or static, the *volksmoeder* ideal celebrated maternal piety and female passivity, obedience to men, in addition to economic self-reliance (Brink 1990). Women's child-rearing was a holy duty, and women were framed as custodians of their children's souls. Domestic labors were glorified as the health of the home was linked to the health of the [white] nation. Through women's welfare societies like the Afrikaanse Christelike Vroue Vereniging (ACVV), white middle-class volunteers and quasi social workers provided girls from poor families a conservative sex education and training to be competent "housemothers" (Du Toit 2003). These efforts were an attempt to stave off the dangers of girls choosing factory work (seen as public and less respectable) over domestic service and urban girls' tendency to engage in sexually "amoral behavior" such as premarital or cross-racial sex that ultimately "made them unsuitable for motherhood" (Du Toit 1996, 278). Private welfare societies and later state-supported social workers sought to convert *armmoeders* (poor white mothers) into *volksmoeders* through the mechanism of welfare (Du Toit 1996). This intervention was envisioned as a nation-building project, as political groups argued, "We need good citizens; and without healthy, courageous mothers it is impossible to get good citizens" (Du Toit 1992). Reforming white motherhood was a nationalist endeavor.

It was in this period that welfare was solidified as a right to which some groups demanded inclusion and as a form of regulation that others attempted to skirt. During and following World War II, a radical new concept of citizenship took form, inspired by the 1942 Beveridge Report, in which the state's role was to guarantee certain "rights," including social entitlements, to all people, regardless of their level of civilization (Dubow and Jeeves 2005). Indeed, in their drafting of "The Atlantic Charter from the African's Point of View," in 1943, black African political elites argued that their "claim to full citizenship" entailed the "recognition of the sanctity or inviolability of the home as a right of every family" and inclusion in the welfare system "on an equal basis with Europeans" (African National Congress 1943; Seekings 2000). In the years leading up to the 1948 National Party win, South Africans of all races were provided noncontributory old-age pension, invalidity pensions, and unemployment insurance (Seekings

2007). In 1947, all race groups except black Africans were offered family allowances designed to compensate for the insufficiency of wages to meet the needs of raising families (Patterson 1953, 116).[27] The inclusion brought about by these policies was tempered by the continued differentiation of payment amounts by perceived civilizational need.[28] Yet, they were deeply symbolic of state recognition in the social community; as one parliamentarian noted, "the amounts involved are not large, but they have a greater value than mere money, in that they are a recognition of the citizenship of the African, bringing with it the right to share in the General Revenue of the Union, for his uplift and his old age" (cited in Posel 2005, 80). Such statements reflect an understanding shared by both legislators and activists about the link between state support for social reproduction and feelings of national belonging. From roughly 1940 to 1960—the last years of segregation and the first decade of apartheid rule—urban white, coloured, and black African women were part of a racially stratified project of social assistance that would involve a diverse group of white magistrates, black and white volunteers from child-welfare societies, and the first generations of formally trained black and white social workers, all of whose political sympathies did not map cleanly onto race or class.

The enhanced notion of state responsibility was also linked to the expansion of state power and regulation of the family to ensure a normative familial life and preserve the social order (Posel 2005). In keeping with the larger European political shift of governance *of* the family to governance *through* the family, mothers in particular became "an agent for transmitting the norms of the state into the private sphere" (Teppo 2004, 37). At the most basic level, families were expected to be economically self-sufficient and not become a "parasite to society." When families failed to meet this expectation—as all poor families did—they would be subject to surveillance and policing by a newly professionalized class of state agents: social workers (Donzelot 1979). Social workers ensured that children's upbringing was in accordance with "modern" standards and addressed overriding concerns with maternal inadequacy through education and discipline. They administered a variety of poverty relief cum social engineering programs—overwhelmingly targeted at white women—such as free meals for expectant mothers, summertime baby camps, dental clinics, and mothercraft training (Berger 1983). A key example is the response to mothers engaged in the sexual economy, as most single mothers were presumed to be. White women and their progeny were lifted out of poverty through direct welfare relief, labor laws that reserved well-paying jobs for whites, and massive investment in white education secured their dominance in the labor market for decades (Freed 1949). A critical source of aid was the State Maintenance Grants (SMG) designed to help single mothers raising children without seeking employment outside of the home and to keep their children from being removed to state institutions. The grants were subject to strict and often moralized regulation by social workers seeking to ensure that monies were spent on child-rearing necessities rather than so-called luxury goods (Muirhead 2012).[29] Though the grants were ostensibly available to low-income women of all races, access was challenging and payments were highly unequal (Clark 1999). For example, in 1948 the maximum monthly payment for the maintenance grants was £23L for whites, £11,10s for coloureds, £9L for Indians, and £4L for black Africans (Patterson 1953, 119). Oftentimes Indian and coloured single mothers, who were labeled as prostitutes regardless of their practices, were denied grants and instead given counseling in moral reform. Black African mothers who were found to be in towns without husbands or formal jobs were frequently sent to the rural areas to be supported and reformed by their families.

Apartheid—"The Most Extensive Welfare System in Africa"

The elaboration of apartheid following the 1948 election of the National Party (NP) included both continuities and ruptures from the welfarist thinking of previous decades. As Iliffe suggests, in the following decades, the NP created "the most extensive welfare system in Africa" (1987, 142). Apartheid involved a refashioning of state reach and state obligation that "drew directly on a welfarist logic of regulation—even if for different political and ideological ends" (Posel 2005, 64). Unlike welfare states of the North putatively premised on some form of equality, the basis of the apartheid welfare system was to support and maintain racial hierarchy. The notion of cross-racial entitlement to state support developed earlier was swiftly discarded. Across the decades, welfare provisions for whites became more expansive and redistributive whereas those for other racial groups were contracted or phased out.[30] State leaders argued that eligibility for support should not be extended to black Africans lest the black African majority become a burden on a white minority-led state (Sagner 2000). The Population Registration Act of 1950 classified the population into four racial categories, which determined not only differentiated access to voting rights but also to welfare benefits.[31] In 1949, the Department of Social Welfare spent the overwhelming majority of its budget on social assistance to whites who comprised 20 percent of the population.[32] Whites had access to benefits such as free public education and public health care, subsidized housing, rent control, social grants, and community services such as luncheon clubs for the elderly, residential care, and rehabilitative social services (Patel 2011). In the city of Durban, inequality was felt all the more starkly because of the municipal government's dogged refusal to spend more than what the beerhalls generated on services for Africans. Within the voluntary organizations that provided direct welfare services (75 percent of which catered to whites only) the national government mandated differences in salary, allocations of equipment and transport, and even diets for residents in welfare institutions on the basis of racial category. As one coloured social worker working in the Durban Child Welfare Society in the 1960s bitterly joked, "We worked in the same building doing the same things, but every last thing was separated. Even their [the white employees'] toilet paper was softer." Though social spending on other racial groups increased gradually over time—such as through the building of townships in the late 1950s and early 1960s—the motivation was frequently less to include Indians, coloureds and black Africans into the social citizenry and more an effort to exert control or mitigate potential conflict (Sagner 2000).

Alongside the increasing elaboration of segregationist legislation, the period between 1945 and 1960 was a time of fervent political action. Durban saw the 1946 march against the Ghetto Act, the 1949 race riots that among other things centered on claims to land in Cato Manor, 1952 Defiance Campaign, the 1959 beerhall protests and dockworkers slowdown, and the 1960 riots in Cato Manor, to name a few. While all of these involved protest over state control and often included demands for state support, of particular note here are women's antipass protests across the 1950s and their contribution the 1955 Freedom Charter, which envisioned rights to social and economic support for all races. As laws controlling the movement of black African women into the cities tightened, cross-racial groups of women heightened their activist response, often framing the problem of passes in terms of their harmful effects on children and families by regulating women as mothers (Healy-Clancy 2012; Gaitskell and Unterhalter 1989; Gasa 2007; Wells 1993; Magubane 2010; Walker 1991). At a fiery speech at a 1953 protest, Dora Tamana, ANC Women's League member and founding member of the Federation of South African Women (FEDSAW) said, "We [African] women will never carry these passes . . . We have seen unemployment, lack of accommodation and families broken because of passes. We have seen it with our men. Who will look after our children when we go to jail for . . . not having a pass?" ("History" n.d.). A year later, Tamana and others would form FEDSAW, a national cross-racial women's organization, and establish the Women's Charter. When the Congress Alliance's Congress of the People issued its Freedom Charter in 1955, it was inspired by the Women's Charter, including the section "What Women Demand" that FEDSAW contributed. These demands included "four months of paid maternity leave, antenatal and child care, nursery schools, and contraceptive access" in addition to rights for children's health and education, and rights to housing, infrastructure, and food "FOR ALL PEOPLE OF ALL RACES" (Healy-Clancy 2017, 857). As Shireen Hassim has noted, FEDSAW's "concrete demands went beyond a general political call for the extension of political citizenship and reflected the importance placed by women on the creation of an inclusive welfare state" (Hassim 2005, 626). However, until 1994, black African, Indian, and coloured women would remain largely excluded from state support except for areas where state support furthered the apartheid project, such as with the expansion of townships.

Apartheid policy expanded the welfare state through massive investment in racially segregated townships for Indians, coloureds, and black Africans. This was an effort to inexpensively address the massive urban housing shortage while also physically controlling an increasingly restless populations (Bozzoli 1991). One of the primary technologies of control was the township house, allocated only to married men, as a means of disciplining the workforce and refocusing labor to support a nuclear family (Hunter 2010). Among black Africans, responses to the relocation to township houses was uneven. Most often well-employed men accepted the transition because it gave them an opportunity to claim section 10 rights—the right to permanent residence in the city and the opportunity to apply for a (rental) house and other social welfare supports.[33] Men who relied more on the shantytown community for their trade were less enthusiastic because it cut them off from important economic opportunities. Black African women, whose primary economic activities were tied to an illegal economy, suffered the transitions the most because they lost not only their livelihoods but also their tenuous hold on urban residence, as they could not claim a house without attachment to a working man (Sambureni 1997).

The differing effects of the township relocation reflects the divergent effects of the relative prosperity of the 1950s and 1960s. Despite growth in employment opportunities and consumer options, the benefits were distributed unequally. The distribution was hardened by years of unequal investment in education and the legal prohibition of particularly black Africans from urban centers: "For people with the skills, qualifications, racial classification, or pass law status to be able to secure employment in the expanding, better-paying classes, the period was one of rising prosperity. For people competing for the stagnant number of unskilled jobs, the period was one of continuing or deepening hardship" (Nattrass and Seekings 2010, 40). A small group of black Africans did experience class mobility. They were the children of the urban black Christian elite whose partial claim to the city had been recognized and who had received a mission education. This group was able to step into the newer, better-paying jobs and take advantage of new consumption opportunities (Thomas 2019). Even this relatively privileged group was not protected from the harsh effects of racist rule. The 1952 Native Law Amendment Act required every African woman, man, and child who stayed in the city over seventy-two hours to carry a pass, and black African homes were subject to frequent police raids in search of pass violators. In an oral history interview about black urban life in the 1950s, Louisa Metwana reported,

> The raids create anxiety in many households and children are not spared from witnessing ill treatment of their parents. They see the powerlessness of their fathers and the indignities they suffer as a result of the inspection of men's income. Within a few minutes of inspection, a family could be literally ejected into the streets should the man's income be deemed not high enough to cover the rent . . . this can happen in the dead of the night, in the early hours of the morning . . . while it is still dark outside, the family is thrown out, their belongings scattered in the street. (Quoted in Gasa 2007)

For most black Africans, this was a period of deepening poverty and contracting state support, and the majority of households survived on incomes
well below subsistence levels.[34] Life in the rural reserves had grown increasingly impoverished, leading to a large growth in the urban black African
population from about 2.2 million in 1951 to 5.6 million by 1980, many of
whom were women (Simkins quoted in Nattrass and Seekings 2010, 42).
This growth only exacerbated the pervasive lack of low-skilled jobs and inexpensive housing, little improved by the massive construction of houses
in the race-segregated townships. Further, single motherhood was becoming increasingly more common for black African women, but section 10
rules made it difficult for unmarried black mothers like Grace, whose case
is discussed in the next chapter, to access such housing (Watts and Lamond
1966). Wait-lists for housing in the townships were long, and housing was
only available through a [male] spouse or through a job, which, in turn,
often precluded care for a child. Some women entered informal "kipita"
(*ukukipita* means "to keep" in isiZulu) marriages in town with migrating
men who were supporting a primary family in the reserves. While the
terms of these marriages differed by couple—who paid for rent or food,
duration of relationship, and such—women frequently remained responsible for the children's needs such as clothing and school fees. They often
faced childcare challenges because there were fewer extended kin networks
in the townships to help, and, frequently, neighbors charged high rates for
child-minding (Watts and Lamond 1966). In the event that the relationship
with the man ended, they often could not call on his family for help with
the children. Though women in kipita marriages were often solely responsible for supporting children they were not eligible for a State Maintenance
Grant because of the peculiarities of their marital status.[35] For those women
who did manage to secure a grant, the payments were very low relative to
other race groups, at levels consistently below the most conservative poverty line.[36] As one researcher pointedly stated:

> in the case of Bantu families where the mother has to support her children
> on the basis of maintenance grant figures alone . . . her children would be
> ill or dead within a few months—the gap is too wide for even the most
> intelligent and the most competent housekeeper to even have the most
> remote chance of coping. (Watts and Lamond 1966, 123)

The impact of poverty took a particularly heavy toll on black African children who were found to have numerous poverty-related health issues such as malnutrition and gastroenteritis. Further, as apartheid became more elaborated, many of the meager welfare services to black Africans were cut: black Africans were removed from eligibility for free milk in 1951, the 1953 Bantu Education Act brought an end to school feeding schemes, and by 1960 all the Durban nursery schools had shut down due to lack of funding. In a particularly cruel twist of fate, the beerhall protests in the early 1960s decreased the income to Durban's native revenue account, resulting in deep cuts to welfare expenditures for black Africans in 1961 and 1962 (Watts and Lamond 1966). In a 1966 survey of children living in the black African township of KwaMashu outside of Durban, 90 percent were found to be living in poverty (Watts and Lamond 1966). Various groups such as the Durban Municipal Welfare Clinics, Durban Bantu Child Welfare Creches, Kupugani, Our Daily Bread, the KwaMashu Community Health Centre, and Cato Manor Welfare Huts provided a patchy network of aid that attempted to mitigate poverty's harsh effects.

Indian and coloured communities also experienced the prosperity of this period unevenly. On the one hand, they enjoyed improved access to public education at the secondary and tertiary levels. The expansion of white-collar employment in general created opportunities for Indian and coloured workers to move into better-paying jobs, especially in industries seeking to divide up higher-paid jobs reserved for whites into lower-wage jobs for Indians and coloureds (Davies 1979). These economic shifts led to large gains in health, particularly children's health (Eberstadt 1995). However, this mobility was crosscut by wage discrimination and the massive disruption to wealth accumulation created by the forced removals to newly constructed townships as a result of the Group Areas Act. In terms of governmental support, from the 1960s onward, the largest number of beneficiaries of State Maintenance Grants were in the coloured and Indian race groups whose populations were larger than the white population and who had greater proportion of families living in poverty, though the grant amounts they received were far less than their white counterparts. Indian and coloured communities responded to the dramatically smaller scale of national welfare spending through activism via community and religious-based private welfare organizations, some of which became the social face

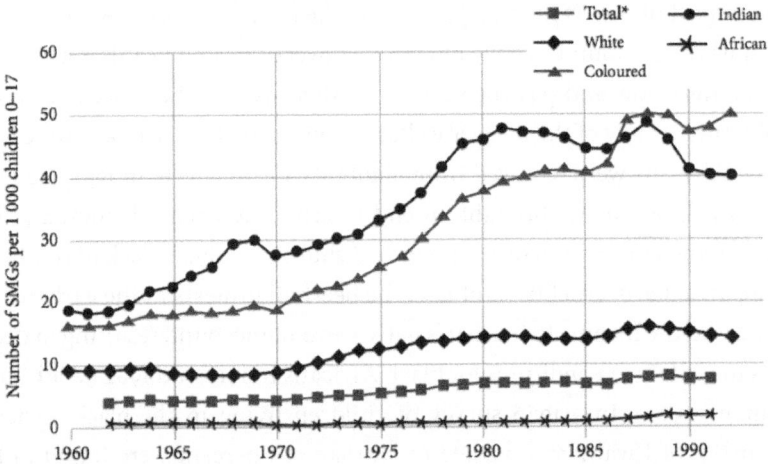

Source: RSA (1996: 11), based on figures supplied by Servaas van der Berg
Note: * The average rate for the whole population, all races included.

FIGURE 2.1   Number of Maintenance Grants per thousand children aged zero to seventeen years. Source: RSA (1996, 11).

of more overtly political organizations that were banned following the Sharpville massacre in the 1960s.[37] While often poor, these urban communities had robust family and neighbor networks that were critical lifelines for residents.

By the late 1950s, the poor whites around which the welfare system had been built were largely thought to no longer exist. However, as Magdalena's case in the next chapter reveals, the nightmare of the 1930s "poor white problem" continued to haunt the social imaginary. As apartheid became more entrenched and the boundaries of proper whiteness hardened, the more the remaining poor whites conflicted with the prevailing order and the more marginal and less respectable they became (Teppo 2004). White incomes more than doubled in a generation, leading to increased consumptions expectations for white middle-class lifestyles, leaving poor whites further behind (Nattrass and Seekings 2010). Despite deepening unemployment among the lower-skilled populations, unemployed white men like Magdalena's husband, Mr. Amos, were viewed as "work shy" and an indefensible deviations from the norm of the hard-working white man. Poor whites in this period "became anomalies in a social order that increasingly rejected the possibility of their existence" (Teppo 2004, 167; see also Hyslop 2000). As such, they were subject to ever-increasing stigmatization and regulation predominantly through an expansive welfare system designed to eliminate white poverty.

———

So it was that by the time Magdalena, Rosemary, and Grace encountered the social welfare system, it had become highly differentiated and fractured. The vision of welfare had moved from that of a human right to that of emergency relief in the framework of assumed self-development. Indeed, as the former Deputy Secretary of Social Welfare said,

> the responsibility of every citizen's social security rests with the citizen himself. Only if his own efforts prove inadequate is the state prepared to step in with help and guidance. The independence of the individual, the family, and the community must be maintained and encouraged. (Quoted in Brummer 1964, 3)

Yet, the notion of "independence" in this statement belied the many forms of intervention the state made to control the lives of black African, coloured, and Indian people and to shape the families of all races into particular kinds of social units. Critically, women's maternal identity—how it was expressed and interpreted—sat at the nexus of "help and guidance" in the form of aid or discipline. Mothers of the nation were worthy of investment, though who counted was consistently under debate. The standards applied to each race group were highly differentiated and reflected the purposeful partitioning of citizenship along racial lines, an ambiguity that could prove useful and harmful to women like Magdalena, Rosemary, and Grace.

3 "SHE IS NOT CONSCIOUS OF HER MATERNAL ROLE"

Kinshipping in the Welfare Office

IN THE EARLY 1960S, THREE women racially classified as white, black African, and coloured, struggled to raise their children under conditions of dire poverty in the city of Durban. As part of these efforts, these women sought aid from various institutions, including the Durban Child Welfare Society. Magdalena, a white woman, received some food, clothing, and housing assistance, but, despite her vehement protests, her children were eventually removed to state institutions. Grace, a black woman, also received food and clothing, and her child, this time at her request, was eventually taken into foster care and subsequently adopted. Rosemary, a coloured woman, received extensive support of not only food and clothing, but also a State Maintenance Grant and a township house. She also fought with the society social workers over the removal of her children, which occurred a number of times over the years. In her case, they were always returned within weeks of their removal.

These women, carving out lives for themselves amid deepening poverty and hardening racial regulation, were likely not members of the period's robust women's political movements adeptly discussed by other historians.[1] At the same time, their domestic lives and practices of mothering—oftentimes glossed as private—were decidedly public and of critical concern to the white supremacist project of the state. A fragment of their lives and their ambitions are captured in the historical record by virtue of their inter-action with state-employed social workers, a relationship over which they had some, if limited, control. These records show how these women's claims to state support, their attempts to "get by," affected state allocations and helped to outline the contours of their very different forms of citizenship (for a discussion of similar negotiations by black women in the US Recon-struction era, see Kandaswamy 2021).

In the one sense these cases are particular, their outcomes the result of idiosyncratic interactions between individual poor women and equally sin-gular social workers. At another level, when analyzed alongside other cases from this period and oral history interviews, they reveal how motherhood as both a lived experience and as a mode of claim-making operated during a critical period of state-making and political activism. In South Africa, the 1950s to 1970s was a period of intense contestation over the increasingly regulatory reach of the state that further hardened the race-based exclu-sions of coloured, Indian, and black Africans from the citizenship whites enjoyed. This manifested in increasingly violent state crackdowns on pro-tests and brutal policing of communities of color. Another mechanism of violent control, less robustly examined, was the welfare system, designed to preserve white supremacy and manage black African, coloured, and Indian populations through state intervention into social reproduction. By this period, discourses of motherhood (albeit quite divergent) were embedded in white nationalist projects and various black African groups' demands to inclusion in the national community.[2] Public motherhood—women's com-munity involvement as grounded in maternal authority—was a growing part of multiracial women's antiapartheid activism "to fight for women's rights and for the full economic citizenship of all" (quoted in Gasa 2007, 216; Healy-Clancy 2017). At the same time, maternal care practices were also a primary site of intervention for social workers increasingly embold-ened to ensure to protection of (overwhelmingly white) children.

Public motherhood is a relatively new term developed by historians of west and east Africa to name women's grounding of their community work and participation "on the basis of literal or symbolic maternal authority" (Healy-Clancy 2017, 845; Semley 2010, 2012; Stephens 2013). It operates in contrast to the analytic framework of "maternalist politics" previously used by historians of South Africa who wrote about how women drew on their "private" roles as mothers to inform activism against state policy (Semley 2012). Instead, public motherhood is informed by black feminism and feminists from the Global South who emphasize how African maternal identities were never solely defined by the domestic realm and that women's activism involves a range of actions beyond direct confrontation with the state. Rather, women's actions are "informed by their prevailing conditions and the nature of the patriarchal oppression they are experiencing" and might just as often involve working around oppressive states—as many public mothers under apartheid did—to advance their political goals (Gasa 2007, 2; Healy-Clancy 2017; Oyewumi 2000).

Across the three cases considered here, these women's maternal status enabled them to make claims for resources and also attracted unwanted intervention for purportedly having "failed to realise [their] maternal role." As the previous chapter detailed, discourses about idealized maternal roles evolved in response to changing state priorities and social pressures driven by rapid urbanization and industrialization. Between the formation of the Union of South Africa in 1910 and the apartheid era, the conditions of mothering dramatically changed for all race groups as subsistence farming became untenable, mass urbanization and industrialization occurred alongside growing racial segregation, and the migrant labor system intensified. Walker captures the changes succinctly: "one need only contrast the experience of feeding, educating and nurturing children . . . the actual work involved, the degree to which the social expectations could be met, and the choices women were being forced to make in relation to this role, would have been radically different" (1995, 429). The period also saw a rise in the different groups concerned with supporting and disciplining practices of mothering, often to different ends. For black African women, and to a degree Indian and coloured women, mothering qua social reproduction became a privilege they had to fight for in the midst of an increasingly oppressive state. This history informs my analysis of the 1960s case files and outlines the stakes for poor women of different races invoking motherhood as a means of defense and claim-making. They do so in a context in which their racial and class statuses mark them as deviants in the eyes of the state.

I am concerned with how motherhood as a particularly political identity has been linked to both activism and state control. My use of political identity is informed by Walker's analytic separation of three dimensions of motherhood—the practice of mothering as embodied action, the dominant and oppositional discourses on ideal motherhood, and women's own social identity (1995). However, political identity, as I use it, differs from Walker's social identity in that it attends to women's uses of both discourse and practices as a form of claim-making (G'sell 2020). The discursive power of maternal language arises from the fact that motherhood operates as both a multivalent and condensing term. By multivalent I mean that motherhood as a singular term can be used in many different settings to mean quite different things. Motherhood, as it is invoked and enacted by the women in this chapter, and as it is understood and enforced by surveilling authorities, capaciously draws bodily comportments, material and social practices, normative understandings of social reproduction, and labor all under its moral umbrella. As it does so, it condenses the different elements into a single concept, juxtaposing them such that they are rendered malleable and porous, open to slippery entanglements, misrecognitions, and elisions. As the women in this chapter came to realize, such a seemingly self-evident, yet changeable signifier had enormous, but often unwieldy, political potential. Carefully crafted invocations of proper motherhood all too easily could get away from you.

During the 1950s and '60s, there were abrupt changes in the ways in which motherhood was experienced, interpreted, and expressed by women of different races in South Africa (Healy-Clancy 2017). As has been deftly covered by feminist historians, cross-racially, women's use of maternal discourses was an important part of overt activism against racist rule in both the segregationist and apartheid eras (Du Toit 2018; Hassim 1993, 2006; Healy-Clancy 2017; Gaitskell and Unterhalter 1989; Gasa 2007; Walker 1991, 1995).[3] Public motherhood, in varying forms, was used to protest the pass laws for black Africans in the 1910s, 1930s, and 1950s; to challenge labor laws and the migrant labor system in beerhall protests in the 1930s and 1950s; and to make claims on the state for improved health care, welfare, and education for their children and themselves.[4] By the 1950s, organizations such as the Daughters of Africa or the Federation of South African Women used public motherhood as a means to give women of diverse backgrounds and agendas a unified identity and a grounded moral legitimacy for their activism in formal politics (Healy-Clancy 2017). Whether they had children or not, women drew on a maternal identity in order to accomplish a variety of goals because it was a position afforded respect, regardless of race (Walker 1991). They leveraged discourses of motherhood to claim not just political citizenship but a national recognition for their gendered labor (Hassim 2005). In each case, the choice to foreground a maternal identity was neither random nor the inevitable result of the gendered division of labor. Instead, it reflected the strategic work of actors attempting to forward their political projects in terms that were meaningful and effective. The salience of motherhood as a recognizable political category was more thoroughgoing than just overt political activism and permeated multiple scales. Women like Magdalena, Grace, and Rosemary—not activists or even community leaders—also relied on a maternal identity to make individual claims in their case for deserving support. However, like their activist counterparts, they found that invoking motherhood was both enabling and constraining to their ultimate goals (Hassim 2006).

This chapter considers the mobilization of maternal identity from a different viewpoint than previous scholarship. Instead of examining overt political activism, I examine the everyday efforts of women like Magdalena, Grace, and Rosemary, women attempting to care for children under conditions of poverty and racist rule. I focus on these quotidian processes of kinshipping in order to argue that the labor of "getting by," of ensuring the reproduction of vital relations through daily activity, not only lays the foundation for more traditionally conceived forms of political engagement but is, in itself, a form of political action. In one sense this is because the domestic and political domains are co-constitutive, as feminist scholars have long espoused. In another sense, this is driven by the recognition that black African, coloured, and Indian women's homes and ability to care for their children were directly and purposefully attacked by successive oppressive states (Hassim 1993). Nomboniso Gasa reminds us that for decades "African women were homeless by state design" due to both their gender and their race (2007, 214). Under conditions of white supremacy, women excluded from the privileges of whiteness practiced daily acts of survival that were just as much the stuff of politics as mass protests. As differently raced actors under racist rule, the claims to national inclusion that Magdalena, Grace, and Rosemary made were each distinct. Nevertheless, an analysis of their files reveals how making claims for domestic security are deeply political acts. Further, intersecting forms of racial and gendered oppression shaped these women's conditions for getting by and the political potential of their maternal claims.

Motherhood as a political identity is effective precisely because motherhood is a multivalent term that condenses differing experiences into a unified conception. When someone invokes motherhood, those present assume they know and agree on what is being discussed, despite often widely varying understandings. This condensation is possible, in part, because the indexical and symbolic assumptions about what motherhood means seem to have remarkable historical consistency in the English-speaking world. These assumptions make motherhood *appear* to be a seemingly self-evident concept—the rearing of children—enabling the identity category to bridge differences of race or nationality in ways that are politically useful. Key to this efficacy is the moral authority motherhood affords to the projects that can be incorporated under its umbrella. The moral status of maternal care rests on a set of popular assumptions that can be summarized in three nested equivalencies: namely, caring for = caring about; good caregiving = feminine; carework = moral good.[5] These equivalencies reach their apex in the social conception of the mother as the paradigmatic, selfless caregiver. Thus, women can often imbue their actions and concerns with moral legitimacy if they can successfully subsume them under the heading of maternal care. For the women in my research, this meant kinshipping, or narrating their needs—for food, for housing, for income—to social workers and judges as needs to support their maternal care. Even when their actions were readily evaluated as deviant, the women called those actions maternal in hopes that the patina of the professed ideals of motherhood would rub off on them. However, as the experiences of Magdalena, Rosemary, and Grace reveal, the seeming moral unity of maternal care is precarious at best, vulnerable to its own capaciousness and the vagaries of an often-mercurial interpretation grounded in racial ideologies. Indeed, the invocation of putatively universal motherhood can quickly break down when that care is quite differently valued depending on race.

I argue that as motherhood became increasingly politicized both in South Africa and on an international scale, women's mobilization of maternal identity to make claims must be reconceptualized as more than identity politics. Instead, we must think of it as a strategic discursive action of claim-making—as an attempt to make motherhood work. By invoking motherhood, women drew on this presumed unified concept to make themselves legible as social actors and to make arguments that they deserved assistance. In other words, they engaged in kinshipping. However, the multivalence of motherhood as an interpretive concept also posed challenges. Women labored to retain control over the meaning and translation of motherhood as they used it, and their relative power was constrained by their poverty, gender, and place within a racial hierarchy. Attending to the unpredictable interpretations of motherhood is historiographically important. I show that the outcome of cases often sat at the intersection of legitimating ideologies handed down through Commissions of Inquiry, legislation, and social work education and the idiosyncratic proclivities of the social workers and judges the women encountered (Ashforth 1990). By considering these events in the early 1960s, I contribute to the scholarship that seeks to track how apartheid became elaborated not through a grand ideological blueprint, but through an uneven and often contradictory negotiation between street-level bureaucrats and everyday citizens (Posel 1992; Roos 2015). The close reading of the welfare files of Magdalena, Rosemary, and Grace reveals that while national discourse was uniformly concerned with reforming motherhood, the political meaning and potential of that identity was shaped by the racial ideologies of the moment, the activism of different women's liberation groups, and the longer history of state interventions into mothering practices.

Motherhood on File

The women whose experiences populate this chapter were classified according to the four apartheid racial categories: white (also called European); Indian (Asiatic); coloured; and African (native/Bantu). They lived or worked in the Point neighborhood and their lives entered the archival record because, by choice or by fortune, they interacted with South Africa's child welfare system, and their maternal caregiving was subject to evaluation by neighbors, landlords, teachers, social workers, and, finally, a magistrate. These social workers and court officials were not only gatekeepers to critical resources such as grocery vouchers, rent subsidies, or a monthly government grant, they also decided whether women's maternal projects were worthy of support or required reform or termination by removal of their children.

This chapter draws from a sampling of Children's Court cases from 1949 to 1998 in which the participants' primary residence—or workplace in the case of black Africans—was in the Point. Under apartheid, the Point, like all urban centers, was deemed a whites-only neighborhood. Whites were viewed as the legitimate face of the neighborhood despite the presence of black men laboring in the neighborhood's railyard and shipyard, black women who cleaned the neighborhood buildings, Indian restaurant and shop owners, and the coloured nurses who staffed the neighborhood hospital. The majority of those whites living in the Point were either poor or working class—a highly stigmatized social category in the midcentury and today—and many sought assistance from a social welfare infrastructure that had been created for their virtually sole benefit.

Prior to 1998, in order for a caregiver to receive state funds, the child had to be declared "in need of care" by a commissioner of Child Welfare, usually a magistrate. Records of these Children's Court cases contain a host of documents that argue for or against a variety of interventions, from receipt of a State Maintenance Grant (the predecessor to today's Child Support Grant) to removal of the child to a state institution or foster care. The documents include reports and letters produced by social workers in the Durban office of the Department of Social Welfare and Pensions and Durban Child Welfare Society; transcripts of trial hearings that include testimony from social workers, parents, and neighbors or friends; and letters or statements composed by school principals, neighbors, and the parents or children themselves. These documents can be read as evidence for what constituted normatively desirable (and undesirable) family life in various times. Further, the surveillance to which poor families' lives were subjected produced abundant data—albeit through a particular lens—on the intimate life of families in the Point.

Making Motherhood in Apartheid South Africa

Rosemary Dunn was a thirty-two-year-old single mother racially classified as coloured. She reached out to the Durban Child Welfare Society (DCWS) in April of 1962,[6] a year after her husband, Michael, had died, according to her report, and had left Rosemary, unemployed, with three young children: Christopher, approximately eight years old; Linda, four; and Ernest, two.[7] She was referred to the Department of Coloured Affairs to apply for public assistance and a maintenance grant. However she never received the money because she did not provide the appropriate documentation for the children—their birth certificates—and moved before the application could be processed, leaving no forwarding address. She was a client of the DCWS off and on from 1962 to 1970 working with two social workers, Mrs. Smith and Mrs. Walljee. Over the course of that time, her children were removed from her care and sent to a children's home four times for the violation of abandonment. These removals occurred first in 1962, for leaving her children all day "without supervision and food" and in the care of the neighbors in order to work, and second in 1963 when she gave birth to an illegitimate son, Peter, and again in 1964 and 1969 when she was imprisoned for theft and fraud for listing the DCWS as a guarantor for her purchase of furniture on credit.[8]

Despite these transgressions, and despite Rosemary's noncompliance, often hiding the children from the social workers and refusing to produce necessary documentation, the society offered Rosemary a great deal of support. The social workers frequently organized grocery donations and household furniture and arranged for Rosemary to receive a monthly State Maintenance Grant. This was in keeping with a national trend in which coloured mothers were the largest group of maintenance grant recipients. Upon her release from prison in 1964, the DCWS procured her a house in a newly created coloured township on the outskirts of the city and arranged for the rent to be paid by the local Catholic Church, even retaining the house for her when she was reimprisoned in 1969 (Chari 2006). Additionally, in each case, Rosemary's children were returned to her custody within weeks of their removal.

Rosemary's case reveals a complex relationship between the DCWS and its clients. Rosemary was brought under case management because she transgressed from the ideal paradigm of white middle-class motherhood. However, the arguments made for the substantial support provided for by the society were done in the name of her actions *as a good mother*. It is worth considering what attributions of problematic and beneficial motherhood were called out by the social workers and how they were weighed against one another to legitimate intervention into Rosemary's family life.

One of Rosemary's primary transgressions was her inability to "maintain a proper home environment." In the report from her first visit with Rosemary, the social worker, Ms. Smith, devoted many lines to an evaluation of the housing conditions in which Rosemary was living.[9] She described them by saying, "the room is maintained in a filthy condition and there is no furniture. The family sleeps on the floor—there are two threadbare, filthy blankets and four pillows. There are no cooking facilities and no pots or crockery. . . . Communal toilet facilities of the pail system are provided." Also, there was no outdoor space for family recreation.

These critiques of Rosemary's home arose out of a larger conflation of living space with social habits that characterized government intervention in South Africa in the 1960s.[10] While single-family homes were thought to foster discipline and responsibility, apartments were seen as too "easy" and "spoiled" families by encouraging them to go out on the town instead of engaging in family activities at home.[11] Apartments and their lack of outdoor recreation space were even cited by one government commission as a cause of inadequate care and upbringing of children: "Here we have in mind such factors as inferior living conditions in the slums and unsightly industrial areas, migration from rural areas to cities, the effects of flat living on the child, coupled with the lack of space for playing and recreation within reach of the child's home."[12] Given these concerns, the social workers went to great length to restructure Rosemary's home environment in terms of her housing. In contrast to her prior space, the housing that the DCWS found Rosemary included running water and flush toilets. Ms. Smith noted, "The room is large and well-ventilated . . . [and is] maintained in a neat and clean manner."[13] Also, an outdoor space was available for the children to play in. The refiguring of space was seen to have helped to discipline Rosemary into becoming a more ideal mother.

A second cause of Rosemary's improper care of her children was her "inadequate spiritual care and the absence of positive religious convictions."[14] Ms. Smith initially criticized the lack of religious involvement in the life of the Dunn family. But, after intensive casework, Rosemary was reported to be going to church regularly—indeed, the same church that was paying her rent—and Ms. Smith continuously emphasized Rosemary's reinvigorated religious spirit as evidence of the progress Rosemary was making. Ms. Smith used Rosemary's realization of her "religious duties and moral obligations" as one of the key rationales for returning the children to their mother's care.[15]

A third concern was that Rosemary initially attempted to work to support her children. As part of maintaining the imagined ideal home environment, women were not supposed to "needlessly" work and leave their children without a maternal presence during the day. Indeed, it was because Rosemary left her children with neighbors during the day that the DCWS renewed contact with the Dunn family. As a single mother with no family support, the proscription to stay at home was more complicated. The society "assisted and encouraged" Rosemary to find employment, but she was frequently listed as being unemployed. Instead, the society arranged for groceries, rent payments, and furniture. At the close of the case, Rosemary was granted a State Maintenance Grant, the amount of which would have been roughly equivalent to the salary of a menial job such as a hotel maid. It would not have been sufficient on its own to support the family without the help of the DCWS, but it did allow Rosemary not to work and thereby to mimic middle-class female respectability. Indeed, as one commission report noted, "The main object of the introduction of maintenance grants was to enable mothers or foster-mothers to look after their children without being forced to seek employment away from home and in the open labour market."[16] In this way, with the society acting as provider, Rosemary could maintain the proscribed gender role of the full-time mother.

A key maternal success that was celebrated across Rosemary's file was the affective bond she shared with her children. Following each of the times that the children were removed to a children's home, Ms. Smith noted that Rosemary "begged that the children be returned to her and the children were obviously anxious to return to her."[17] Despite the fact that Rosemary had deceived Ms. Smith by hiding the children before they could be removed, in her list of "positive factors" of Rosemary's character, Ms. Smith included Rosemary's "refusal to part with the children and her anxiety to have them returned to her" and "the strong bond of affection between mother and the children."[18] This perceived bond formed an integral part of Ms. Smith's argument that Rosemary be allowed to keep her children. It was effective, in part, because it resonated with prevailing beliefs that mothers should feel intense love and attachment to their children and that their good care as mothers would arise out of this emotional bond.[19]

Despite her deviance from the maternal ideal, we see that the social workers used Rosemary's successes to legitimate continued support and cast her as a woman capable of learning to be a competent mother. Such an argument was no small task. She was known to have abandoned her children without food and care during the day and had maintained a squalid home. On at least two occasions she was imprisoned for theft and fraud, including using the DCWS as a guarantor for debts. In addition, she was continuously duplicitous in her dealings with the society. Yet, the social worker reframed her time in prison as a removal from the negative influence of friends and a form of rehabilitation. Her theft and fraud was labeled not as criminal but as a problem of "living beyond her means," rectifiable through further counseling. A change in her housing was noted to have brought about improvements in her housekeeping. And, critically, the emotional bond between her and her children was continuously emphasized. With these arguments in place, the social worker concluded:

> The case history reveals the mother to be an unsatisfactory and unfit person to exercise control over her children. However, this does not mean that the children would benefit from removal from her custody . . . this mother can be helped to care for her children. Therefore, she should be given the opportunity to keep her children.[20]

It is notable that in the face of numerous transgressions, the social worker argued that Rosemary was reformable and deserving of support. Not all mothers were deemed worthy of such investment.

In 1949, Magdalena Amos, a white Afrikaans mother, approached the DCWS for assistance with food and clothing. Her husband, who was a casual laborer on the docks, had not brought home any money in a month, and Magdalena and her four children were desperate. Since 1937, Magdalena had had a long history of coming to the society for assistance, always at intervals spaced 6 months or more apart. This time, though the society assisted her, they also began more intensive casework and were displeased with what their investigations revealed. The social workers levied critiques of fiscal mismanagement and overindulgence in liquor alongside accusations of parental neglect. What began as a case to argue against further assistance for the family ended with the children's removal to state institutions. Across seventeen years, in letters and court testimonies, Magdalena mobilized her maternal identity to simultaneously make a case for her need and defend against her children's removal.

Magdalena was well-versed in the welfare landscape of Durban and how best to frame her appeals for support. Due to her race and ethnicity, she was able to seek aid from a number of different agencies, such as the Benevolent Society, the Dutch Reformed Church, and, due to her husband's job, the Railway Welfare. For scheduled visits, social workers were sure to find a tidy home, with Magdalena present and presiding over the children. Often on days when the social worker had visited her home, Magdalena would visit the DCWS office unannounced to report another woman for a possible case of neglect. In one instance, she reportedly did this while drunk.[21] In moments such as these, Magdalena positioned herself as the defender of child welfare and the arbiter of good motherhood, thereby attempting to remove herself from possible rebuke.

Magdalena's carefully calibrated relationship with the society was disrupted when an intimate neighbor reported her as neglecting her children. The reporter was Agatha, a recent divorcée, whom Magdalena had taken in, along with her three children, as a subletter to help with the rent. The women shared and frequently fought over the childcare responsibilities and domestic labor. After a particularly raucous fight, which ended in blows, over whose responsibility it was to remove the washing from the bathtub, Agatha retaliated by calling two welfare agencies to report Magdalena for neglect. Not only did Agatha report Magdalena, but she testified at the Children's Court hearing as to Magdalena's inadequacy as a mother. Magdalena vehemently refuted these allegations and in letters, testimony, and visits with the social worker, she sought to recast her actions as reflective of good motherhood. In a 1951 letter, she pleaded, "Please don't take my children away from me they are my whole life to me . . . give me the chance to proof [sic] to you that what was said against me was all a lot of deliberate lies and jealousy." Her inability to do so ultimately resulted in the court's removal of the children to state institutions.

A primary domain in which Magdalena's conduct deviated from that of the ideal mother was in the social life she cultivated beyond the house. Maternal caregivers in the 1950s and 60s were expected to remain home, taking care of the domestic duties of cooking, cleaning, and child-rearing.

A mother's life was supposed to be an interiorly oriented one to provide the basis of support for a man engaged in the public role of income generation. This housebound requirement was an especially difficult burden for poor women. Even in the case of Magdalena's family, where a male breadwinner was present, wages often did not support all of a family's needs. However, women's work outside the home was still seen as unnecessary. As was true for Rosemary, mothers who left their children to "needlessly" work were considered negligent (Clowes 1994).

The social worker, Miss Glynn, viewed Magdalena's activities outside of the house as conflicting with her expected role as wife and mother. She characterized Magdalena as being "more interested in outside activities than her children."[22] Likely knowledgeable about these domestic expectations, in her trial testimony, Agatha testified that Magdalena went out all day and sometimes part of the night while her children remained at home. These accusations brought up concerns of maternal negligence and broader respectability. To suggest that Magdalena was out at night was to suggest that she was consorting with men who were not her husband and, because of the hour, served as a subtle hint that Magdalena might be engaging in prostitution.

In her letters and testimony, Magdalena worked to bridge the discrepancies between the activities she engaged in outside of the home and the interiorly oriented ideal of the wife and mother invoked by the social worker and Agatha. She argued that her activities outside were a critical part of her household duties and an extension of her maternal responsibilities, not neglect of them. She said she did not go out an "unnecessary" amount, but instead needed to go out to take care of shopping and to "see to business" to run the household.[23] In a court testimony she responded to the bundled accusations of the late-night sojourns, "I have never neglected my children in any way. In regards to going out, I went out with my husband I used to visit him around 8 pm and stay with him on the boat until 9 pm on the tug (name unreadable) on which he was working. Then I would stand on the wharf and I would talk to him."[24] Here she sought to reinscribe her potentially adulterous actions under the banner of matrimonial loyalty.

Magdalena was also critiqued for her choice of caregivers when she was out. Agatha testified that Magdalena left her children "just in the care of native servants, who lay on the floor of the kitchen and went to sleep."[25] This criticism was a slippery one that speaks to the complex relationship between white mistresses and domestic employees of other races. On the one hand, there was a long tradition in South Africa of black men and women assisting in the child-rearing and domestic labors in white homes (Cock 1989). It was also noted in the social worker's critique of Rosemary's untidy home that she did not keep a "domestic servant." The presence of such staff was seen as essential for reproducing racial hierarchies in which black labor, viewed as more suitable for "lower" level jobs, freed up particularly white labor for high-skilled work (Ginsburg 2011). White mistresses were conscripted to educate black staff in the respectability of white domestic life (Cock 1989). Magdalena's family, with their tenuous hold on working class status, would have felt the need for such racial distinction acutely.

On the other hand, black domestic caregivers were also seen as an insufficient and inappropriate substitute for white maternal care. Food was a decisive arena for marking the boundaries of care practices because it indexed maternal care, and thus meal planning had to be overseen by the mother. There was a great deal of social anxiety about the "damaging influence of the native nursemaid" on the health of white children, especially among poor whites who were seen as already too intimate with black lives (Stoler 2001, 850–51). Good white mothers, then, were to have help, but also were expected to closely supervise the contact between those domestic servants and their charges (Cock 1989). In this way, Magdalena's behavior was viewed as doubly problematic. First, she was shirking her duties to educate and chaperone her black staff and, in the process, affirm white racial superiority. And, second, she left her children to the vagaries of what was seen as semicivilized care. In response, Magdalena sought to do away with the complicated labor relations altogether by arguing that her children were left in the care of her nineteen-year-old daughter, Joanna. A white woman and elder kinswoman, there was little room to dispute the acceptability of Joanna as a caregiver.

Magdalena was also criticized for feeding her children inadequately. Agatha testified that the children were given "only milk and bread" and were regularly undernourished. She went on to say:

On several occasions, I had to give Magdalena's children food when Mrs. Amos was away because she left no food in the house and the children were hungry. She often told me she had given her boy money to buy food for the children, but I don't know what he did with it or if he ever got it . . . I was just renting part of the dining room. . . . There was never any arrangement that I would look after Magdalena's children during her absence.[26]

This quotation reveals a trifecta of maternal critique. Magdalena spent time outside of the house. While she was away, where she purportedly should not have been, her children were hungry. To allow one's children to go hungry was the ultimate maternal transgression. Magdalena attempted to turn this criticism into a testament of her own money management. She responded, "I pay all my household commodities as I can afford them. When I have money, I buy groceries. When I have no money, we don't buy anything." In this statement, Magdalena worked to position herself as a fiscally responsible woman with well-aligned priorities living under conditions of duress.

Magdalena went on to deny that Agatha fed her children regularly and instead argued that she fed Agatha's children. It is likely that both women fed each other's children. However, by this point in the trial, Agatha held more influence in the courtroom. Magdalena attempted to defend herself by reasserting herself as an attentive mother and by discrediting Agatha. She argued that she gave her children milk and bread because they preferred it—thereby setting herself up as more attuned to her children's preferences—and that she regularly bought vegetables—signaling she knew about proper nutrition. Additionally, Magdalena continued, she not only cared for the welfare of her own children, but also ensured the welfare of Agatha's children:

I would not have taken her [Agatha] in but for the sake of her children, for they were put out of a house and had nowhere to go, so I took them in though it was making the house crowded. . . . Agatha for one has such a lot to say about my home why couldn't she keep her home together.[27]

Here Magdalena attempted to undercut Agatha as morally superior, saying that it was Magdalena who saved Agatha, a divorcée, and her children from a life on the street as a result of Agatha's inability to maintain a nuptial home.

A final domain of Magdalena's maternal failure was around the consumption of alcohol. Respectable, Christian mothers were expected to abstain from alcohol or to only sip demurely on holidays or festive occasions. The evidence suggests that Agatha and Magdalena regularly drank alcohol together and with mixed company in their house. These parties would have reduced the social isolation, common in poorer, more transient neighborhoods like the Point, that left families more vulnerable to changes in life circumstance (Gordon 1988). In addition to being pleasurable, such sessions helped forge important relationships with other men or women who could be called on later for favors or resources. Though frowned on, the court may have been persuaded to overlook Magdalena's consumption of alcohol when socializing with adults at home. However, Agatha and the social workers contended that Magdalena was noticeably drunk during the day while interacting with social workers and in full view of her children. Such conduct was seen as evidence of Magdalena's inadequacy as a mother.

Magdalena's testimony and letters to the magistrate make visible her attempts to leverage the capaciousness of motherhood to serve her needs. Magdalena continuously argued that even as an impoverished woman, she engaged in many of the practices of the ideal white, middle-class mother. Further, she worked to recast many of her deviant behaviors as being in service of achieving this ideal. For years, Magdalena successfully managed her relationship with the DCWS, but Agatha's report shifted the terrain of negotiation. Though Agatha was clearly not a paragon of white respectability either, her report and testimony in the Children's Court case gave fodder to the state assessment of Magdalena's mothering that Magdalena could not successfully reframe. The end result was that Magdalena's children—aged seventeen, sixteen, fourteen, eleven, and eight—were all removed to institutions in 1962 until they aged (or married) out of the system.

From the data available in the case files, Rosemary and Magdalena appear to be quite similar women. The files, which are constructed to provide evidence for the evaluation of their characters, show that both engaged in activities deemed irresponsible for women and mothers at the time. Yet the responses to these indiscretions was markedly different. Both women were recorded as socializing with men who were not their husbands. Both women had children by multiple men in and out of marriage. Neither woman retained suitable housing for any length of time, and both left their children unattended. Rosemary committed theft and fraud—crimes for which she was jailed for a few months. Magdalena was known to drink, however, she argued,

> In all the time that I stay down here the Point Police can verify that I have never been locked up for being drunk or that I have had to go to jail for causing a disturbance. I have never stolen anything from anybody. I have never committeed [*sic*] a murder. What did I do?[28]

Magdalena's defensiveness is all the more poignant in a situation where her actions prompted an outpouring of moralizing language whereas Rosemary's did not. Magdalena was characterized as a "disreputable woman" whose actions contributed to an "environment of drink and indecent living."[29] Her use of alcohol is important given that in the 1950s and early 1960s there was a national frenzy over white women's alcohol use as an antecedent to moral degeneration and miscegenation.[30] However, in contrast, Rosemary's other transgressions receive little evaluation. In the case of Rosemary's sexual relationship, this is especially surprising given, as others have suggested, the intense policing of coloured women's sexuality that took place within the coloured community (Erasmus 2001). Indeed, because people classified as coloured were often spoken about in ways that associated them with immorality, sexual promiscuity, impurity, and untrustworthiness, state interaction with the coloured community frequently involved the disciplining of sexual relations (Erasmus 2001). Under these conditions, it would have been likely that Ms. Smith, herself classified as coloured, would have been highly critical of Rosemary's sexuality in ways that do not appear in the reports.

The relative credibility that is afforded to Rosemary and Magdalena is also quite divergent. Like Rosemary, Magdalena withheld information from the social worker and frequently made testimony that was later documented to be false. We know this because the social workers who handled Magdalena's case sought out corroboration. They interviewed principals, neighbors, and social workers from other institutions, sought court records, and collected police reports. Very little of these investigative efforts were made on Rosemary's case. Magdalena's file is exceptional because of the amount of self-advocacy she did—writing letters, producing elaborate testimony, and even soliciting letters from former neighbors in support of her. However, this evidence was given very little weight in the final conclusion and oftentimes was used against her.

Also like Rosemary, Magdalena did not have enough money to support her children. But, whereas Rosemary was given groceries, furniture, housing arrangements, and ultimately a State Maintenance Grant, Magdalena was offered far less support. Part of this was due to the fact that Magdalena had a husband who occasionally worked. In many respects, the fact that the Amoses more closely resembled the nuclear family ideal, could have been used to legitimate support. But, even when Mr. Amos was unemployed or when his working wage was insufficient to cover the costs of rent and food, the DCWS did not assist. This is not because of the family makeup. The society provided food and clothing (or support referrals) in the years prior to intensive supervision, but from 1959 to 1963, when social workers visited the home an average of ten times a year, no resources were offered. Instead, once the three elder children were sent to institutions, the court spent a great deal of time and resources attempting to extract a contribution from Mr. Amos that amounted to almost two-thirds of his monthly salary, which the report suggests was never paid. Yet, he was never offered counsel in finding more remunerative work, a common form of assistance at this time. Though a consistent critique of Magdalena was that she spent too much time outside the home—quite possibly engaging in social and illicitly remunerative activities—little aid was offered to ensure she did not work or need to seek support elsewhere.

Critically, what was at stake in the cases was how Rosemary and Magdalena were perceived as mothers. Much of this hinged on caregiving and race. The case against Magdalena was that she was a "neglectful mother." The files suggest that both women lived at times in conditions that the social workers found "dirty" and "overcrowded," and that their children were found to be "thin and unkempt."[31] Magdalena (and likely Rosemary) knew the import of care to the evaluations of her and throughout her trial reiterated how she nursed one of her children back from the grave, how she regularly took them to the clinic, and how she "sat and sewed til [sic] early hours of the morning" making clothes for them.[32] Rosemary's hiding of her children from the social worker was taken as a testament to her laudable attachment. When Magdalena hid her children and "kicked up such a row" at the social worker's attempts at removal, she wasn't perceived as bonded to her children, but as "aggressive" and "abusive," and the social worker called the police.[33] To a certain degree, these differences in approach may be attributable to social worker idiosyncrasies. But across various social workers, the case files reveal that Rosemary's issues were seen as remediable while Magdalena's were not. Notably, for three decades prior to her case, the state had invested substantial resources into disciplining poor white women like Magdalena out of existence. The survival of women like her and particularly her Afrikaans background would have been a nagging embarrassment and an economic and social threat in a historic moment when the state needed whites to be skilled and educated. This is most starkly visible when Mrs. Knipe and Mr. Shapero, who Magdalena describes as "a South African [who] speaks Afrikaans like myself," take over the case from Miss Glynn. Their tone and criticism is markedly harsher than that of other social workers, remarking that "the social workers warned her to change their ways or the children will be taken away and it has had no effect. She did not follow advice but had her own agenda. Her excuses have not been convincing and suggest she is unable to provide care for children. It is considered that it is in the best interests of the children to be removed without delay." Though Magdalena thought that reassignment to Afrikaans-speaking social workers would help her case, what she received was far more intense criticism from her fellow white ethnics.[34]

Magdalena's and Rosemary's children also had very different perceived values in the future of the nation. In the case of Rosemary, she was deemed an "unfit" mother, yet the social worker concluded, "but that does not mean the children should be taken away."[35] Classified as coloured, the children's relative status in society would not be substantially diminished by less than ideal care. In the case of Magdalena, the social worker concluded that "with proper care, these children should develop into worthy citizens." In the example of another case, the social worker went on to describe the positive impact a children's home could have on wayward white children, "an institution of group living will afford her the opportunity through which the rights and abilities of others may be recognized and where she would experience regularity of personal habits, consistent disciplines and wholesome group competition. This should help her to reach greater social acceptability."[36] For white children like Magdalena's, that care was to be grounded in the best practices of the day and managed by the state, not left to Magdalena.[37]

Many of the similarities of Magdalena's and Rosemary's cases fall away when we turn to consider the experience of Grace Mkhize, a Zulu woman from the rural area of Eshowe. On July 9, 1963, Grace gave birth to a baby boy, Themba, her third child. Shortly afterward, likely in part because of the pregnancy and birth, Grace lost her job as a domestic servant where she lived with and worked for a mixed-race family. As a black woman, her termination meant that, under apartheid laws, she was no longer legally allowed to be present in the neighborhood designated for coloured persons on the edges of Durban proper.

During her first pregnancy, Grace had been working in Point and living as a subtenant in Cato Manor. However, since that time, the area where Grace had lived was cleared and informal housing was scarce. Grace found herself, as another black African woman in the same situation described, with "no home, hiding from the police, living like wild people" (Callinicos 2007, 172). Hopping from one backyard room to another, Grace and her newborn lived off the hospitality of other domestic servants willing to offer them food and possibly shelter for the night. On those lucky nights, they had to creep out from the yard early in the morning before the family discovered them. But if the baby cried, or Grace woke too late, fellow domestics risked losing their own jobs, so such offers were infrequent. Grace had to walk for hours, ducking into alleys to dodge the police looking for curfew violators and catching a few hours' sleep in a public toilet.

After three months of this, Grace approached a coloured woman, Mrs. Bonhomme, asking her to adopt Themba. Mrs. Bonhomme took the pair to the DCWS to process the adoption. While Mrs. Bonhomme did not become Themba's adoptive mother, DCWS did offer aid. This is particularly surprising because the society's mandate at the time was to promote the welfare of children and families of only the white and coloured populations. Deviance from this mandate in Grace's case was partially due to pity. When they arrived, the social worker, Miss Saunders, described Grace as appearing "in a state of neglect . . . dirty, poorly dressed, and malnourished. Her face reveals symptoms of fatigue."[38] However, the society had for thirty years resisted calls to extend their services into impoverished black communities. Furthermore, the inclusion of coloured families was only due to the higher status afforded to this group under apartheid racial hierarchy and was an uneven inclusion at best. Thus, there was an institutional limit to charitable sentiment (Du Toit 2014). More than pity, then, the society's willingness to give Grace food and to provide Themba milk, medical care, and eventually an adoptive family was the result of Grace's successful manipulation of the flexible racial category of colouredness.

At two months, Themba's skin was lighter than his mother's. Because of this, it was conceivable that Mrs. Bonhomme could adopt him. Though Grace had former ties to the Bantu Child Welfare Society—the society designated to serve black Africans—from her previous two children, she allowed Mrs. Bonhomme to take her and Themba to the better-resourced Durban Child Welfare Society. There, she completed forms about Themba's father, giving the same first name as the father of her other children, but did not include his recognizably Zulu last name of Ngcobo. Instead, she said, Themba's father was coloured. Despite the fact that Grace had already registered Themba a black "bantu" child, she went with DCWS social workers to the Population Registrar to have him registered as coloured. She then took Themba to the Durban Children's Hospital in Point—which only treated white and coloured children—for treatment of malnutrition and exposure.

Prior to her contact with the DCWS, Grace's experience is concurrent with what scholars have told us about the lives of urban black African women in the 1960s. She had two children, Sipho, age three, and Sylvia, age two, with Elias Ngcobo, a police constable in Pinetown. As a man with a relatively good government job, it is likely that Elias was married with another wife and children living in a township house.[39] His relationship with Grace, while not unusual, would not have been welcomed by his family. In September 1962, Grace was reported to have "abandoned" the children with him. Elias would have made more money as a police constable than Grace as a domestic laborer, and two small children would have made her work life a challenge if not impossible. We can imagine her "abandonment" as an effort to coerce Elias into offering more support, though he quickly committed them to Othandweni Infants Home in the black township of Lamontville. The children did not stay at the children's home long, however. By 1963, they were under the care of a maternal aunt in Lamontville. We don't know if this aunt was a blood relation, but Lamontville was an older township with comparatively wealthier residents. It is possible this was a caregiver who Grace would not have had to pay to house the children. Grace's mother was also a domestic servant living on her employer's premises in

Pietermaritzburg, a city an hour from Durban. Not surprisingly, when the DCWS contacted her, she refused to take Themba or the other children, a decision that would have threatened her job. In her refusal, she criticized Grace, saying she was "irresponsible and over indulged in liquor."[40]

The social workers also did not have a high opinion of Grace. In one assessment of her, Miss Saunders wrote:

> The mother was unemployed and . . . she and the child lived illegally in the servants quarters of various Coloured owned homes. . . . The mother does not play a prominent part on the Bantu community. She is a Bantu Domestic Servant of inferior status. Although she states that she is a member of the Roman Catholic Church, she does not appear to be aware of the church's doctrine. She does not participate in her religious duties and has not even had her baby baptized. Her main interest centers around visiting other Bantu Servants and abusing liquor. She does not appear to attach much importance to moral values. She is not conscious of her maternal roles. She abandoned her two older children and openly rejected the child Themba. She has been unreliable and uncooperative.[41]

Grace was seen to have failed in cultivating moral values of religious participation and temperance. She had failed in creating economic security and stable housing. Though she was deeply constrained from at-home care by her work and had made provisions for her other children, she was seen as having abandoned them and negated her emotional bond. Her lateness to appointments with the social workers was interpreted as noncooperation. Despite these negative assessments, Grace still managed to secure assistance for Themba. While Themba was in the hospital receiving treatment, Grace signed the papers consenting to his adoption. However, she did not wait to hear if a family could be found. Instead, she disappeared. Shortly after, Themba, renamed as Clive, was fostered and eventually adopted into a coloured family in Cape Town.

Discipline and Support: Furthering the Project of "Getting By"

In all three of these cases, Rosemary, Magdalena, and Grace sought out the assistance of the Durban Child Welfare Society to support their children. I place all these efforts under the frame of "getting by," or the project of survival and social reproduction. These women invoked their status as mothers to needy children to make claims on resources and, in the case of Grace, institutional power. Motherhood was an available resource for their claim-making both due to a long history of maternalist politics and from the particular social and political salience of motherhood in South Africa in the 1960s. In the domain of social welfare, underlying ideologies of moral responsibility had shifted away from ideas that social ills arose from individual moral and character flaws. Instead, there was a greater recognition of the influence of relationships, which opened a space wherein family system could be targeted for intervention. In this period, problems such as juvenile delinquency, crime, or prostitution were addressed with interventions into the family and child-rearing practices as the wellspring from which such issues arose (Ferguson 2015). Maternal care operated as the source of problems for the ills of society and also as the powerful solution (Donzelot 1979). However, while motherhood as a unified category held enormous potency, the "problems" that maternal care was thought to beget or address were figured quite differently for different racial groups. Thus, the stakes for coloured, black, or white women invoking motherhood as a form of claim-making were quite disparate.

In accounting for the difference in the outcomes of the three cases, we must acknowledge the important role that the social workers played as complex mediators between mothers and the state. On the one hand, social workers are part of a broad category of reformers—missionaries, aid workers, domestic arts teachers, and the like—who worked to refashion family life and gender roles in accordance with the dominant ideology of the day. On the other, while a power differential often exists between social workers and their clients, it is not totalizing. Defining desirable motherhood is a negotiated process that involves the client's active response to and reformulation of the social worker's proscriptions (Gordon 1990; 1994). Nevertheless, while both parties may be involved in these negotiations, they do not participate equally. Social workers can be authors but are unlikely to be subjected to their enforcement to the degree that clients are.

Historically, social work in 1960s South Africa produced conditions under which white social workers shared a striking number attributes with their white clients, undoubtably shaping their interactions. Research on the profession in the 1950s and 1960s reveals that, like many of their clients, social workers employed in South Africa's child welfare organizations were also white, young women who were lower middle class.[42] The majority of them were married, and their time employed in various social welfare institutions represented a brief foray into the working world before they left to begin families of their own. This meant that many of the welfare organizations were a revolving door of young white women—in their early twenties, fresh out of university, who had become experts in "scientific motherhood" but not yet mothers themselves.[43] In the cases here, Rosemary was thirty-two when she first came in contact with DCWS, Maureen was thirty-seven, and it was estimated Grace was twenty-five. Thus it is likely that the social workers involved in their cases were younger than their clients, and at times, significantly so. In a letter to the judge, Magdalena tried to simultaneously discredit Miss Glynn for not having experienced motherhood or poverty and to uplift her own maternal legitimacy: "Miss Glynn has never had a child in her life and doesn't know what it is like to sit and pray at a sick child's bedside and she has never known hardship, so she wouldn't understand." However, In Magdalena's case it had little traction. Pia Kemble, a white social worker who began what would be an unusually long social work career at Durban Child Welfare Society in the early 1970s, noted that that when she arrived as a "young 20-year old," work with clients was challenging:

> PK—There were difficult people, some of the parents, they'd say, "You're too young, what do you know?" which I guess could be valid . . . I mean, obviously I was young [she laughs] . . . It's, much easier now if I'm engaged with the family now. It's very different.
>
> BG—What would you even say in those moments?
>
> PK—Well, the thing is, you know, I was qualified as a social worker and I had a job to do and you try to listen and empathize and do your job.

Depending on the social worker, this might have prompted overconfidence and emphasis on their scholarly expertise or, alternatively, cautiousness based in their inexperience. Rachel Abrams, a coloured social worker, who also worked in child welfare in the 1970s, discussed moments like those exhibited in both Rosemary and Maureen's cases: "That was heart-breaking to see, these parents really resisted letting go of their children, they were really swearing and they were *hard* and the children cried, and I thought, there *must* be an alternative." But, especially in the early years of her work, when family separation was more the standard of practice, suggesting the family stay together was risky, "For us, for young social workers, I think we were too afraid. What if the child dies? What might happen to the child?, you know. So the safest was to actually remove the child at the time. 'Cause we were not really *that* in power [original emphasis]." Rachel and Pia offer insight into the situatedness of social workers' decision-making. They were at once experts—trained professionals in a position of authority—but often young and inexperienced and burdened with the responsibility of making high-stakes decision about the lives of vulnerable families. It is no surprise then that their recommendations could be highly variable.

Social workers were the gatekeepers to a robust system of resources and restrictions. They were actors with a great deal of disciplinary power, but they were also constrained within a larger system. Until the late 1970s, caseloads at DCWS were racially divided—white social workers worked with white or coloured clients and coloured social workers only worked with coloured clients.[44] In a contingency that worked to Rosemary's benefit, it is altogether possible that her statements were not subject to as much intensive investigation as Magdalena's because coloured social workers like Ms. Smith were not given the same resources of transportation, time, and police escorts as white social workers like Miss Glynn. These conditions also shaped the ways they understood their position and that of their clients in relation to a racist state. Pia Kemble reflected on her stance, "I am not sure I was being an activist, I think I was a bit, you just did what you could within the system. I don't know, the risk, those old days, you were at such a risk if you stepped outside the system." This was somewhat different for Rachel Abrams who, as a young coloured woman, experienced state oppression more directly and already understood herself in opposition to apartheid. She became a target of police attention for her participation in Black Consciousness meetings and, due to police pressure, had to leave her post at a coloured child welfare agency in a Durban township and move to the racially mixed DCWS. Her activism was not without its own sense of fear of retaliation, "It was also at the time [the early '70s] when they started picking people up. You know, um, disappearing them and things like that.

But you just became overly, overly cautious. And I think that is what happened at [Durban] child welfare, probably the same type of thing." This is a critical backdrop in which to consider the actions of Miss Saunders in Grace's case. Her title of Miss suggested she was likely young; she would have been overseen by a supervisor to whom she had to justify her actions. Yet, she was also complicit in having Themba classified as coloured, despite many questionable data points that could have thwarted that effort. We can understand her action as both bold and as doing what she could within the system.

In addition to their structural conditions, social workers were also people with temperament and proclivities. Pia Kemble noted the complexities of trying to review a fat file with notes from multiple social workers, "Social workers work very differently and you'll see it in the filing entries, you know, their personalities, their attitudes. And so you might put great store on some things and others leave those details out, but you, you want the whole story." The social worker who successfully removed Magdalena's children stands out in the files as having unusually harsh language and judgment. In contrast, Miss Saunders, who oversaw Grace's case, used very sympathetic language both in her report on Grace and the few times she also offered input on Magdalena's case. Alternatively a social worker's approach might change from person to person or even across time. In an interview, Pia reflected on a case from the 1980s when a Point woman shut the door in her face, "I don't think I had a chance with her, actually . . . my approach to somebody like that would be so different now. I would have a better understanding, I think, or more openness to understand. . . . I can get people to trust me better than I would've managed earlier." For both Pia and Rachel—social workers with uniquely long careers—time and experience transformed their orientation to their clients. They each told stories of notable cases—interestingly, both Point mothers—who profoundly changed their social work practice by teaching them about the importance of respect for even the most stigmatized of mothers and the transformative potential of comprehensive support.[45] Of course what that support could look like was changeable.

The outcomes of Magdalena's, Rosemary's, and Grace's cases were also deeply shaped by the divergent interpretations of the women's maternal status. Though Magdalena's and Rosemary's circumstances were similar, their motherhood and maternal successes or failures were given different social meaning based on their racial categorization. Rosemary's transgressions were framed as issues of material need. This is, likely in part, because she was not described as exhibiting the social ills negatively associated with coloured women—hypersexuality, drinking, and irresponsibility.[46] Practices that could have been framed as moral weaknesses (e.g., theft) were instead posited as evidence of economic want, as the assistance provided to her reflected. Magdalena's conduct, however, was framed as evidence of an improper "attitude towards life" and a lack of "proper values" when it came to family care.[47] Given the national concern over these moral ills that were seen to be plaguing the white population, social workers were given a strong mandate to inculcate their clients with a set of values that placed children above material gain. Magdalena's case managers worked to do just that. Despite the ongoing presence of poor whites such as Magdalena, their categorical existence was continually denied. As one 1961 commission of inquiry noted, "whites are not suffering material want" and, "material want is incidental."[48] Under these terms, Magdalena's poverty was an anomaly, and the means to her reform was not economic assistance, as it was with Rosemary, but a value-based rehabilitation to impress on her that she needed to foster a stable nuclear family for her children. Speaking about maternal evaluations in the 1970s and the high levels of child removal, Rachel noted, "I have the feeling that in the white communities they had a higher standard of 'how our children must be reared.' That if you don't have that, then you're not a good enough parent." White households like Magdalena's were to be the foundation for the future success of the white population.

For black African women like Grace, her motherhood and the value of her children had quite a different meaning. Her motherhood was secondary, necessary only insofar as social reproduction ensured a continued labor force; her value was her *labor*, essential to the state's attempts to solve the labor question by ensuring that there was enough black labor in cities while curbing the massive influx that was well underway by the 1960s. Black women were expected to assist in this project in three critical ways. First, by staying out of the cities. But for the small numbers of women employed in formal jobs in the city, black women were an unwanted presence. Since early in the twentieth century, the presence of unattached black women in the city had been the source of tremendous national anxiety. By

1963 the apartheid government would succeed in making the presence of women like Grace—unemployed and destitute—illegal, punishable by fines or expulsion. Prior to that, however, the illegal presence of black women in the city was thought to breed lawlessness, prostitution, immorality, and of course, an overindulgence of liquor. As an unemployed, unmarried woman, Grace's condition only fed into these fears. Her history of alcohol use did not help her case.

Black women's second role was to enable the migration of male laborers into the city by remaining in the reserves. It was the imagined role of rural black women maintaining the homestead that undergirded apartheid state arguments against providing black men a family wage or offering black youth in the city poverty relief. Women's labor in the rural reserves, "provided a form of indigenous pension which enabled them to support the aged and destitute Africans" (Kaseke 2002, 222–23; see also Iliffe 1987, 206). In short, black women *were* the welfare system for the black African population. Under this logic, the destitution of black women like Grace did not prompt the extension of support, but instead became a justification for removal from the city. Instead of supporting a migrant labor system, Grace's poverty was a drain on it. Grace's decision to run away from the social workers (and their police escorts) when they visited her, as well as her disappearance, are all the more legible in this context.

The third important responsibility of black women was to raise black children to occupy the social position afforded to their race. By not rearing her two younger children herself, Grace deviated from the important role of labor reproduction qua social reproduction that undergirded the state's welfare logic. Instead, Grace's file reveals glimpses into the many ways she (and other black women) cultivated a "black interior" away from and in opposition to the authoritative reach of the state. That black interior, Hartman writes, "is a space for thought and action, for study and vandalism, for love and trouble" that has revolutionary potential (Hartman 2021, 23). They made and drank alcohol, they had sex beyond the strictures of marriage, they hosted and helped one another, and they had children. "Unattached" women like Grace stoked white fears around unregulated black female desire. Their children's familial nonconformity was read as pathology and delinquency that would wreak social havoc and cost the government important resources. In their persistent unruliness, women like Grace carved out freedoms and enacted alternative forms of black maternal-ness beyond the those validated and valued by the state (Hodgson and McCurdy 1996; Kandaswamy 2021; Haarmann 1998).

Herein lies a critical difference to the cases of Magdalena and Grace. Though both were able to locate their actions under the moral umbrella of maternal care, their mothering was subject to different valuation due to their race in ways that powerfully affected their daily efforts of social reproduction. Magdalena's children were viewed as future citizens. As such, her care for them was supported until it was deemed so insufficient it could not be remedied. Only at that point were her children sent to state institutions, but again, to be rehabilitated into productive members of the nation. Grace's child was, a priori, a noncitizen, viewed as a burden on an already strained urban welfare infrastructure. Had she remained in contact, it is likely that both mother and child would be sent to the reserves where their poverty would be no less pressing but decidedly less visible to white leadership. Instead, Grace dodged this fate. Her actions suggest that she was savvy to the different racial valuations of maternal care and their political power. The father she named for Themba had the same first name as the father of her younger children, with the notable difference of being mixed race instead of black. She said she had no information as to his whereabouts as they only slept together once, thereby forcing the social worker to rely on her word. By recasting Themba as mixed race, Grace was able to raise his social status and make claims on a better resourced welfare institution. In short, she was able to persist in the project of getting by and the provision for Themba, even—and indeed because of—her maternal absence.

———

This close examination of three 1960s Children's Court cases of women of different races shows the intermingling of domestic, welfare, and racial ideologies as they worked out in practice. In each case, the women made claims to welfare resources on the basis of their maternal status as a powerful yet unstable identity. I view these efforts as part of a larger practice of "making motherhood work," by which I mean mobilizing the legitimacy and moral authority afforded to the social category of mother to enable the project of social reproduction, or getting by. Implicit across this chapter is also the argument that from the nineteenth century through the 1960s, state support for social reproduction outlined the contours of citizenship in ways that were at every point crosscut by race, class, gender, and geography. Interpretations of proper family life and maternal practice were consistently refracted through racial ideology and heteropatriarchy.

Across the apartheid era, the ability to claim state support grew increasingly important. In the early years, when there was a skilled labor shortage, households were poor if they did not have a member or a link to someone of working age or, in rare cases such as Magdalena's, if the wage earner worked in a low-wage occupation. As the economy transitioned from one of labor shortage to one of labor surplus and apartheid policies further solidified inequality, creating an underclass of "landless, unskilled, unemployed" persons, state support marked the difference between poverty and working-class status (Nattrass and Seekings 2010, 47). By 1994, most poor households had members who could work, but could not find jobs. Old age pensions lifted households with older members out of deep poverty. The poorest households—often headed by women in their forties and fifties— were those who could not make any claims on kin or the state for support (Nattrass and Seekings 2010).

The category of mother had such potency to make claims on the state because in popular discourse, motherhood functions as a symbol that subsumes very different meanings, identities, and experiences under a single referent. It is seen as a self-evident concept with tremendous social weight that affords the social position both great authority and great vulnerability to critique. Female activists across the century have drawn on this symbolic power and used public motherhood to contest state policy. The capacious reach of motherhood as symbolic concept allowed various women's groups to transcend yawning differences in ideology and social position. This chapter argues that, in a similar vein, poor women drew on the potency of motherhood for their own political actions. However, they also confronted the ways in which motherhood is subject to very different meanings.

The South African welfare system, like its counterparts in other countries, developed an ideal type of motherhood that was used to evaluate and shape the lives of the families who encountered the system. Amid state-led white supremacy, the dominant ideal was that of the white middle-class homemaker who devoted full-time efforts to child-rearing, meal prep, cleaning, and (usually Christian-inflected) spiritual uplift. In many ways, a similar ideal was promoted within the coloured race groups with a greater emphasis also placed on service to the community (Erasmus 2001). Social workers also recruited poor coloured women to be a part of a project of national moral uplift by eschewing the negative qualities associated with their race, such as promiscuity, untrustworthiness, criminality, drug and alcohol abuse, and vulgarity (Erasmus 2001). Rural black African women were less subject to a domestic ideology based on the nuclear ideal because they were understood to be living in adherence to very different cultural norms and because they were not recognizably part of an industrial class (Gaitskell 1983). However, their urban counterparts lived under the disciplinary technology of influx control and the township house that attempted to make them into full-time mothers of a nuclear household. Further, groups from the overtly political Inkatha Women's Brigade or the Federation of South African Women to Christian church groups and sewing clubs promoted black African respectability through nuclear, and overtly patriarchal, families. Oftentimes social welfare agencies remained doggedly committed to these ideals regardless of how inaccessible they were for impoverished mothers.

For the women in this chapter, motherhood lost its symbolic coherence when it encountered the hard borders of racial ideology. How the maternal idea was defined and how deviance from it was regulated shaped the differing experiences of these three women. White women such as Magdalena were first and foremost deviant because of their poverty. A higher standard of living was seen as the marker of white civilization and ascendance. Improper practices such as too much time spent outside the home, multiple sexual liaisons, inadequate disciplining of native servants, and overconsumption of alcohol were only further evidence of how her internal sensibilities needed to be brought in line with the motives of thrift, piety, and discretion, more befitting of her gender and race. In contrast, Rosemary's poverty was seen as less of a moral failure and more an obstacle to proper child-rearing. Her primary deviance was as a single mother who sought work outside of the household instead of attending to the care of her children. Comparatively, Grace's poverty was also less an issue of personal failure—although the report suggests she lost her job by virtue of improper conduct—as much as it was a violation of the role assigned to black women. The cause of her poverty was less a concern to state social workers as much as its whereabouts. Women like her were not to be supported by the state but relocated back to the reserves where they could be aided by an imagined kin network. In her presence in the city, she was failing in her role to ensure the reproduction of the migrant labor system and in her responsibility to produce the next generation of laborers. Importantly, these ideals and deviations were not formed in isolation, but were co-constituted through practices of differentiation and distinction. Likewise, social workers, aid workers, missionaries, teachers, and church women's groups all engaged in the project of shaping domestic life and contributed to the conversation of what the ideal family should entail.

The files make clear—most visibly in Grace's case—that in their claim-making, these women were aware of the dynamic, mobile nature of motherhood—as singular symbol and as multivalent signifier. They worked hard to maintain control over how the meaning of motherhood was translated in a given context, most evident in Magdalena's multiple letters. The efficacy of making motherhood work relied on this duality and was threatened by it. However, not only was the singularity of motherhood subject to differentiated meanings based on race (and class), its meanings also shifted over time. The women in this chapter are the metaphorical mothers and grandmothers of the women I met in Point in 2014, and their histories shape the contours of how motherhood operated quite differently in the decades following democratic transition.[49] The next chapter turns to those women.

4 "WE ARE MOTHERS, WE ARE HUSTLERS"

Kinshipping in the Community

BRONWYN AND MARYANN WERE IN another fight. It was 2014 and we were standing in the open-air corridor outside the small, adjacent rooms where Bronwyn and Maryann lived with their children. These public spaces were where most interactions between tenants—angry or otherwise—took place. The prior week Maryann's refrigerator had broken. She had stored leftover chicken in Bronwyn's fridge while she saved for repairs. However, Bronwyn betrayed her own fridge-hospitality when she used Maryann's meat. When Maryann learned of this, she'd hurled accusations of theft and selfishness at Bronwyn—words with dangerous implications in most parts of South Africa—before storming out of the building. Bronwyn turned and animatedly defended herself to me, justifying her actions through a liberal critique of Maryann. Bronwyn argued the chicken was being wasted because Maryann was "lazy to cook." "Me," she boasted, "I make my children a hot meal every night. Many nights her kids eat just butter and rolls." I tried to suppress my smile, aware of Maryann's notorious hatred of cooking. "You know," Bronwyn said conspiratorially, "the girls are getting poor marks"—referring to Maryann's daughters, newly enrolled in the neighborhood school—"they will probably have to repeat. I told Maryann to go over

129

their work with them, but she is lazy to do it. That's what I did with [my son] and his marks are good."

In my research, I encountered many women like Bronwyn and Maryann, not formally married or employed, who supported themselves and their children by cobbling together resources from a range of sources. Maryann's meat offers a key example of how a chicken was not only a source of nourishment but also part of a vital economy where gendered performances of caregiving were evaluated and either rewarded or policed.

Sometime before the poultry was purloined, I had visited Maryann and found her drinking tea in her room with an Indian woman, Jamila. Jamila worked for a well-endowed white church that ran an aid program out of the neighborhood school. Unusually racially integrated for Durban, the school's population identified predominantly with black African and coloured racial groups and partially with white and Indian race groups. Coloured women like Bronwyn and Maryann considered themselves different from women like Jamila both in terms of race and a broadly defined notion of "culture." There was also an added dimension of social power. Though she lacked formal training, most residents referred to Jamila as "the school social worker." Jamila's neighborhood role was to counsel troubled kids—and their problematic parents—and to distribute resources from the church such as groceries, clothes, school supplies, and, on that particular day, the small luxuries of fresh milk and sugar.

As I entered, Maryann offered me tea—a regular ritual—gesturing casually to the milk and sugar, displayed artfully in new dishes balanced on an overturned orange bucket. I mentioned that the room smelled good, glancing, with some surprise, at the pots bubbling on the hot plate. Jamila laughed and explained. Maryann had just recounted that on her recent trip to the shop, she capitalized on a two-for-one sale on chicken by persuading another, white, customer to give her one. Maryann grinned, gesturing broadly with her cigarette: "Oh yes, I just said 'Are you going to say no to these children? . . . It's not for me.' The girls said, 'Mommy do you know that man from work?' I said, 'No my darlings, he is just a very nice man.'" We all laughed at Maryann's cleverness. Jamila turned to me and wrinkled her nose, "She is so naughty." Bolstered by the laughter, Maryann shrugged casually and said, "My family must have their meat. What must I do? I made a plan."

Here I consider the processes by which women "make a plan" to secure resources, the conditions under which they do or do not succeed, and the meaning of that support. An analysis of these kinshipping efforts, I suggest, has implications for understanding how women rework their citizenship in the new South Africa. As the previous chapters detailed, the boundaries of inclusion in the nation have long been marked by whose social reproduction the South African state was willing to support and in what ways.

During white minority rule, white citizen families could receive robust support from the welfare state. This was fiscally possible because the white population was small and because job reservation for whites and almost full employment ensured that state assistance was often temporary relief amid frequent periods of work. Though South Africa's economy shifted to one of labor surplus in the 1970s, the structure of welfare as short-term aid persisted, and waged labor continued to be held up as the most morally reputable way of gaining the resources to enable social reproduction. A key tenet of the antiapartheid struggle and the democratic state that followed was that jobs be liberated from the racially discriminatory and exploitative structures of the past to allow all South Africans to work their way into prosperity. But when the wage labor market collapsed instead of expanded, those who had gained juro-political citizenship at transition were left without the most venerated means of achieving relational citizenship. In an attempt to redress the inequities of the past, the welfare system that had previously ensured white families' relational citizenship was reformed to be more inclusive. However, the effects were ambiguous at best. On the one hand, all race groups were eligible for support and, for the Child Support Grant (CSG) in particular, the collecting caregivers were not subject to the scrutiny and regulation endured by Magdalena, Rosemary, and Grace in the 1960s. On the other hand, grant amounts were far smaller (not enough to live on) and the caregiver portion of the State Maintenance Grant that Magdalena and Rosemary received was stripped away in the CSG. In other words, though all race groups were equally eligible, the democratic state only recognized its obligation to support those deemed legitimately external to the labor market, namely, children, people with disabilities, and pensioners. Able-bodied women and men who were unemployed lacked mechanisms to make claims for support of their own projects of living. Critically, claims to deservingness for support in 2014 continued to operate as claims to belonging in the new nation. For Point women they also served as demands for recognition that their caregiving labor mattered and that they, as caregivers, deserved support.

Mothers like Bronwyn and Maryann used kinshipping to assemble and make claims on broad support networks of multiple people and institutions—neighbors, friends, family, boyfriends, fathers, state agencies, or chicken-benefactors. This involved leveraging widely held social beliefs and legislative commitments that children are a unique category of persons entitled to support.[1] In their kinshipping, Point women enacted performances of motherhood to affirm their relationship to a deserving child and claim support and recognition for their mothering.

Motherhood as a repertoire of claim-making operated differently in 2014 than it did for Magdalena, Rosemary, and Grace. Point mothers in 2014 shared with their foremothers a fraught position in the long-standing moral panic over mothering as both cause and solution to the social degradation of the citizenry (Donzelot 1979). The particular form these concerns take under democracy is as widespread alarm about "family disintegration" indexed by children growing up in female-headed households and the prevalence of fathers who do not participate in their children's lives physically or financially. Female-headed households are pathologized for their poverty, for their dependence on government grants, and for their deviance from a nuclear ideal that was made virtually impossible for black families. Their poverty is attributed to laziness and unwillingness to work—critiques with long histories—and linked to new accusations that women, particularly teenage girls, become pregnant in order to access government grants. At the same time, an ideal of the self-sacrificing, tireless, impoverished black mother who is able to make something from nothing is also lauded and celebrated in popular discourse. This veneration of the poor, black superwoman is not without its own drawbacks as it is often used by black and white women alike to critique black and coloured women who are seen to misspend the children's grant monies (for example, on fancy hairstyles or expensive cell phones). Thus, in their claims, Point women had to tread a narrow path between avoiding the deviant forms of motherhood that would render them ineligible and invoking the maternal ideals that their audiences value.

This chapter accounts for the embeddedness of maternal performances in particular political economies. In the Point, talk about mothering and actions of caregiving were performative, meaning they had social effects beyond just care (Austin 2018). They were a means of claiming resources from more powerful audiences. Drawing on sociolinguistics and performativity theory, I trace how women performed what I term *adequate motherhood* and the conditions under which these performances garnered material support. Performances of adequate motherhood included ways of speaking and acting that, in different contexts, were viewed by an audience as indicating an unobjectionable—neither "ideal" nor "deviant"—and deserving maternal status (see Silva 1996). These performances took place in what linguistic anthropologist Summerson Carr terms a "semiotic economy," wherein differing values, both moral and material, were assigned to various practices and talk (2011, 82; Keane 2007). However, the varied audiences from which my interlocutors sought aid (social workers, imams, pastors, boyfriends, neighbors) held different and often competing definitions of what constituted adequate motherhood. Whereas neighbors praised the prostitute mother for putting food on the table through hard work, pastors rewarded the chaste Christian mother who relied on the church's soup kitchen. Women only received support when their performances aligned with an audience's values. Here I track how women applied effective ways of speaking and acting to attract support.

Shifting Maternal Repertoires in the Point

In 2014 the social and economic landscape of the Point had changed remarkably from that of the 1960s. Neighborhood residents were still predominantly poor, but following the repeal of influx control laws in the 1980s, black African, Indian, and coloured families now lived alongside white families in the converted boardinghouse rooms once reserved for white workers, such as the old Blenheim Hotel. All race groups could enjoy the neighborhood's many resources—the beachfront, the large government hospital, and the formerly white primary school. The Greek and Portuguese immigrant groups that had once dominated the neighborhood were now replaced by immigrants from the African continent. Racial intermingling, however, had not undone decades of racial tensions. Black residents complained of mistreatment by Indian nurses at the hospital. Coloured mothers who did not speak isiZulu were suspicious that their black African neighbors were gossiping about them. The transience of most neighborhood residents and people's reliance on morally ambiguous forms of deception and chicanery (e.g., hustling or *phanda*-ing for isiZulu speakers) to afford the high cost of living also impeded a sense of community cohesion and contributed to the deep-seated mistrust people had of many of their neighbors.

The lives of Point residents reflected the ambiguous gains of the poor following the end of apartheid. Neighborhood residents often complained about the relentless demands imposed by a cash-based economy that contrasted markedly with the nostalgia many held for rural life. Cross-racially, Point residents expressed a profound sense of disappointment and exclusion from the changes they attributed to democratic transition as well as exhaustion from persistent economic insecurity in a milieu where stable employment was the stuff of fantasy. They all decried the lack of jobs, a decline that actually began well before 1994, blaming it on (black) governmental mismanagement, corruption, and the presence of "too many foreigners." Critiques of nepotistic allocation of employment when made by white, coloured and Indian residents described what they viewed as racist exclusion from privileges many had come to expect, and when made by black Africans, named what they saw as the fragmentary nature of the transition.[2] They argued that providing for their families was far more difficult than what they felt it should be in the era of democracy and that the fault for these challenges lay squarely on the shoulders of the government.

Point women were notably dissatisfied with the deracialized version of state welfare. They remembered well the robust welfare provisions whites enjoyed in the 1960s and 1970s. Many of the white and coloured women had grown up in households where regular visits by the Durban Child Welfare Society social workers ensured that the family received State Maintenance Grants (SMGs) and grocery parcels. A number of black African women had older relatives or friends who had worked as "domestics" for poor white families, their paltry wages paid out of the generous SMG. They also remembered that black women received little if any support from social workers and were constantly scrambling to house themselves and feed their children. So it was that black and coloured women were particularly incensed that, even under democracy and with state aid, their lives were not much improved from that of their foremothers and in some ways were economically more insecure.

In, 2014, housing in Point was much more expensive than elsewhere in the city, meaning that few women could afford to live alone and support their children. Together with a man—often a child's father—these women rented a portion of a room, a room, or a studio apartment in one of the multiunit buildings that dominate the neighborhood. Their boyfriends worked at odd jobs or as car guards, directing drivers into parking spots and protecting cars from theft in exchange for small tips. A few men had higher earnings as truck drivers and security officers, or from dealing drugs, but these were the exception. Men usually earned enough to pay rent, and women were expected to secure cash, food, clothing, blankets, or other family necessities. Though some worked part-time as waitresses in beachfront cafes, such opportunities were scarce and the high cost of even neighborly child care made such jobs inaccessible. In addition to the do mestic labor of cleaning and cooking, women spent most of their days circulating through neighborhood institutions seeking necessary resources.

The retrenchment of state services and a narrowing of the terms under which they could request aid left poor women in a precarious position (Hassim 2005). The logic of deservingness embodied in the CSG also pervaded community relationships. Although women were expected to translate resources into proper social reproduction, they themselves were not regarded as legitimate aid recipients in their own right. There were widespread and heavily moralized critiques of women's misspending what was supposed to be the "children's money"—the greatest violations being purchases of makeup and hairstyling. Such critiques must be understood as part of a larger "politics of the womb," wherein debates over women's access to resources to support their productive and reproductive labors are part of larger concerns about the gendered ordering of the nation (Thomas 2003). These critiques also have material consequences in elaborating the boundaries of women's control over aid resources. The neighbors, pastors, or school principals from whom Point women sought aid saw children as the only worthy recipients. Thus, successful performances of motherhood were the primary means to access support.

Herein lies the stakes in Maryann and Bronwyn's performances of motherhood to one another and to me. It is a pressing concern that poor women have no mechanism to achieve state recognition other than through their status as mothers. However, this lack of recognition does not only exist at the level of the state. Women's recognition from their own community members and sometimes their own household is also predicated on successfully embodying shifting and contradictory performances of deserving motherhood. This is a rather tenuous hold on belonging indeed.

In 2014, it was no longer just social workers or the state that evaluated deserving motherhood. It was something that everyone had taken up, from the volunteer dishing out plates at the soup kitchen to the neighbor in the stairwell. These audiences were pervasively present and overlapping. And now, more than ever, their opinions matter. Neighborly critiques—as seen with Bronwyn and with Agatha and Magdalena in the previous chapter— have long been present, but in a context where formal employment is no longer a given and even more rarely an option, the stakes of these ever-present audiences have changed. While the gossip of a neighbor no longer results in the removal of a child, it can cut a mother off from critical resources and information and thereby heighten her economic and social

FIGURE 4.1   Dishing up a steaming plate of curry at a Point soup kitchen. Photo by Cedric Nunn.

insecurity. In the Point, successfully learning, enacting, and managing performances of motherhood is a critical means to survival.

This chapter draws on ethnography with fifteen women who rented rooms in the Blenheim building. I observed how they talked about their own and others' mothering practices and took note of how their caregiving actions and talk differed based on with whom they were interacting. These differences were not random, but clustered into repertoires of verbal and nonverbal expression that are the objects of my analysis. Words and actions convey meaning to observers because they press into service conventions of signification existing in a society (Cameron and Kulick 2008). The aggregate of sociolinguistic resources—ways of speaking, gesturing, walking, dressing—that can be used to perform, say, adequate motherhood is a repertoire. Repertoires, like scripts, "contain the rules and roles of performances" that delimit the interpretive range of action within which a performance will be effective, meaning intelligible (Carr 2011, 192; also Bauman 1996; Silverstein and Urban 1996). While innovation and improvisation are possible, and sometimes desirable, repertoires are effective because they are coherent, reproducing, and reproducible. Thus, people such as Point women can learn and reproduce them and scholars can examine and compare them across time and space (Tilly 2008). Attention to the sociolinguistic resources used to perform adequate motherhood is critical because what resources are available in a given context shape our understanding of what someone is (or what they should be) doing when they do motherhood. In other words, available repertoires of language and practice significantly influence what is possible mothering.

The repertoires available to differently raced Point women to perform adequate motherhood were informed by a long history of welfare officers' evaluations of motherhood such as those discussed in the previous chapter (Erasmus 2001; Gaitskell 1983; Meer 1972). Across South Africa's history of segregated welfare, racist stereotypes shaped which repertoires were materially rewarded (for Durban, see Watts and Lamond 1966). White mothers were historically expected to demonstrate sobriety, thrift, Christian piety, respect for patriarchal dominance, and, importantly, an awareness of white racial superiority (Teppo 2004). Poor coloured families were often associated with promiscuity, criminality, and drug and alcohol abuse (Erasmus 2001).

Thus, in their interventions, coloured and white social workers promoted repertoires of coloured respectability that eschewed interaction with black Africans and embraced white middle-class norms (Adhikari 2006). In contrast, repertoires valued by volunteers at the Durban Indian Child Welfare Society valorized the Indian mother as the keeper of a specifically Indian tradition against a hostile foreign—read, white—environment (Kuper 1960; Nowbath 1978). Indian women were encouraged to be submissive to their husbands and to strictly discipline daughters while showering affection on sons (Meer 1972). For urban black mothers, in the apartheid era, traditional African child-rearing practices were viewed by social workers as a sign of backwardness (Du Toit 2014). The repertoires of deserving black motherhood, thus, emphasized a woman's ability to shed her rural roots and rear her children in "modern" ways—ensuring regular medical checkups and inoculations, buying western clothing and shoes, and teaching them English or Afrikaans (Gaitskell 1983). These are broad summaries of what, in practice, were quite malleable understandings of deserving motherhood. Nevertheless, they had afterlives in the democratic era. The majority of the coloured and white women I knew in Point had grown up regularly interacting with social workers intervening into their family (in three instances I had Children's Court files for them or their siblings). Through these experiences, they internalized successful repertoires of interacting with gatekeepers to resources such as social workers. Additionally, those providing aid on Point—the prayer group leaders, the soup kitchen volunteers, the aid association members—often had either come out of a long lineage of voluntary welfare programs that also employed the aforementioned maternal ideals or had also grown up dependent on state welfare.

Where seeking aid in the 1960s involved a more limited range of interactions mostly with social workers, in 2014 the audiences were more varied and diverse and their interactions far less formal and routinized. A key effect of the narrowed welfare system under democracy was that sources of aid and definitions of deservingness multiplied and became far more diverse and divergent. The presumed unified concept of motherhood that women like Magdalena, Rosemary, and Grace had leveraged, had fractured into multiple maternities. The various potential sources of support often had different and conflicting definitions of adequate (and deserving) motherhood. For instance, the terms of interaction with the church soup kitchen's volunteers bore little resemblance to either the ritual confessions expected at an informal prayer group or the home visits of 1960s social workers. Only through continued and repeated participation in these various settings did Point women learn the "contextualization cues" that suggested what actions would be valued in a given interaction (Gumperz 1982). It is not surprising, then, that women's abilities to successfully perform motherhood varied enormously. Some were quicker studies, while others were more adept at acclimating their performances to different contexts. Furthermore, not all people could enact all repertoires of adequate motherhood. Each woman's race, language skills (e.g., knowledge of English or Afrikaans), or history of interactions shaped the repertoires she could access. These differences in skill and personal attributes marked the boundaries of who succeeded—and who didn't—in the semiotic economy of the Point.

Doing Motherhood

In this chapter, "motherhood" incorporates two domains: the labor and practices of mothering, and the discourses and norms of motherhood—often evaluations of that mothering work—that circulate in a particular social group (Walker 1995). In doing so, my analysis brings together once more the distinction feminist scholarship has long made between motherhood and mothering.[3] A motherhood performance comprises both women's embodied practices as they care for a child (such as food preparation, bathing, clothing, or discipline) and the ways in which they narrate or critique those action to different audiences—their children included—to have themselves understood as a mother.

Here I attend to what social effects performances of motherhood have regardless, or even in spite of, the intentions behind them. This is in contrast to scholarship on activism and identity construction that emphasizes the conscious, intentional means by which people perform (or conceal) certain identities (Cameron and Kulick 2003). I am not suggesting that intentions are irrelevant. The distinction between whether Bronwyn took Maryann's meat in order to feed her family or to make Maryann look bad—though not mutually exclusive—is, of course, meaningful. However, as I will discuss, what Point women understood themselves to be doing when they were doing adequate motherhood is not data to which I have access. Instead, I focus on the repertoires of speech and action that women drew on to perform adequate motherhood and the situations in which they did and did not elicit support from the audience.

My analysis uses performativity theory, which is concerned with how language and communicative practices do things in the world, how they convey meaning to the audiences who witness them (Austin 1962; Derrida 1995). In the domain of gender, a performative analysis can consider the conventions of signification—shared ideas of meaning—that allow for a person who dresses, talks, walks, and gestures in accordance with a particular repertoire to be understood as a particular gender or another (Butler 1990). Performativity is concerned with the conditions under which performances are intelligible—the conventions of signification, or shared ideas of meaning. This means that regardless of whether, for example, one puts on a dress in a self-conscious drag act, as part of an unconscious morning routine, or avoids dresses altogether so as not to be misconstrued as female, the conventions of signification in circulation that equate dresses with femininity enable audiences to interpret dress-wearing as feminine. This is not to say that the dress-wearer's intentions don't affect the audience—there are a number of ways one can indicate, for example, "I am wearing this dress as a joke." However, the interpretation of dress-wearing as feminine does not *depend on* the wearer's intentions (Cameron and Kulick 2003). The audience makes their own connections between what they witness and the conventions of interpretation (Derrida 1995). Audiences are knowledgeable about these conventions because they are, indeed, conventional. They have been repeated many times and in various contexts. This is how the concept of a "strict, disciplinarian mother"—conjures up clusters of words and actions that could or could not be enacted. These repertories are the rules of acting and speaking that enable repetitive reenactments to be consistently interpreted (Bauman 1996; Jackson 2005). Actors can alter the available repertoires, improvise, or refuse the assigned role altogether, but such deviation threatens the reliability of how the performance will be interpreted (Austin 2018; Briggs 2007). In short, motherhood can be many things, but not everything goes at any given time.

I focus on the performativity of motherhood in order to also account for power. While the term *performance* may evoke play or, at least, interpretive creativity, the boundaries of that play are limited by hierarchies of authority. Not all people have equal power to do work with words, and the relative power of an actor vis-à-vis an audience shapes what repertories an actor can access or the degree to which she can change them (Brada 2013). For Point women, their performances of motherhood were most frequently done for a more powerful audience that was evaluating and assessing if they were, indeed, adequate. They were constrained by the available repertoires and lacked the power to define what maternal practices would be viewed as deserving of material support. However, what Point women did have was repeatability. For the women, much of the day, every day, was spent interacting with people from whom they sought resources. By tracking what actions were rewarded and which were sanctioned, they could learn the "contextualization cues" that signaled what repertoires were valued in which context (Gumperz 1982). They also learned how a woman's racial, ethnic, and class identity shaped what an audience expected from her. For instance, given their poverty and lack of high-class *habitus*, none of the Point women could successfully perform the repertoires of the idealized middle-class mother. Even if such repertoires were performable, to do so would have limited their eligibility for aid. Rather, the repertoires that attracted support were those of *adequate* motherhood, neither stellar nor problematic. Worthy, but needy. This might involve dressing children in meticulously ironed, yet stained, secondhand clothes, or speaking about homemade remedies to forgo expensive medicine. Thus, the power that women held was their ability to discern what repertoires would be effective and to attune their maternal performance to these expectations.

The fact that repertoires of adequate motherhood could be learned and reproduced has the potential to induce anxiety about authenticity and faking. Among people in the Point, there are widespread concerns about how to assess the sincerity of actions. On a different level, questions about insincerity and truth have methodological implications. The colloquial understanding of performance creates an opposition between an "act" and a "real" self who engages in intentional speech and action. This orientation assumes that personhood precedes speech and action; that there is a self, what Butler terms the "epistemological subject," that intentionally decides what to say or do (1990, 144). Within this framework, an understanding of motherhood as something that could be performed creates a methodological conundrum as to how to distinguish between reality and play-acting. While an important consideration in any context, this is especially pertinent for my research with Point women. As a white, American researcher who was accurately perceived to be more economically advantaged, women often made claims on me for resources or job contacts. Further, neighborhood residents consistently misinterpreted me as a social worker who, theoretically, could remove their children. Thus, women had high stakes reasons to ensure that I only witnessed well-curated performances of motherhood. My use of performativity theory addresses the impossible task of differentiating between purportedly authentic, unmotivated actions and intentional performances.

A foundational premise of performativity theory is that no self exists prior to social interaction (Austin 2018; Butler 1990; Goffman 1959, 1981). Selfhood in this view is not an internal, stable entity that is somehow separate from the cultural field that encompasses it. Instead, selfhood is brought about through the process of social interaction (Briggs 2007). While there are intentional and unintentional actions, identity—in this case, motherhood—is a performative *result* of speech and actions, not the originating motivation (Cameron and Kulick 2003). This shifts the theoretical questions away from what actors intend to do with their actions—phenomena to which researchers often do not have reliable access—and toward questions about what meaningful social effects their actions have.

This shift in orientation is not only important methodologically but also politically. Within feminist scholarship there is precedent for viewing mothering as performative (e.g., O'Reilly on feminist mothering or work on the "lactivists" who publicly breastfeed to protests misogynist bodily regulation (2004; Carpenter 2006). These are cases in which intention is usually made explicit. However, in the instances where motivations are more ambiguous, strategic actions are often seen as antithetical to sincerity and to love. It is well-trod ground that there is great cultural discomfort with analysis that imply that mothers may not love their children (Scheper-Hughes 1993). In my case, the question of whether Point women *really* loved their children is neither my focus nor within my ability to answer. Instead, what I have access to are actions and their reception. Maryann's wiping of her son's nose was as strategic as how she cooked the chicken for Jamila. She might wipe to show her son love or to relieve discomfort. Or, she might wipe to show a pastor that her child was well-cared for and that she was the kind of mother who attends to things like runny noses. These multiple interpretations are not incommensurate; one does not negate the presence of the other. As a researcher, I attended to how Maryann's son and the other audiences to her wiping responded to the action and the outcomes that arose from it. My analysis need not be fettered by an attempt to discern what women really intended to be doing and instead is concerned with what social effects their performances of motherhood actually had. I demonstrate that within the semiotic economy of the Point, there were important contexts in which acts such as nose wiping were rewarded with critically needed support.

To Be a Mother Is to Be a Hustler: Managing Authenticity Anxieties

Point women performed motherhood in circumstances of unequal power. More powerful teachers, social workers, and neighbors assessed whether women's words and actions aligned with valued repertoires of adequate motherhood. However, two simultaneously held ideological regimes complicated these evaluations. First, in everyday life, interactive performances were regularly expected and disciplined. To not clean your house on the day the social worker came to visit provoked criticism, as did the failure to greet your neighbor. Second, South Africans, like Euro-Americans, held a language ideology—a collective understanding about how language works—that words and actions were sincere reflections of an actor's inner state (Carr 2011). Therefore, clean houses and hellos should arise out of personal desire for tidiness and hospitality. The idea that someone might be performing in the colloquial sense of "putting on an act" would mean that actions did not come from sincere intentions, but from strategic, and therefore duplicitous, motivations. However, no one was naive enough to think that the Point was a community uniquely populated with overly clean or friendly people. This produced what linguistic anthropologist Judith Irvine terms a "sincerity problem" or an inability to assess the authenticity of intention (1982). High levels of mistrust and anxiety resulted throughout the neighborhood as residents guarded against insincere performances with little epistemological grounding for assessment.

Due to the Point neighborhood's small size and density, pervasive suspicions of insincerity caused a further complication. Women's performances of motherhood were often witnessed by multiple audiences simultaneously. As a woman walked along the streets, stairwells, or beachfront, she was vis-

FIGURE 4.2   A moment of rest before heading out for the afternoon. Photo by Brady G'sell.

ible to other pedestrians, taxi passengers, and apartment residents hanging out of windows, who often would shout a greeting or a catcall. Frequently, these overlapping audiences valued quite contradictory repertoires of adequate motherhood. For instance, one Pentecostal prayer group leader who was cultivating a worship group of mothers saw some of her followers in line at the Episcopal Church soup kitchen as she drove her Mercedes out of the neighborhood. She later accused the women of "religion shopping," implying they lacked a sincere commitment to the spiritual transformation she was leading them towards. In another case, a woman was seen on the beachfront selling the toddler shoes she had received as a donation from the refugee center, and the center manager accused her of misrepresenting her need. The visibility of women performing multiple, contradictory maternal repertoires challenged the ideology that words and actions arose from sincere intention. Revealing the performative nature of motherhood destabilized the mechanisms by which audience members evaluate a performance's efficacy. Women's sincerity was put into question, and they were subject to moral critiques of lying and deception.

Aware of their audiences' suspicions, women managed this anxiety over authenticity through metalinguistic commentary, meaning talk that described talk. They used the term "the hustle" to acknowledge that there were important times when one's words and actions did not transparently reflect one's interior self. Take for example a conversation I witnessed while waiting outside with a group of women to walk to a Christian prayer meeting:

BG: Where is Claudette?

M: [crossly] I called her. I dunno what she's doing.

P: [laughing] She's taking off her Muslim clothes . . . she can't go to church with Muslim clothes so she's put jeans on. [all laugh] Those people that live a double life. Hey, but when you are a mother, what must we do?

S: Ja, that's the life, we are mothers, we are hustlers. That's what we do. We are hustling. . . . That's how we survive.

L: [laughing] Double jobs.

P: A double life. I must do this, do that. . . . In the day I am a Muslim, in the night I must be a febe [prostitute].

This is the same joke Maryann shared with Jamila when she told the story about "making a plan" to get the chicken. The ability to hustle—to successfully align your maternal repertoires to audience expectations—was a source of pride, a skill. It was part of being a mother. Here women shared in a collective recognition that some performances did not necessarily refer to inner states, but could, nonetheless, be effective.

Point women used the notion of the hustle as a descriptive label to delineate between sincere and insincere talk and action (e.g., "there I was just hustlin'") in an effort to reestablish their credibility to their audiences. It allowed women to attribute contradictory actions to different epistemological orders (Mol 2002). By invoking the hustle, women could call out one performance as insincere in contrast to an implied "real" self from which the speaker spoke. In doing so, they worked to again produce a cohesive image of themselves—a single self among multiple maternities—that made the contradictory practices appear to "hang together" (Mol 2002).

In the case of the Pentecostal prayer group, Ann, one of the accused "religion shoppers," later told the leader that she was hustling for her sick sister, who had no food at home. She had gone to the soup kitchen, she argued, with Tupperware in hand but with a nonbelieving heart. Through her use of the term, Ann reframed her presence at the soup kitchen as an insincere request and her involvement in the prayer group as committed belief. In doing so, Ann reconstituted herself as a trustworthy, and therefore deserving, mother. Importantly, this ability to successfully perform a multiplicity of repertoires and to manage the anxieties their contradictions produced paid dividends within the semiotic economy. As one woman, Vijy, said, "We walk the crooked way we come right, we walk straight nothing comes right." Women's descriptive usage of the term "hustle" allowed them to tread a narrow ethical line between engaging in actions deemed morally suspect because they involved forms of deception and performing actions considered morally legitimate because they were done out of economic necessity. However, as powerful as a usage of these terms could be, they could not explain away all contradictions.

Performing Multiple Maternities

Performing adequate motherhood was both the stuff of everyday life and a highly cultivated expertise for Point women. Success relied on what Carr calls "anticipatory interpellation," or one's ability to forecast a more powerful audience's expectations of their actions (2009). Some women had life experiences that had honed their skills. Before having children, Maryann had been a waitress at a bar where patrons could also wager on horse races. She proudly regaled me with stories of how she would flirt with the men, goading them into ordering stronger and more expensive drinks that often resulted in higher tips, or how she would advise them on bets until they would trust her to place the wagers and she could skim off what they gave her. When she was caught, which was rare, she often beguiled them into contributing to her "mad money" fund. Asanda also prided herself on giving people "what they want to see." Before her second child was born, she had worked as an escort, serving clients at the beachfront hotels. She talked about how European tourists wanted a "real eMzanzi girl," (eMzanzi meaning South African)[4] displayed by a hospitable, modest, and grateful black femininity, whereas the black businessmen down from Johannesburg sought a "Durban chill" experience with a sophisticated and fashionable woman who could dance in the clubs until dawn. In their claim-making, both Maryann and Asanda moved smoothly among very different groups and quickly learned what actions were rewarded and which were sanctioned. Bronwyn, though, had a more difficult time.

Bronwyn grew up in a household that heavily relied on assistance from the Johannesburg Child Welfare Society. Though the family, the six siblings who accompanied Bronwyn, saw numerous social workers over the years, the expectations for conduct did not change dramatically. In the Point, Bronwyn often accompanied Maryann on visits to soup kitchens, storefront Pentecostal churches, or school "service" days, but complained that she found it exhausting and distasteful. She had a challenging time assessing the very different repertoires expected in each interaction and didn't pivot as smoothly as Maryann. She spoke about her "husband" in meetings ostensibly for single mothers or brought her eldest, a teenage son who many thought should have a job —to places catering to young children. The ability to calibrate their performances to the appropriate audience and to make these diverse performances hang together into a cohesive maternal self was a skill Point women regularly practiced and also, even among the most adept, occasionally blundered.

Social workers were still an important part of the landscape of Point welfare, though it looked different from the 1960s. While the social workers who were regularly in the neighborhood in 2014 were not employees of any state agencies that could remove children, they were gatekeepers to aid such as groceries or school uniforms. Many Point women knew well social workers' repertoires for deserving motherhood. They would clean their small rooms meticulously, place a pot of beans to boil on the stove to demonstrate their thrift and work ethic, and would set out milk and sugar for the tea to exhibit hospitality. For those not formally married, they would remove any evidence of a man (who might be giving them money or invite inquiries about their sex lives). Luxury items such as hair creams or body sprays, which raised doubts as to their poverty or sexual purity, would be squirreled away into cupboards. The children's fresh-pressed uniforms were hung on display. Children themselves were counseled to stay in the room and not play with the neighbors' children who might be perceived as a bad influence. They were expected to be respectful—greeting the social worker and pouring tea—and disciplined—sitting quietly during the interview and only answering questions as directed.

In contrast, the many informal prayer groups and churches that offered

FIGURE 4.3   A tidy Point room visible from the door. Photo by Brady G'sell.

aid to the community's children demanded a slightly different repertoire. In these spaces, children were often encouraged to "be free" and engage in more rambunctious play, and their requests for more cake or sweets were often met with indulgent kindness. Mothers coached them to recite the opening of the Lord's Prayer and to ask for extras "for my baby sister at home," regardless of whether such a sibling existed. Women would come equipped with memorized Bible verses to describe their poverty in Christian idioms of graceful suffering. Maryann was known to be quite successful at soliciting support from Christian prayer groups and mission societies. The refrigerator, whose demise instigated the meat-incident, had been a donation from one such group. Maryann dressed much more modestly than many of the other women and, during her outings, her children always had shoes and clean faces and hands, making them stand out as exceptional. Many prayer group leaders told me they especially liked giving resources to Maryann because it was clear she "used them well," as suggested by the children's dress and conduct. In one group, women were asked to testify weekly about the challenges to their faith they had encountered in the intervening days. Maryann solicited my help in crafting a three-page speech that used every verse the group leader had quoted in her most recent sermon. Her "commitment to her faith," as the prayer group leader described it, was rewarded with a week's supply of groceries.

Boyfriends, too, demanded certain conduct in order for the women to enjoy the privilege of the cash they brought home. Their repertoires included sexual and domestic labors, as well as protocols for the treatment of the children, many of whom had different fathers. Women had to be careful not to be seen as spending the boyfriend's money on another man's child. Conversely, in the event of a generous donation of shoes or clothing, they had to ensure that the children from another father did not appear to be better resourced than the boyfriend's own. This meant a delicate and rarely successful calibration of the desires and opinions of boyfriends, children, donors, and of course the women themselves. In one case, Thuli traded her neighbor a pair of shoes she had been given by an aid agency for a bag of rice because the shoes were far nicer than those of her other children. When Thuli's son was seen barefoot at the next meeting, the aid agency director accused Thuli of misusing the donation for her own benefit. However, her act also allowed Thuli to avoid an argument with her boyfriend over unequal treatment of the children that, last time, had resulted in his refusing to work.

Some women also made claims on various Muslim associations for aid. This required that women know the rules of fasting, Arabic greetings, and prayers for maternal piety. Only women with particular social capital could perform these repertoires. Their children were enrolled in madrassa and had Muslim names whose genealogies the women could recite. Wearing the hijab was a highly visible marker of identification with a Muslim audience, but it did not protect women from suspicions of insincerity. There was a circulating discourse disparaging black African women who, during Ramadan, would "put on hijab and go running" to receive zakat money. Zulu and Xhosa women who had married Burundian men and converted to Islam, like those in chapter 6, complained of these critiques as irritating and hurtful. These women experienced the converse of the "sincerity problem" wherein they felt they lacked the means to demonstrate their genuineness.

In contrast, Claudette, who smoothly moved between Christian and Muslim maternal repertoires, felt less personally attacked by such accusations. She had grown up in a Christian-based children's home for coloured children and thus knew well key prayers, songs, and idioms demanded by those aid societies. Later in life she had met an Indian man, the father of most of her children, who had encouraged her to give up her "wild ways" of partying and fighting. He had also prompted her conversion to Islam. She appreciated the very different orientation of the Muslim aid societies, which she described as less moralizing and proselytizing than their Christian counterparts, but complained that they demanded a higher burden of proof of religious observance. As a new convert, she said, her Arabic should not be held to such high standards. She also bristled at the idea that any one group should demand her exclusive commitment in exchange for what amounted to only partial support. Instead, she continued to move back and forth between multiple societies, her success depending on her ability to keep those two audiences separate. If she were to encounter a church pastor on the street while wearing the hijab, reframing its interpretation was almost impossible. Her performance of both repertoires also depended on her maintaining good relationships with neighbors by sharing the spoils of her work. A disgruntled neighbor was a threat who could bring the contradictions between these two repertoires to the fore. Instead, Claudette's performance skills provoked mostly praise and amusement from her peers.

The most complicated performances of motherhood by far were those for women's most proximate neighbors, such as between Bronwyn and Maryann. Neighbors' generosity was the lifeblood of survival of Point women. Neighbors provided everything from cooking oil to loan payments when someone was short, short-term childcare for a trip to the store or job interview, or access to much-needed appliances. Importantly, neighbors were a source of vital information about who was passing out biryani, when a new church opened its doors and its donation bins, or when a much-coveted flat became vacant. These exchanges embedded women in complicated webs of reciprocity and obligation where neighbors were constantly tallying their credits and debts. Women sought to cultivate a delicate balance between appearing generous enough with their time and resources to inspire other neighbors to be the same, but not so generous as to invite too many requests. One of the Muslim aid societies distributed in the last week of the month, which was a lean time for most families. After receiving a parcel, Claudette would fill her own canisters with rice, flour, and sugar and then go door to door in the building distributing the rest. The rest of the month, however, she rarely gave things away. In contrast, Maryann often provoked the ire of others in the building because her redistribution was uneven. Her success with aid societies was well known, but when she was feeling cross, she often responded to neighborly requests with a negative "I don't have." She even went so far as to write on the door of her room, "this welfare is closed"—a statement interpreted as a refusal of her embeddedness in the building's community.

Women likewise cultivated closeness with neighbors through their own and others' children—caring for them, feeding them, offering friendly advice. Success was a fragile balancing of demonstrating one's own skill against the potential of appearing to be "too proud" or superior to others. If not handled deftly, actions such as prohibiting children from playing with the neighbor's children when the social worker visited could quickly backfire and alienate neighborly allies. Vijy's son was known to skip school often and had been caught many times shoplifting in neighborhood stores. For a number of weeks, Vijy hid in her room, pretending to be out when Jamila was in the building. When the family ran out of bread, she opened the door to a conversation about her son's school conduct that might also bring in some food. When Jamila arrived, she loudly and forcibly told her son to "stay away" from the family in the room next door who were widely

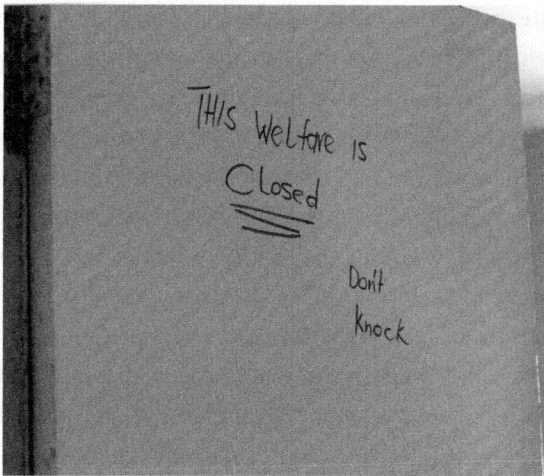

FIGURE 4.4   A statement about distribution written in marker on Maryann's door. Photo by Brady G'sell.

thought to be physically unclean and hosts of "tummy bugs." Later, after Jamila had left and Vijy had learned that the next-door children would be enrolling in school, Vijy tried to explain to the skeptical mother that Vijy hadn't wanted her son's tarnished reputation to rub off on the neighbor's kids. However, the family never spoke to Vijy after that.

In addition to the resources and labor that neighbors provided, the collusion of neighbors was necessary to maintaining cohesion across contradictory repertoires of motherhood. Neighbors' assistance could support a narrative that differentiated between "the hustle" and sincere action. Ann's reframing of her attendance at the church soup kitchen as a caretaking act for her sister was accepted in part because she had a history of active participation in the prayer group and in part because she brought a neighbor to the group to pose as her sister, which both verified the story and increased the leader's following. Conversely, an alienated neighbor could sabotage a performance by calling attention to the discrepancies between repertoires.

Maryann continued to go to the Pentecostal prayer group long after the others had stopped attending. She had garnered the leader's favor and received a regular supply of groceries and lotions. These resources she refused to share with the other women, arguing that they were rewards for pious adherence that her neighbors did not deserve. Fed up one day by what she saw as Maryann's stinginess and pride, Bronwyn unexpectedly returned to the group and told the leader that Maryann had spent the previous Sunday drinking with a man on the beachfront, not watching her young daughters. "And you know those girls have green eyes and would be snatched by anyone," Bronwyn noted, adding another layer to the transgression. Indeed, Maryann had been on the beachfront socializing with a friend who, later, bought Maryann's daughters new clothes, a boon for their family. It is likely that invoking the hustle would not have helped Maryann explain her weekend performance because that particular group leader was known to find talk of hustling distasteful and sinful instead of entrepreneurial, as others did. Maryann instead argued that it wasn't her on the beach, but her sister who, from a distance, resembled her. Yet, in this interaction, Maryann lacked the power to reframe the interpretation or, like Ann, the social capital to bring a friend to corroborate. Unconvinced, the prayer group leader lectured Maryann on her maternal responsibilities and dismissed her from the group.

The successful performance of multiple repertoires of motherhood to different audiences often depended on women's ability to make multiple repertoires hang together in a comprehensible way. As much as the notion of the hustle was one tool for such work, so too was the cultivation of amicable relationships with neighbors. A performance's success relied on the collusion of children and neighbors. Discord with these supporting actors could undermine a performance or undo the tenuous cohesion women build across multiple maternal repertoires. An angered Bronwyn highlighted the contradictions between Maryann's actions as a party girl/socialite and the expected conduct of a Christian mother. Despite Maryann's skills, without neighborly collaboration, she could not regain the performative authority to reframe the contradictory repertoires. The result was that she was cut off from a lucrative source of aid.

———

The past four decades in South Africa have seen democratic transition coupled with an evacuation of the low-skilled labor market. While juropolitical citizenship and the rights it confers was universalized, employment has remained a primary requirement for inclusion and relational citizenship, thereby reproducing stratified belonging at the very moment of incorporation (Barchiesi 2011). At the same time, though state assistance is now available to all race groups, government discourse promotes work-citizenship and minimizes state obligations to support any but the limited categories of persons deemed unable to work. Indeed, the landscape of welfare assistance in South Africa has changed dramatically since the 1960s and with it the terrain in which women can claim support for raising children. The children's homes in which Claudette, Maryann, and many of Bronwyn's siblings grew up by 2014 were filled with AIDS orphans who had no kin instead of children whose home lives were deemed problematic. The State Maintenance Grants on which white and coloured mothers and children previously lived were converted to a CSG that now reaches over 60 percent of children but can purchase little more than a package of diapers (Patel et al. 2012).

In the absence of state welfare services that provide sufficient resources for survival, poor mothers draw on a large network of persons for resources, labor, and assistance. Since claims for their own needs are not recognized as legitimate, poor women's requests take the form of performances of adequate motherhood, carefully aligned to the values of particular audiences. Using a performative analysis, this chapter has shown how women learn the appropriate repertoires for each interactive context as well as how those rules map on to their particularly racialized body. In the Point, women must also attend the presence of multiple audiences, frequently with different values. Performances that contradict each other make visible the performative element of motherhood and incite suspicions that Point women engage in acts that are false and insincere. Women manage this anxiety— brought about through the multiple maternities they must embody—by marking certain performances as strategic and others as authentic with the term *the hustle*. However, this ability to reframe the meaning of action—to make their multiple maternities hang together in a cohesive narrative—is dependent on the collusion of supporting actors, often children and neighbors. Without the support of these collaborators, Point women can be left without a stage to stand on.

Much as I have focused on how women use performances of motherhood to shape the distribution of resources, also at play is the issue of what political theorists call "recognition" that, in this case, are also claims to redistribution (e.g., Fraser 2000). By performing motherhood, women make demands that various community members are obligated to meet their needs. In other words, they make an argument for recognition and belonging. This local case offers a different vantage point on enduring feminist debates about the political value of maternalism. On the one hand, this and the previous chapter have revealed that though potent resources, performances of motherhood are shifting, multiple, and offer a precarious claim to social recognition. On the other, political recognition that acknowledges the inherently relational (as in social) quality of caregiving may offer new potential for caregiving labor to be both respected and remunerated. Attending to performances of motherhood as a claim-making process reveals the contours of citizenship not as a given but as a lived and fluid sense of belonging. In short, I have tracked how citizenship is reworked in everyday practices such as the wiping of noses and the cooking of meat.

5 "ME AND HIM WE ONLY HAVE A CHILD TOGETHER, NOTHING MORE"

Kinshipping in the Court

CEBO SAT WITH HER BODY held tensely upright, furiously texting and restlessly sweeping her eyes around the rows of chairs filled with women, waiting. A smartly dressed black African woman in her thirties, Cebo was one of eighty women that day who, with luck, would have their cases heard by one of the four maintenance officers in Durban's Maintenance Court. These courts bring estranged, unmarried parents together for the purpose of enforcing the Maintenance Act, which legally requires both biological parents of a child, regardless of their marriage relationship, to contribute financially to the raising of that child.[1] Maintenance policy is almost a century old in South Africa, and it has been applied unevenly to different race groups. Now universally applicable, should people choose to invoke it, the law has taken on new significance in the present-day context where couples frequently have children outside of marriage processes and at a greater physical and emotional distance from larger kin networks.

Among black Africans, many culturally ascribe to the idea that the obligation to support a child is held by the members of the lineage to which the child belongs. Children are assumed to belong to their mother's lineage until the father or his family undergoes ritual payments of either *ilobolo* (bridewealth) or *inhlawulo* (damages for extramarital pregnancy), which serves to incorporate the child into their father's line. Blood is not essential to lineage membership as nonbiological fathers can assimilate children of their wife by another man through similar payments (Armstrong 1994; Krige 1936; Preston-Whyte 1974, 1993; Schapera 1940). In a rural subsistence economy, this was less of an issue of providership obligation as much as outlining which lineage would receive the labor and esteem of a child and which *amadlozi* (ancestors) the child would honor. Theoretically, a child always belongs to a lineage and that lineage holds responsibility for their care. This is part of the logic deployed by successive white governments to claim that the African extended family provided a sufficient social safety net for black communities, discussed more extensively in chapter 3. However, both historically and presently, the lived reality is always more complicated.

Few men today can afford *ilobolo* or *inhlawulo* and childbearing outside of marriage is a ubiquitous, if stigmatized practice.[2] Many young couples I know fervently hope that the relationships that bore extramarital children would eventually become nuptial unions. However, the challenges of poverty and practices of infidelity often lead to separation. Unemployed men who cannot *ilobola* also struggle to send money to support their children, who are overwhelmingly (69 percent in the case of black Africans) raised by maternal kin (Hall, Meintjes, and Sambu 2014). Extended maternal kin, and occasionally (nonmarital) in-laws, often provide support, but they too are often financially strapped (Mosoetsa 2011). Women, especially urban women like Cebo, living far from extended kin, assemble a network of relationships to support themselves and their children—in other words, a functional family. These relationships are often part of broader economies of intimacy—systems of exchange that include money, affection, labor, and sex that women and men negotiate (Cole 2009). The Maintenance Court, concerned with the financial obligation of biological parents, is one of many strategies for getting by to which mothers turn. However, women recognize that maintenance monies are not just cash but have important bearings on their broader exchange relationships. As such, decisions about how and whether to use the court are guided by far more than financial interests.

Cebo had had two young children with her previous boyfriend, Fikile, who lived in Cape Town with his parents. At one point, Cebo, too, had lived with them, cared for his parents, and contributed her domestic labor to the home. Three years ago, though, the couple separated after the birth of their second child, and Fikile stopped contributing money to the children's care. Unemployed and now homeless, with two small children, Cebo took Fikile to the Maintenance Court to compel him to help. For eight months, until Fikile lost his job, the security company where he worked deducted payments from his wages. After the payments ceased, Cebo moved back to Durban to live with her mother, who could help with the children. A year went by in which Cebo found a job and moved to a flat of her own, near her mother. At that time, she and Fikile reconciled, and he moved into her flat, but after a few months, the couple separated again, and Fikile moved back to his parents' home and sought work there. Angry at the breakup and Fikile's distance, Cebo returned to the court, where I met her, to renew the three-year-old maintenance order.

Over time, Cebo's goals for her family had changed, and with it, her relationship to the court. In her first trip to the court, she explained, she was desperate, suddenly finding herself with two children and no income or home of her own and, still in Cape Town, far from her family. Though Fikile no longer spoke to her, she could still occasionally call on his family for help with child care or to transport the older child to school. Together with the maintenance payments, this help made the situation livable for her. Later, when the payments ended, relations with Fikile's family soured because they blamed her wage garnishing for tarnishing his reputation and causing his job loss. Seeking help from her own family, she found enough support that she felt that the hassle and acrimony weren't worth the possible monetary gain of pursuing a maintenance claim from Fikile's family in his stead. After Fikile moved back in with her, he still did not pay maintenance, but their burgeoning relationship, his assistance with child care, and the income from her own job, kept her out of the court. Over time, the couple began to argue over what she felt was an unfair double burden of her wage earning and domestic labor. When their relationship ended, she returned to the court, enraged and seeking to make sure he "took on his fair share" of child-rearing duty.

This chapter considers the decisions that women like Cebo—unmarried, poor or working poor, and black African—make about whether to use, threaten using, or avoid the Maintenance Court. I argue that women's decisions are shaped by larger projects of child rearing and family making that must be understood as part of their efforts to establish membership in the new South Africa. The experiences of Grace in chapter 3 and her foremothers remind us that secure social reproduction has long been a privilege for which black South African women have had to fight. Aware of this history, the women I met in the 2010s held up their continued struggle to support their children as evidence of the incompleteness of their citizenship under democracy. At the same time, posttransition public discourse pathologizes the expanding demographic category of the "female headed household," attributing it to a decline in "family values." Such arguments, steeped in nostalgia for an imagined past, erase the sustained attempts of white governments to undermine black family life (Budlender and Lund 2011). In this milieu, the Maintenance Court, and women's use of it, operates as an important tool in the South African state's efforts to discipline parents (and notably men) into becoming responsible citizens. This chapter turns to the democratic state's projects of "family strengthening" that are a response to national concerns about the physical, emotional, and economic absence of men in their children's lives (Department of Social Development 2012).

This chapter primarily draws on fieldwork at Durban's Maintenance Court, observing intake interviews, mediation sessions with maintenance officers, hearings with the magistrate, counseling sessions between clients and attorneys, and—often the most revelatory—the conversations of women during long periods of waiting in the court's halls. These observations were contrasted with fifty-three in-depth interviews with intake counselors, maintenance officers, attorneys, legal aid staff, and a core group of twenty-five black African women who either were seeking maintenance or had decided not to pursue cases. (Those who did not use the court were a subset of my lager group of interlocutors whose experiences are traced in this book.) These twenty-five women were notable because they had children with comparably wealthier men who were often formally employed, at least for some period, meaning they could conceivably use the court, if they chose to do so. In the Point neighborhood, most women lived with other women or new boyfriends. The former partner frequently was not a resident of the neighborhood. The demographics of the mothers here reflect the population in the court in 2014: poor, young (between the ages of eighteen and forty), and black African, mirroring what other Maintenance Court researchers found in other parts of the country (Khunou 2012; Mills 2004). Only four of the twenty-five held formal part-time jobs.

The Maintenance Court operates as one tool among a range of possibilities that women like Cebo use for assembling a network of kin, friends, patrons, and lovers in an attempt to constitute a supportive family for themselves and their children. I situate this work within the longer history of state reliance on the uncompensated labor of black women to ensure social reproduction in the face of impossible obstacles (Hassim 2005). In the migrant labor system, women's adherence to a "patriarchal bargain" in which they sustained a rural household in exchange for the economic support and social status provided by a migrating husband, shored up African families in the midst of intense social and economic tension (Bozzoli 1991; Hunter 2009; Mayer 1961; Murray 1981; Preston-Whyte 1978). Presently, impoverished predominantly black women are expected to translate Child Support Grants (CSG) into successful child-rearing without any resources to meet their own needs. In the Maintenance Court, women's work to bring cases, when cases are successful, serves broader state goals of disciplining nonpaying men and keeping families off state grants. As with the CSG, women's labor assists the state in meeting its constitutional obligation to provide for the basic needs of children. But to what extent does the court meet the various needs of women?

It is widely known in South Africa that the Maintenance Court is plagued with problems and is often ineffective, especially when fathers are unemployed or do not receive a pay slip. The court cannot mandate that an unemployed man must contribute, and his friends or family can easily sign the required documents that attest he is looking for work. In these situations, the Maintenance Act stipulates that the duty of support can pass on to his parents, and the mother may lodge a maintenance claim against them; however, I have only ever seen women threaten such an action (Reynolds 2016). Often aware of these challenges, many women continue to view the courts as an important part of their tool kit to achieve ends that are not solely about maintenance money. I show that the reciprocal effect of money on sexual and affective relationships is critical to understanding black women's use of the Maintenance Court. By tracing the temporal, relational, and institutional complexities women take into account as they make decisions about the court, I show how these at times align, divert, and occasionally contradict policy goals in an effort to serve women's own needs. This serves to move away from an idea of women or even black African women as a group who share undifferentiated relationships to the South African state and the fathers of their children. Instead, it moves toward a recognition of women as agentive actors who, in the midst of their gendered, classed, and racialized positions, negotiate the boundaries of state authority and male control to (attempt to) serve their own ends.

Family Strengthening and a "Culture of Nonpayment"

The Maintenance Court is a critical part of democratic South Africa's family policy framework. This framework seeks to address "family disintegration" by "strengthening families," specifically, by making them more economically solvent (Department of Social Development 2012, 3, 23). The language of family decline, by no means new, is currently concerned with black children growing up in households headed by unmarried women and the prevalence of "absentee fathers" who do not contribute money or labor to their children's care (Department of Social Development 2012, 18). This privileging of a middle-class nuclear family model reflects an ahistorical misrecognition of both the flexibility of family forms and the labors—primarily of African women—to shore up families, often in the absence of men (Delius and Glaser 2002; Hunt 1999; Hunter 2010; Krige 1936; Mager 1999; Moore and Vaughan 1994). Recall the experience of Grace in chapter 3, an unmarried mother with a nonsupporting former partner. Her efforts to compel her previous partner to contribute were taken as disregard for and abandonment of her children. In contrast, in 2014, the recognition of family diversity beyond a heteronormative, nuclear model had permeated many spheres of policy making in the democratic state. However, this more nuanced understanding was often irregularly applied (Knijn and Patel 2018; Rabe 2017). Regardless of the familial orientation, poor single mothers were often interpreted as both the victims of hypersexual and negligent men and irresponsible in their birth control choices. In response, policy papers framed the Maintenance Court as a tool to capacitate women to realize their rights and correct the ills of family decline.

A well-functioning Maintenance Court, which ensures that men financially support their offspring, is framed as essential in South African policy for two reasons. First, it empowers women to demand men share the fi-

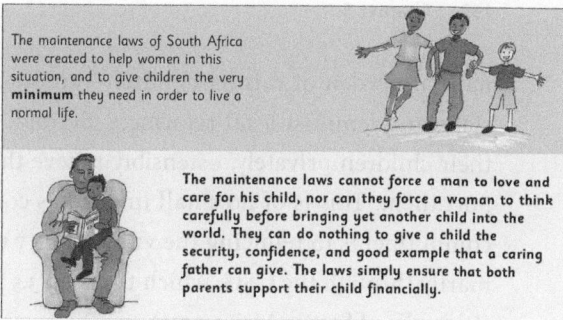

FIGURE 5.1 Excerpts from the brochure "Maintenance and Child Support: A Shared Responsibility." Developed by Educational Support Services Trust and the Department of Justice and Constitutional Development in 2003.

nancial burden of raising children—an outcome desired by mothers, the state, and feminist legal reformers. Second, fathers compelled to support their children privately, ostensibly relieve the burden on the state to support them. This is of no small import, as constitutional and international commitments to reducing the vulnerability of children have been met primarily through the CSG, which takes up 3.5 percent of the national budget (Republic of South Africa 2015).

Despite the extent of the democratic state's social assistance spending—about a third of the population receives a state grant—government officials have remained at best ambivalent about the system (Dawson and Fouksman 2020; Nattrass and Seekings 2010). The ANC publicly celebrates the poverty reduction brought about through state grants (African National Congress 2009). At the same time, developmentalist logics pervade the state, and ministers warn that "too much" spending on social assistance might "entrench the culture of entitlement" the poor are thought to have (DSD 2006; Meth 2004; Molewa 2010). Work membership—or citizenship as achieved through self-reliance on one's own labor—remains the most legitimate (if inaccessible) means to inclusion (Ferguson 2013).

Over the past two decades, a series of cost-recovery plans to compel people to pay for public services have been launched in an effort to lower the economic costs and mitigate the purported ideological pitfalls of extensive social spending. In some cases, the technologies were quite material, such as the pay-per-use water meters that discipline poor South Africans into water-conserving and rates-paying citizens (von Schnitzler 2008). Others were more ideological, such as the *Masakhane* ("let us build together") campaign launched nationally in 1995, which sought to reform a perceived "culture of nonpayment" associated with thirty years of apartheid-era resistance that involved a refusal to pay taxes, rents, and utility bills. The campaign focused on educating people on their rights and responsibilities as citizens by retooling the payment of taxes and utilities to signify patriotism and democratic participation. But this retooling took place alongside what for many was a decline in their economic position, and few changed their payment habits. The national *Masakhane* campaign was largely considered a failure, though a number of provinces and municipalities have launched campaigns of their own (e.g., Mngomezulu 2006; Fjeldstad 2003).

Nevertheless the logic of payment as indexing good citizenship and fears about a widespread "culture of nonpayment" have endured (Corrigan 2023).

The emphasis on economic participation as civic duty is also part of the new government's policy on families. Again, previous chapters revealed that while this fiscal emphasis takes a particular form in the democratic era, the orientation is not itself new. The policy goals as articulated in the 2012 White Paper on Families is to foster families to be "economically self-sustaining" so that their "members are able to contribute effectively to the overall development of the country" (DSD 2012, 8). State welfare is envisioned to afford citizens, "the opportunity to play an active role in promoting their own well-being" (DOW 1997, 59). This orientation is quite different from a redistributive model as articulated in the antiapartheid struggle's guiding document, the Freedom Charter, which states, "The people shall share in the country's wealth!" Instead, in democratic welfare policy, impoverished families are problematic because they are dependent on government grants instead of contributing to development, as proper citizens should.

Both the notions of "family disintegration" and a "culture of nonpayment" are highly racialized and gendered (DSD 2012, 3). Concerns about marital decline are directed less at the 67 percent marriage rate among whites than at the 24 percent marriage rate among black Africans (Posel et al. 2011). While characters of multiple races are represented in the comic in figure 5.1, the primary story depicts the plights of Nomvu, a recognizably black African woman and her racially ambiguous lover, Mike. In policy documents and countless incendiary news stories, black fathers are described as "absent," not simply because they do not live with their children—as many have not done for the past hundred years of labor migration—but because they do not *pay* for their children (DSD 2012, 19; Chauke and Khunou 2014). Under these terms, the solution to the problem of unsupported children becomes an enforcement of the presumed support obligation of biological parents by obliging mothers to bring fathers into the court and by compelling fathers to pay.

Historically, the State Maintenance Grant (SMG) and the Maintenance Court were closely connected and understood as two prongs of a single system. Women were not eligible for a SMG unless they could prove they had tried and failed to obtain maintenance through the court. The CSG does not have such requirements, and efforts have been made to delink it from the Maintenance Court (Lund 2008). However, as we have seen, the two remain closely intertwined in policy. In 2002, the Committee of Inquiry into a Comprehensive System of Social Security reported that:

> despite being plagued by problems, . . . the private maintenance system is an important system and as a result it should not be discarded. There is a legal and moral duty on the part of both parents to provide for their child[ren]. . . . The state's duty to provide enters the picture only when parents are unable to provide—not because they do not want to. (Taylor 2002, 58)

The committee's report reveals a widely held assumption—that fathers' nonpayment arises not out of economic constraint, but out of personal inclination, interpreted as a moral failure (Chauke and Khunou 2014). Here, the Maintenance Court is seen as an important stopgap to ensure that the state does not end up footing the bill for the irresponsible choices of fathers. Yet, the disciplinary potential of the court depends on the motivation and persistence of women to bring a case.

Maintenance in South Africa: Background and Process

As a result of the sustained work of the women's movement, in various instantiations, the framework for the democratic transition promotes a legislative commitment to addressing gender inequity. This has resulted in the dramatic increase of political representation for women and the removal of gender discrimination from legal language, though, as Shireen Hassim potently states, substantive socioeconomic power redistribution "remains a tenuous dream" (2014, 17; Walker 2013). Early on, reform of the private maintenance system—widely known to be ineffective, racially discriminatory, and burdensome for women—was seen as a key step in realizing women's rights (Burman and Berger 1988a, 1988b; Lund 2008). Policy interventions, led by groups such as the Black Sash, the South African Law Commission, the Maintenance Action Group, and the South African Human Rights Commission sought to improve the maintenance court processes as a means of reducing women's reliance on unreliable and arduous kinshipping practices such as those seen across this book.[3] For the feminist activists, reform of the maintenance system offered an opportunity to simultaneously and substantively address women's disempowerment in the home and within state structures. In 1998 (and again in 2015), the Maintenance Act was amended to improve equitability and to ensure it complied with the 1996 constitution and South Africa's international commitments to the rights of women and children.[4] These acts are meant to facilitate the legal enforcement of parents' duty to contribute financially—proportionate to their incomes—to their dependents' food, clothing, accommodation, medical care, and education. Legislatively, the courts are intended to be a "user-friendly, one-stop" site for unmarried women to seek maintenance without the need of a lawyer (Department of Justice and Constitutional Development 2003). Unsurprisingly, the realities are quite different.

In many ways, the process of seeking maintenance remains the same today as it was in 1963. The claimant, henceforth, the mother, must submit to the court clerk an application for a maintenance order, often requiring translation of both the legalistic language and the English text (Singh, Naidoo, and Mokolobate 2004).[5] This form requires that she have the father's full name, identification number, home or work address (preferably both), and telephone number—no small feat, given the estrangement that invariably precedes a claim (Budlender and Moyo 2004). Upon receipt of the application, the court sets a date and notifies the father. In some courts, the mother must notify the father herself, sometimes risking personal injury; in others, the mother can point out the father to an accompanying police officer who will actually serve the subpoena (CASE 2012). On the appointed date, provided both parties are present and possess the necessary documentation of their assets and expenses, they will meet with a maintenance officer to determine the financial responsibilities of each parent for the approved expenses for the child. If the parties can agree on a maintenance amount, it is outlined in a maintenance order—a legally binding document signed by both parties. If the parents do not agree, or if the father does not appear on the appointed day, the case goes before a magistrate for a formal hearing, where both parents will give evidence regarding their financial situation. In the case of a father's continued absence, the magistrate can issue a warrant for his arrest (often not enforced without pressure from the mother), or, after ten days of nonpayment, can enforce a maintenance order by garnishing his wages or attaching his property and debts. The result may be that, for a time, the man complies with an order through regular payments. In the likely event that he fails to pay, he may be subject to a fine and imprisonment for up to a year; however, the mother must report and document the default and initiate a separate court process, often lasting several months. Understandably, it is not uncommon that maintenance arrears often reach into the thousands of Rands, with little hope of payment (Witbooi 2002).

Recent reforms have attempted to address the most inequitable elements of the system—the burden of proof women shoulder to lodge a claim and the woefully inadequate enforcement of maintenance orders (Budlender and Moyo 2004; South African Law Commission 1997). Now many courts (such as Durban's) employ maintenance investigators, who investigate fathers' whereabouts, financial position (businesses or property he might have registered in someone else's name), or reasons for a change in status (such as job loss), and who can take statements from relevant witnesses. Additionally, maintenance orders can now be granted by default in the likely event that men do not attend the hearing. The court can now enforce an order through attachments of property, debts, and garnishment of wages, however, property attachment still requires that claimants pay a hefty fee (South African Law Commission 2014). Further, wage garnishment is only possible when fathers have a job that documents their pay. For those such as taxi owners, who may make a sizeable income but collect no pay slips, wages cannot be garnished. Finally, maintenance payments can now be made through Electronic Funds Transfer (EFT), freeing mothers from another trip to the court and long lines, and reducing burdens on court staff time.

Despite these reform efforts, the Maintenance Court remains fairly ineffective (Coutts 2014; De Jong 2009; Mamashela 2006; Singh, Naidoo, and Mokolobate 2004; South African Law Commission 1997, 2014). While the 1998 act enlarged the powers of the court, problems of procedural ambiguity, insufficient training, resources, and manpower, and discrimination against women claimants persist (De Jong 2009; South African Law Commission 2014). Women still bear the overwhelming labor burdens in lodging a claim for payments that are consistently below their needs and are frequently defaulted on (CASE 2012). Indeed, in 2003, the Constitutional Court ruled that the logistical problems in the Maintenance Court constituted a failure by the state to meet its constitutional obligation to protect the rights of women and the best interests of children (*Bannatyne v. Banna-tyne*; Clark 2005). Research and efforts to improve the system are ongoing.[6]

Given the numerous challenges with the private maintenance system, it is not surprising that many women find it an exercise in futility and are reluctant to engage with it. In research and public discourse, the relative success or failure of a case is often narrowly measured in terms of whether or how much money was transferred. Instead, I draw on what Cole calls economies of intimacy—the interrelationship of sex, money, affect, and power—to show how Maintenance Court processes have far larger relational effects that women account for in their evaluations (Cole 2009). In doing so, I bring attention to the court as, in Hassim's terms, a performative public sphere of democracy that women can use to build families and forge belonging to the national community the court was designed to support (2009).

Economies of Intimacy

Asanda was like many South African women today, raising her baby in a context in which neither the income from work nor the support from a partner can be counted on to be exclusive or enduring. Like her peers she adamantly sought a family built around a monogamous marriage grounded in romantic love that adhered to normative gender roles of male economic provision and female domestic care (Ashforth 1999; Hunter 2009, 2010). Also like others, she was frequently disappointed. Asanda was unusual among my interlocutors because she did not live with a man. Rather, she split the comparatively high cost of her room in Point with two other young women, one of whom also had a baby. None of the three had formal jobs, but the childless one had staked a claim on a spot on the sidewalk downtown and sold trinkets, used clothing, and hair braiding. On days when it was likely there would be more customers, Asanda or her roommate would join her to help, but these earnings never amounted to much. Instead, Asanda met her needs of economic stability, affective care for herself and her baby, and sexual fulfillment, through a host of relationships with both men and women. All of these relationships were bound together by reciprocal obligations—"ties of dependence"—that included various assemblages of money or gifts, emotional support and affection, domestic labor, or sex (Swidler and Watkins 2007; Verheijen 2013). For example, she would often swap child care with her other roommate so that the other woman could go visit her boyfriends or pick up a job she had come across. If she had a particularly lucrative month, the roommate would cover part of Asanda's portion of the rent or buy food for both of them. The babies were close in age, and the women would often trade clothes and, while they were still breastfeeding, feeding responsibilities. While the babies did not have the extended family network that Asanda had growing up in rural Eastern Cape, they were cuddled, carried, fed, and sung to by the three roommates and many other women in the building, including an intermittent anthropologist.

Asanda was very attractive and also never lacked for attention from men. Of her many suitors, only a few earned the status of boyfriend. She often came home with gifts of new clothing, cell phone minutes, perfume, or lotion from one of her various male admirers. In this economy of intimacy the expectation was that such gifts, most often by a man to a woman, obligated the receiver to reciprocate, usually sexually (Cole 2009; Hunter 2009). Conversely, sexual favors in addition to other "comforts of home," such as cooking cleaning, or emotional support, also valued practices, demand the reciprocal sharing of material resources from those who enjoyed them (Leclerc-Madlala 2003; White 1990). In some cases this would look like a man taking Asanda out to lunch after enjoying a walk on the beach with a beautiful woman on his arm. Or Asanda would visit a man's room when his roommates were out to relieve his stress with a massage, taking home the lotion. In other cases, she sent many flirtatious voice notes to a gift-giver, but could not find the time to see him in person. Unlike some other women, Asanda did not have a Ben Ten—a man whose explicit role was for the pleasure of the sexual experience.[7] But she did have boyfriends with whom she had a stronger emotional attachment and to whom she would take her baby to visit. Exchanges with those men in particular revealed how variable and complex the economy of intimacy was and the delicacy involved in negotiating it.

Asanda's exchanges fall under the broad category of what has been called transactional sex, a term that sets such practices apart from prostitution and its common associations with female immorality and victimhood (Hunter 2002; Leclerc-Madlala 2003). Women like Asanda also mark this distinction, describing herself as *isifazane oqomayo* (a woman who chooses, or a dating woman) as opposed to *isifebe* (a prostitute). Despite her economic precarity, Asanda was not engaging in sex solely for survival but also for consumption and to satisfy other desires she may have (Leclerc-Madlala 2003). She did so in a milieu in which men held both economic and sexual privilege. For men, giving of resources to multiple partners affords prestige and an elevated masculine social status and moral legitimacy for their redistribution of resources (Ashforth 1999; Hunter 2005, 2010; Verheijen 2013). In the process, they often receive sexual satisfaction, domestic caregiving, and social insurance in the form of multiple dependents they can call on in the future (Ashforth 2005; Swidler and Watkins 2007; White 1990). Black women like Asanda face very different gendered requirements. Women are expected to be partnered—ideally, wed—and to practice or at least conspicuously display monogamy (Rice 2017) Women who have either too many or too few partners attract accusations of disobeying culture, husband-snatching, or prostitution (Rice 2017; Verheijen 2013). Nevertheless, due to the lack of employment that could offer women financial independence and men the ability to pay *ilobolo*, most women, like Asanda, satisfy their needs through multiple partners, making it a common, if not entirely accepted, practice.

For Asanda, many of these complexities came to a head around one of her boyfriends, Bongani. He had also come to the Point having grown up the rural areas and did not yet display the masculine swagger of many of his urban male counterparts. This is not because he wasn't popular with the ladies. Indeed he had a seemingly infinite amount of women who pursued this quiet, somewhat bashful young man who also had a job working security on the port. He and Asanda had connected, and many afternoons—Bongani worked third shift—she could be found with him, often taking her baby along. Over the Easter holidays, Asanda went back to the Eastern Cape for a two-week visit to see family. When she returned, Bongani was different. He was still generous with his time and affections for the baby, but his gifts were more humble. Within economies of intimacy, the values and terms of exchanges are always relationally contingent, and their affective power means that an inappropriate reciprocation can be emotionally hurtful and relationally damaging. The change in the gifts left Asanda sad and confused. Had his feelings changed? Had his affection gone elsewhere? It also left her in a difficult position. Her childless roommate had left and suddenly she was responsible for half of the rent. For the first time, she debated whether she should take her child's father, whom she had not seen in months, to the Maintenance Court.

The Court's Place in the Project of Family Making

Asanda and Bongani's, and Cebo and Fikile's, stories reveal the ways in which the women, men, and children who enter the court are situated in a web of social ties whose bonds are reinforced through exchanges of money, sex, love, and labor. The terrain of this network is always in flux, as jobs are lost and found, family members die, children are born, new boyfriends are brought into the picture, or old relationships break apart. Despite this changeability, the bond between parents, even unmarried ones, is a relatively durable one, which allows women to make claims on the resources of a man far longer than in a solely sexual relationship (Guyer 1994). For example, when asked what relationship she had with her former lover, one woman replied, "Me and him we only have a child together nothing more. We do not have a relationship." Thus, in deciding whether to pursue a Maintenance Court case, my interlocutors accounted for past connections and ruptures, present needs, and future expectations as well as the social meanings of maintenance monies within economies of intimacy.

For the women I know, attempts to secure child support in any form were rarely purely rational calculations, but instead were emotionally fraught, sometimes contradictory attempts to negotiate a broad and shifting relational field. Writing about the negotiation of intimate relationships in India, Sarah Lamb notes similar dimensions: "The popular notion of 'choice'—based as it tends to be on an image of a freely acting agent—does not well capture the sense of ambivalence and constraint in single women's representations of their life paths" (2018, 59). More accurate than choice is the concept of "judicious opportunism," which better represents the adaptability and improvisational nature of women's decision-making (Johnson-Hanks 2005, 370). The rupturing of ties with their children's fathers had usually been painful. Even when their children were not entirely "planned," all the women at some point had embarked with their ex-partner on a shared project of parenting. During that time, his financial support had been an indication of his emotional attachment and commitment to their partnership and their offspring. The loss of affective care and financial support was often taken as a sign that mother and child were deemed unworthy of his love. Decisions about whether to go to court were often steeped in deep-seated longing for reconnection and profound anger at mistreatment. Use of the court proved to be far more successful at addressing the latter than the former.

Engaging the Court

Many women sought a court order, not only out of financial need, but also in the hope that through the process, an amicable relationship could be restored, if just between father and child. Such hopes, though improbable, were not entirely unfounded. Indeed, it is the outcome promoted by court brochures such as in figure 5.1 where compulsory payments lead to paternal interest. These ideas rely on a pervasive logic that monetary gifts are intertwined with emotional commitment—they simultaneously demonstrate and *incite* affective attachment (Hunter 2009). My interlocutor, Nomusa, similarly framed her choice to take her former partner, a teacher, to the court saying, "The child has a right to know. Other children talk with their father and my son doesn't. It is his responsibility to sit with him and share good moments. He is growing up." Her statements invoke a desire for emotional connection between father and son and also reveal anxiety about the lack of engagement in her son's formative years. She describes such care as "a responsibility" that the father has ignored and "a right" to which her child is due. These are not actions mandated by the court, but financial involvement is, so women used the tools available.

Those seeking to promote a relationship between father and child were most often disappointed. In the case of Nomusa, the man never attended any hearings and changed his cell phone number. As Goldblatt notes, "many men and their families regard maintenance claims against them as an attack" (2006, 249). For those who did attend, the court hearings I witnessed were sad, angry affairs, filled with explosive and bitter accusations of infidelity, poor parenting, or lack of visitation. Some maintenance officers saw it their role to counsel couples and reconnect them, but struggled to sideline such emotional battles in an attempt to expedite agreement on payment amounts.[8] Frustrated and wounded, many women left in tears, saying, "I don't understand why he is not paying; he was such a good guy." In interviews after, they expressed shock and hurt at the anger that surfaced in the hearing, as men railed against having any relationship—economic or

otherwise—with them. The hearing concretized women's feelings of abandonment, and many were haunted, later, by the "vicious words" that had
been hurled at them. Some spoke with regret about their choice to go to
court, saying, when the payments stopped coming, as they so often did,
they had been left with neither love nor money:

> Seeking maintenance is . . . time-consuming . . . and emotionally draining,
> and for what? You go up and down, up and down, and what? Now he will
> not answer my calls. [*She sighs.*] What must I do? I do wish we were a com-
> plete family, but I don't sit on it. I don't want to be depressed because of the
> choices I have made.

Arguably, the women who were most satisfied by their use of the court
were those who, as in Cebo's final visit, viewed the court process as a means to
achieve vengeance for perceived mistreatment. This is not to say that monetary need was not a part of their case, but—like their ex-partners—they came
to the hearing angry and many felt empowered by the idea that the law was
on their side. The rage that men exhibited in a court hearing, to them, was
an indication that they were being taught a hard lesson. Women like twenty-
three-year-old Gladness, who had a well-elaborated discourse about women's
rights, saw the court as a disciplining force, which helped reestablish justice
for women. She was purportedly duped into taking on debt to finance her
ex-partner's auto repair business because she held a job as a domestic one day
a week and was thus more creditworthy. The business was supposed to be a
step toward a future she and her partner were building together. But when it
fell on hard times, he took the tools and ran, leaving her and their two-year-
old son at the mercy of a local loan shark, who lived in the neighborhood of
the single room she rented in Point. She said, "These South African men are
running away from responsibility. They want no strings attached. Us girls
suffer the consequences. Us women have to say no or do something." Gladness felt that action—in the form of a court case—was a way of demanding
the respect she felt had been denied her and was necessary, both for reclaim-
ing her own self-worth, and as a lesson for her young son.

Such a sentiment was echoed in 2012 by Phindi, who had felt powerless
within an abusive relationship and found the court to be a forceful correc-
tive to a gendered power imbalance (see Khunou 2012). She had come from a
rural area to live in Durban and had been swept off her feet by her previous

partner, who owned a pawnshop and wooed her with promises of a carefree life. He had been a heavy drinker, and with a complicated pregnancy and subsequent postbirth confinement, she had been less willing and able to keep up with his social and sexual demands. She grew increasingly fearful for her own and her daughter's safety until she moved in with a girlfriend from church, who encouraged her to start a case. She said, "Men always pay with their mouths. To get them to put their hand in their pockets, you must come with a gun." Phindi felt that the impersonal, public space of the court gave her the authority to stand up to her former partner and demand the money she felt was rightfully owed to her daughter.

For women like these, feelings of success often hinged less on the payments than on their experience in court. In the case of Gladness, whose ex-partner never appeared for a hearing, the magistrate garnished his wages, and she left feeling validated and empowered. Phindi, however, felt pressured by the maintenance officer to accept an amount far lower than she needed. Her court hearing left her feeling disappointed and betrayed by a system that failed to protect her.

Dispensing with the Court

Other women, highly cognizant of the emotional estrangement and economic disappointment that often resulted from the court process, chose not to use the court at all or to not return to it after fathers defaulted. Women like Zama were ambivalent about the disciplinary potential, "I thought about maintenance. I am not sure if he is working. Not sure I want to make him pay. It will feel like I am putting my claws into him and making him do something he doesn't want to." Zama's statements suggest that if payments don't arise out of personal initiative, they don't do the emotional work of signifying attachment. For women like Thandi, the thin hope of a future relationship with her child's father shaped her decision. Though he had found work and a new relationship in a distant city, she felt the potential relationship was more valuable than the uncertain economic gains and inevitable emotional discord a maintenance hearing could bring.

BG: Does he give you anything?

T: When I asked him for money, he says, "at the end of the month," but it never comes.

BG: Will you take him to court?

T: Hmmmm, no. I want us to be a family. This other woman, she's not good. . . . When this job is finished, he'll come back, and we can stay nicely together.

BG: Oh?! [*surprised*]

T: [*Laughing*] Yeeesss. But, you know, if I go to the court, there will be no cows [*marriage proceedings*].

This decision was no doubt influenced by the fact that Thandi herself was working, and she was living with her sister, who had a "good job," so she had a modicum of economic security, which left her free to indulge in dreams of marrying her children's father. At another time and under other circumstances, she may have chosen differently. But, more important for this consideration is that women like Thandi echoed what other scholars have found (e.g., Cole 2004; Pauli 2019)—that relationships between un-married mothers and fathers are not simply sexual, but are often seen as potential marriages. As infrequent and inaccessible as marriage was—as affirmed by Thandi's laughter—it remained the sought-after ideal (Hunter 2010). Thandi and others like her worried that initiating a court case might jeopardized that ideal, however unlikely it may be.

Others who avoided the court saw a court case as not only a threat to their future relationship with their children's father but also as an impediment to their child's relationship with his or her father. In these cases, the desire to foster a nurturing relationship between the father and the child kept them away from the courts. When I met Thuli, in her late thirties, she had a new boyfriend, who, though he bought her clothes and cell phone minutes, was uninterested in Nothi, the daughter Thuli had had with Mvu. Mvu had met Nothi a few times when the girl was small, but they had lost contact over the years. Now that Nothi was a teenager, she and Mvu had recently found each other on Facebook and had begun spending time together—a fact about which Thuli was immensely pleased and did not want to disrupt:

He doesn't send money and stuff, [and hasn't for some time,] but I don't force the issue. . . . I want him to have a relationship with her. I didn't have a relationship with my father. I want to be a family and for him to spend time with her. You can't make someone love you or be there if they don't want to.

To Thuli, the making of "a family"—meaning, for her, a warm father-daughter relationship—was something a court case would endanger. Thuli's situation is emblematic of many women who cultivate multiple relationships to serve a variety of ends. With her new boyfriend, she found an element of economic support—which had to be supplemented through other labor and relationships—and a sexual relationship that may have been pleasurable to her, but the new boyfriend did not demonstrate the affective care for Nothi that Thuli prized and that she hoped to retain in Mvu.

A handful of women who could have opened a case, chose not to because they did not want a relationship of any kind with the father of their child. These were often relationships with a history of domestic violence, and, in contrast to Phindi, they did not feel the court would protect them from future abuse (Khunou 2012). As one woman said, "the first one, I could not go [to court] because he would kill us if he saw us; the second [man], I would kill him." Such concerns were by no means unfounded, as there have been incidents where men have violently attacked women during maintenance hearings, and maintenance officers often have the additional role of acting as security. Further, these women often did not want their ex-partner to have any place in their child's life, because he was either a bad influence, or a source of emotional pain, or both. As Nomusa said, "I do not want my son to know him. What might he learn? To have children and abandon them?" Though the payment of maintenance has no legal relationship to privileges of access to the child, my interlocutors expressed that if a man were paying, they would feel compelled to let him visit his child, regardless of how negative an influence he might be. To open a case, these women expressed, was to submit themselves and their children to the likelihood of disappointment and the feeling of rejection all over again.

A final group of women were those who chose not to use the court because to do so would impede their relationship with another man. For these women, or more importantly, for their new partners, the bond created through maintenance payments was understood as a liability that, in principle, could give ex-partners a legitimate claim to sexual favors from the woman. Some women seeking a new partner would send their children to live with other kin, whom fathers could pay so as to not muddy the waters of sexual and financial ties. But that was not always the desired arrangement.

Asanda made a different plan. She told me that despite her rent increase, she would not take her baby's father to the court because she needed to "clear the path" for Bongani. Initially, I was confused. Asanda had been worried that things had cooled with Bongani and she was missing his much-needed support. If anything, it seemed that Bongani had taken another path. However, Asanda corrected me, explaining that this decision was essential to her building a future with Bongani. It is likely that Bongani knew that she had other boyfriends and suitors. However, these were material/emotional/sexual relationships. There were no children involved, thus making them more expendable. Asanda had not seen her baby's father since he left her while she was pregnant. However, if she was to pursue a maintenance order from him, she would have two connections—their child and the money. Because economic support, no matter how achieved, is thought to bear traces of an emotional commitment, Asanda's connection to her former lover would be more than just an economic one (Garey and Townsend 1996; Hunter 2010; Jewkes et al. 2012; Jewkes and Morrell 2011). Given that a man faced few legal repercussions for nonpayment, compliance with payment indicated other motivations, and few people believed it was simply interest in the child. Receipt of gifts—even when they are maintenance money—obligates the recipient to reciprocate. If she pursued a maintenance order, Asanda would have a monthly, public debt to her former lover. By her accounting, the fact that a state body such as the court had mediated these payments did not cleanse the money of its burden of reciprocity. Regardless of whether Asanda had any intention of repaying this debt, her obligation would be viewed as a flagrant threat of infidelity to someone like Bongani who would want to have exclusive sexual access to Asanda, or at least appear to (Ashforth 1999). Asanda had witnessed a version of this with her roommate. Her new boyfriend had disapproved of her spending his money on the baby, who was not his. But diapers were expensive. Though they did not get along, the baby's father, at her request, had sent a small amount of money to help. This had led to days of fighting between the roommate and her new boyfriend, who did not want her taking money from another man due to the sexual obligation it implied. Thus, Asanda decided she needed to sever all possible ties with her ex-lover to move forward in love with Bongani.

Given the interconnectedness of sex, money, and affective commitment, women like Asanda found that the specter of obligation produced by maintenance payments hindered their attempts to build a relationship with another man. Notably, through its provision of grants, the state was often called a de facto father. However, receipt of the CSG created no such obligation. Thus, for women with good prospects elsewhere, seeking maintenance from a previous partner may not be worth the entanglements of debt—whether they intend to fulfill them or not.

———

Since democratic transition, activists and policy makers have upheld the Maintenance Court as an important mechanism for ensuring the rights of women and children. Reform of the Maintenance System has been a key governmental response to the perceived crisis of "family disintegration" (DSD 2012, 3). At the heart of this crisis are black female-headed households who ostensibly have been made dependent on government grants because of the financial (and sexual) irresponsibility of men. Parliamentarians fantasize that women's use of the courts can simultaneously serve to convert men's culture of nonpayment into responsible citizenship. In this fantasy, this would shift impoverished children's economic dependence from state grants, which foster a culture of dependence, to paternal providership, seen as laudable self-sufficiency. Aspirationally, the court is also a means for empowering women to combat the economic mistreatment they have endured in their intimate relationships and realize their rights by wielding the power of the law against errant men. In this way, women's use of the court has the potential to transform various persons languishing in unproductive underdevelopment into productive citizens and contributors to national development.

Of course, women are often well aware of the labor involved in using the court. Doing so requires days standing in line, transport costs, energy spent collecting documents, and the emotional toll of engaging a former lover. For mothers raising children without the financial support of fathers, the Maintenance Court features as one among many possible strategies for getting by. However, their decisions about whether to do so involve far more than simply the potential economic benefit. Maintenance payments are part of larger economies of intimacy that women rely on to secure money, sex, labor, and love. Women often know that even if a court case is effective and they receive payments, receipt of them may negatively affect other relationships. Therefore, women must carefully assess the emotional, economic, and relational impacts of a course case in light of their larger goals of supporting their children and assembling a functional family.

Arguably many of the women I know share with parliamentarians the desire to shift the economic burden of raising children off the shoulders of women and distribute it more evenly among other adults, notably, fathers. To this end, Maintenance Court cases are a resounding failure. When maintenance orders are successfully put in place, they frequently only stand a few years (at best) before the man defaults and women must decide whether to reapply. This is hardly a recipe for self-sufficiency or redistribution.

The women I know view the hardship they face in supporting their children as a simultaneous failure of the state and fathers to meet their obligations to both women and children. This is at the center of statements such as, "I am not a citizen because I cannot support my children." The Maintenance Act affirms women's rights to shared support. The court is a legal tool to enforce the support obligation that biological fathers are assumed to have in a context where other mechanisms of social discipline such as marriage and extended family are less available. However, given that so few cases result in durable support, this affirmation is more rhetorical than material. For women like Phindi and Gladness, who used a court case as retribution, the rhetorical and symbolic power was satisfying and emboldening. The court process functioned as a performative public sphere of democracy—a good enough instantiation of the state working to support some of its most vulnerable citizens—and thus offered them a sense of inclusion (Hassim 2009). However, for many others, the supposed rights that the courts empowered them to secure rang similarly hollow to their sense of national belonging. On paper, they were entitled to support, but they were often left alone with their children once more.

The next chapter considers a rather different strategy of support, namely, South African women's marriage to men who have migrated from other parts of the African continent. These marriages, widely stigmatized, also surprisingly help women achieve key markers of full social citizenship. However, formalized in the midst of intense xenophobia, they come with social costs of additional forms of exclusion. This final example of foreign marriage offers another perspective on how women and men go about their projects of social reproduction in attempts at securing belonging.

6 "WE ARE ABLE TO STAY TOGETHER AS A FAMILY"

Kinshipping at Home

> Foreigners, they come to steal our women and our jobs.
> —*Themba, age thirty-seven, Durban*

ON A COOL BUT SUNNY afternoon, a group of five women from the self-titled Muslim Sisterhood group gathered in the apartment of Zandi and her husband Toussaint. Though the group's name was in jest, these sisters had a rather unusual bond. They met in the madrassa classes for new converts where they differed strikingly from the other attendees because they were black South African women, a demographic rarely seen in such spaces, and because they had quite unconventional marriages.

We sat on the floor sipping tea because Zandi's living room furniture had been carted off to be repaired. Such arrangements were not a hardship. These now very urban women all grew up in rural households where sitting on the floor with guests was commonplace. With the men away working or hauling furniture, the women were free to enjoy the spacious front room and the most optimal patches of sunlight that streamed through the windows. The women removed their headscarves and we unwrapped the babies—my own child among them—allowing the children to explore the room and the next welcoming lap.

Gossip and tea flowed freely, and Zodwa, fresh from an irritating interaction with the family of her husband, began a familiar rant. Switching between English and Zulu, she exclaimed, "We are South African women married to foreigners and hated by both. We are stuck in between two cultures." She had just visited her husband's aunt who had refused to share some spices that were key to making a Burundian dish that Zodwa's husband loved. The spices were hard to find in Durban and Zodwa felt the aunt's parsimonious response was a rejection of Zodwa's embrace of Burundian culture and attempts to integrate into the family as a South African.

Family tensions were a frequent source of vexation for all the women, but they reserved their harshest critiques for what they saw as a denial of their place in South Africa and as poor black African women. "We are South African!" Zodwa continued, "She does not have an RDP house (*pointing at one woman*). She does not have an RDP house (*pointing at another*). She does not have an RDP house (*pointing at Zandi*). And we vote. We are living here with ANC posters up all around us, but we have nothing!" An evocative orator, Zodwa used the "RDP house" as a synecdoche for the larger failures of the ANC-led South African state to live up to its redistributive promises.[1] Many of the women complained that they had "nothing" because they were poor, unemployed, and owned no property. In this way, they were like many of their fellow countrymen whose economic security had not improved with the arrival of democracy. But it was also the frequent discrimination they encountered as wives of foreigners—discrimination that erased their identity as South Africans—that foregrounded their feelings of incomplete belonging in the nation.

Marriages between South Africans and African immigrants were uncommon, and the Muslim Sisters were aware that forging such a union would subject them to prejudice. Thuli, a Zulu-speaking woman also married to a Burundian man, described her initial doubts:

> When he asked me out, I was scared of dating foreigners because, first, I was new in Durban. People used to say terrible things about foreigners, that they are selling drugs or criminals. I never wanted to associate myself with that kind of people. Local people also say bad things about you when you are dating a foreigner. Things like you are a bitch, you are dirty, you like money, you are a prostitute. So, I was afraid of being seen with him.

These everyday indignities also had high-stakes counterparts. Since South Africa opened it borders to immigration in 1994, the country has been racked with a new form of violence and discrimination, this time targeting black bodies from outside the country. Between 2006 and 2012 South Africa accepted the highest number of asylum seekers of any country in the world (UNHCR 2012).[2] In 2011, immigrants made up 4.2 percent of the population, with 71 percent of those coming from the African continent (STATSSA 2012).[3] In addition to the relative economic and political stability South Africa offers, the postapartheid ideals of equality and non-discrimination enshrined in the constitution have produced some of the most progressive asylum laws in the world (Warren 2015). Whereas in other countries refugees are forced into overcrowded camps, in South Africa migrants who have applied for asylum can live and work anywhere in the country until their refugee status is finalized. On paper, asylum seekers and refugees are entitled to the same basic rights as citizens (Landau 2011). Of course, lived reality is much different.

As we are seeing across the globe, in South Africa foreigners have become the scapegoat for the economic and political ills of the country with everything from crime to a lack of public services blamed on their presence (Warren 2015). "African nationals," as they are colloquially termed, are regularly beaten, harassed, their papers torn up, their shops burned, and their communities rounded up for deportation (Amit and Kriger 2014). Spates of xenophobic violence in 2008 and 2015 resulted in the injury and deaths of hundreds of immigrants, those who married them, and those who sought to defend them.

This chapter considers why women like Zandi and Thuli would be willing to tolerate derision and submit their intimate lives to the threats of violence to enter into these binational marriages. How do they understand their partners as husbands or as fathers vis-à-vis South African men? How have these marriages reconfigured their relationships to kin, to their community, and to the state? Though such marriages are still infrequent, answers to these questions reveal the possibilities and limits of black women's citizenship in the new South Africa.

To begin to answer these questions, I offer a key context to the epigraph of this chapter: *Foreigners, they come to steal our women and our jobs.* Like most immigrants around the world, foreigners in South Africa are more frequently employed in more precarious, lower-paying, and hazardous jobs that locals are unwilling to take. This widespread trend is complicated by South African history. A key promise of the democratic government was that employment would be cleansed of its oppressive history and would become "free and uncoerced contractual relationships" through which South Africans could pull themselves out of poverty and build an emancipated and self-sufficient nation (Barchiesi 2011, 14). Thus, black South African refusal to occupy undesirable jobs is in part a protest against a wage labor regime that continues to be repressive and unstable in ways reminiscent of white rule. Under this logic, foreigners who accept such conditions function as scabs who have crossed the picket line. Notably, too, in South Africa, foreigners have a significantly *higher* employment rate—albeit in the informal or gray market—than their local counterparts (Budlender and Fauvelle-Aymar 2012).[4] This relative economic success gives foreigners a contradictory social position. They enjoy greater relative wealth and the prestige of employment (Tafira 2010). Thus, they are doubly vulnerable to the vagaries of state harassment and neighborly anger and jealousy.

Not only are foreigner men able to garner earnings, they sometimes choose to use these earnings to formalize marriages, occasionally, with South African women. Under conditions in which widespread unemployment and low earnings also hinder the solidification of intimate relationships through marriage, nonnationals' employment and marriage to South African women is an obvious source of frustration and jealousy. It is no surprise then that black South African men—overwhelmingly unemployed, poor, and unmarried—voice their frustration and jealousy in the constant critique that foreigners "come to steal our women and our jobs." However, at issue is not simply work and love.

It is a well-worn trope that foreigners plagued by police harassment and political insecurity would seek out marriages with local women to solidify their claims to the polity. However, this does not answer why South African women would agree to be "stolen." I argue that, in a strange reversal, black South African women marry foreign men to gain access to adult status, social inclusion, and, ultimately, a fuller form of citizenship within *their own* nation-state. I contend that in contemporary South Africa, full social citizenship includes an amalgam of newly available forms of state recognition and welfare provisioning undergirded by other forms of social belonging and adult personhood that are unavailable to poor black women and men in the present moment. Thus, as women rework the meaning and access to these various spheres of belonging through their intimate relationships, they also serve to rework the very definition of citizenship in South Africa today. In short, the intimate domains of sex and reproduction are, today, a key site where political belonging is constituted, and in this particular case, black South African women are gaining political belonging through marriage to foreign men. Nonetheless, the forms of inclusion women gain in these transnational marriages comes at the price of other forms of marginalization and exclusion that cannot be overlooked. These tradeoffs reveal the limits of current reworkings of citizenship.

Point Partnerships

Democratic South Africa remains a deeply segregated country. The women of the Muslim Sisterhood met their immigrant husbands because they were living in the Point neighborhood, which has long been a first landing place for immigrants into South Africa. Walking the streets, one is immersed in a cacophony of Hausa, Swahili, Kinyarwanda, and English, alongside the local isiZulu. Though the immigrant population is highly differentiated, it retains a tenuous solidarity, not least of which because the Point is one of the few spaces in Durban where foreigners can safely live and work without the constant threat of xenophobic violence. Thus, when residents from Durban's townships launched anti-immigrant attacks in Point in 2015, the foreigners in the Point united to defend their ability to live and work in the neighborhood.

The South African women I know had come to Point from the rural areas, often as students or as migrants, with few connections to the townships. Though they appreciated the linguistic, racial, and cultural diversity of the neighborhood, as well as its many resources, many disparaged the density and high crime rate, saying it was not a place they wished to raise children. However, because of the transnational nature of their union, they had to continue to live in the neighborhood both to be closer to their husband's work and out of concerns of their husband's safety.

The women in this chapter comprise a subgroup of twelve women out of my larger group of interlocutors. The women range in age from twenty-five to thirty-five, as do their husbands. The women hail from a mix of South

African Zulu and Xhosa backgrounds. The majority (eleven) are married to immigrants from Burundi and converted to their husbands' religion of Islam. The twelfth is married to a Christian Tanzanian. Their husbands predominantly arrived between 2006 and 2010 (in their teens or early twenties). Despite the preponderance of Burundian men in this group, it should not be taken as representative of transnational marriages in Durban or even the Point. Given the high number of Zimbabwean, Malawian, and Mozambican immigrants in the neighborhood, it is likely there are marriages to men in those groups as well. Rather, Burundians dominate this group because many of the husbands knew one another through the close-knit Burundian immigrant network, and the wives came to know one another through the families socializing and from attending madrassa classes together. The Muslim Sisters also intentionally coalesced to form their own informal support network to help one another manage the challenges that came with transnational and black Muslim marriages in Durban.

Burundian migrants to South Africa are a small percentage of total immigrants. The UN estimated a total of 5,227 in South Africa in 2015 (United Nations, Department of Economic and Social Affairs 2015). Furthermore, Muslims comprise only 2.5 percent of the population of Burundi. However, due to a disproportionate level of political ascendance among the Muslim population in Burundi, many more Muslims have felt the effects of the political turmoil of the early 2000s and immigrated. For those that come to South Africa, many seek out Durban as a place to reside, in part, because there is a large, centralized, Muslim population and a mosque within the Point neighborhood. The climate is also more temperate than Johannesburg or Cape Town and thus more familiar to central Africans.

The legal status of the foreigner husbands I know, commonly thought to be the primary motivation for marrying a South African women, did not necessarily shape their claims to belonging. The Department of Home Affairs (DHA), the governmental body in charge of overseeing immigration, has a conflicting stance toward documenting immigrants (Amit and Kriger 2014). On the one hand, the department seeks to keep track of how many migrants are in the country. On the other hand, by documenting their presence, the department imbues migrants with certain rights, which goes against a second goal of limiting the number of migrants through deportation. Thus, many migrants who have presented themselves for registration have been refused documentation so they may be deported later. In 2007, South Africa was a world leader in the number of deportations (Landau 2011, 3).

Documentation also does not ensure protection. Even those who do possess legal documents—documents that entitle them to work and study, to access health care, to open bank accounts, and to a life free from the threat of arrest or detention—have been beaten, harassed, their papers torn up and, deported (Amit and Kriger 2014). The South African state has rejuvenated apartheid-era forms of spatio-ethnic political discrimination once reserved for black South Africans and has deployed them on a new outsider to be denied legal identity: the nonnational (Landau 2011). Like black South Africans under apartheid, African immigrants are regularly excluded from full access to housing and public services to which they are legally due. Denial of these rights maintains their status as cheap, disposable labor on which the South African economy relies (Landau 2011). Indeed, the citizenship claims of poor black South Africans and African immigrants are remarkably similar.

Citizenship, Personhood, Belonging

This chapter presents an unusual case within in migration and marriage scholarship. Here I am concerned with the experiences of women who are the indigenes of a (comparatively) wealthier receiving country who choose to marry a reviled foreigner man. Gender, race, and country of origin have profound implications for how the couples I know navigate their joint projects of social reproduction. Importantly, the couples are committed to building a family in South Africa. This stands in contrast to many migrant marriages wherein men migrate from poorer countries to wealthier countries in order to support marriages and wives they have left in their country of origin (for Africa this includes: Cole and Groes 2016; Hannaford 2017; Ikuomola 2015; Mercer, Page, and Evans 2008). My interlocutors were well aware of the possibility that they could be secondary wives to a primary marriage their husbands had in their natal country. They spent a great deal of energy corresponding with in-laws and members of the sending community in an attempt to confirm the existence of these other families. To date, none have been revealed. Regardless of whether such families become evident, I understand these husbands as making long-term investments in building lives and families that, while inherently transnational, are very much tied to an imagined future in South Africa.

The curious conundrum within the case I offer here is that South African women are marrying lower-status foreigners in order to enhance their status in their own country. In many ways, their actions are comparable to other women in the Global South who, facing limited opportunities at home, marry foreign men in hopes of improving their life. However, overwhelmingly, those are men from a wealthier sending country who themselves have a higher status in the local context (for Africa: Cole 2014a, 2014b, 2014c; Cole and Groes 2016. For other locations: Constable 2003; Faier 2009; Freeman 2011; Fresnoza-Flot 2017; Sirijit 2013; Sirijit and Angeles 2013). What is key to the experiences of the Muslim Sisters is that, though their husbands are considered undesirable, the marriages enable women to raise their children and care for their natal kin in ways their peers cannot. In doing so, they strengthen their feelings of belonging within South Africa.

At the core of this is the link between citizenship and social reproduction. In 2014, when I asked my friend, Sthembile, a longtime political activist, what she wished for in her life, she said simply, "a job where I can be able to get a salary that will be enough to support myself and my family." It matters that Sthembile's greatest wish was for a job *to support her family.* Her desire was articulated not solely as a matter of survival but as a concern of social reproduction. Sthembile was not simply concerned with preventing hunger or cold, illness or death, she was concerned that her parents have security in their old age or that her children could go to a good school. In short, she envisioned a job as a means to shoring up the relationships that were important to her life. It was uncertainty of this reproduction that led Sthembile and other black and coloured women like her to say that they felt excluded from citizenship in the new South Africa. Their citizenship was tenuous because it was constituted through the relationships in which people are embedded, relationships that were insecure.

To take seriously statements like those of Sthembile and others like her requires an understanding of citizenship as relational. This is to say that the transition from minority rule to democracy brought about essential forms of inclusion. Alongside universal suffrage, the new constitution offered to all citizens a radical expansion of rights including the right to nondiscrimination on the basis of race, gender, sexuality, age, culture, in addition to socioeconomic rights to housing, health care, food, water, and social assistance. However, these rights are insufficient given that the majority of South Africans are overwhelmingly poor. Not simply poor, but lacking the very basic housing, health care, food, and water the new constitution guaranteed. In other words, the supposedly universalist character of liberal citizenship was deeply exclusionary of the very persons it purported to include. The state and popular marginalization of poor South Africans leaves them in a tenuous position vis-à-vis their own citizenship. Indeed, short of deportation, many poor South African citizens suffer similar exclusions to that of foreigners: denial of legal status and documentation; harassment, arrest, and detention; and obstructed access to constitutional rights, state services, and legal due process (Landau 2011). Notably, police target people for deportation on the basis of appearance (darkness/lightness of skin), language, and documentation, which has led to the deportation of a significant number of South Africans belonging to linguistic minorities. This has led one scholar to assert, "[the poor] are considered to be less than fully entitled members of the South African polity. What separates non-nationals from citizens is the degree to which exclusion is both bureaucratically institutionalized and socially legitimate" (Landau 2011, 8).

This chapter offers another, more explicit, example of how women are producing relational citizenship through their kinshipping labor. Relational citizenship is constituted through multiple nested and overlapping layers of belonging to groups organized at different scales or terms. Across previous chapters, we have seen how women and men forge belonging through the creation and maintenance of different kinds of social relationships. In this chapter I focus on black women's belonging to a kin group, belonging in a cultural group—here both Xhosa and Zulu, and to the larger nation of South Africa. It is in their efforts to strengthen and regenerate relationships to their extended kin that women forge forms of belonging that then scale up. In short, it is in the space of these intimate relationships that women are reworking citizenship.

Membership through Marriage

In order to understand why someone like Zodwa would choose to marry a foreigner and submit herself to various forms of personal and political violence requires an understanding of how relational citizenship operates in postapartheid South Africa. Across the last century, black women's status in three spheres—kin group, cultural group, and nation—has changed in contour. What has remained remarkably consistent is how their belonging has been mediated by the institutions of marriage and wage labor.

Among Zulu and Xhosa people, marriage marks a critical part of the social transition from adolescence to fully recognized adulthood with the accompanying forms of respect and responsibility (Cook 1931; Guy 1990; Liebenberg 1994). By creating an *umuzi (umzi)* or separate household, sons become *umnumzana,* the head of the household, a man of worth and status (Hunter 2010). These men fulfill their obligation—to their living family and to their ancestors—to continue the lineage through marriage to a *umakoti* (bride/daughter-in-law) who in turn is obligated to care for her husband and mother-in-law and the necessary children.

Prior to colonialism, such marriages were solidified through the exchange of gifts, the most notable being the *ilobolo* or bridewealth of cattle given from the family of the husband to the family of the bride. However, since the early twentieth century, settler land dispossession reduced fathers' capacity to raise and give cattle for sons' marriages. Instead, an increasing dependency on cash drove sons into a wage economy hungry for labor. *Ilobolo* and the marriages it solidified became tied to son's earnings through the migration to cities, upending gendered and generational hierarchies.

In the segregationist and apartheid eras, black women's national belonging was severely limited and linked to the status of working men. Though men were desired in cities for their labor, successive white governments sought to limit men's claims to urban life by granting them only temporary residence in the city and confining them to be housed in single-sex hostels. The critical work of social reproduction—birthing and raising of children, growing of food, caring for the elderly, and honoring the ancestors—was done by women predominantly living on rural reserves. By virtue of their waged labor, black men gained partial membership—the membership available to them—in the polity. Black women, by contrast, faced increasing obstacles for legally residing in cities and in a colonial reworking of customary law, were labeled as legal minors, unable to own property, retain custody of their children, or move without the consent of their husband or tribal elders. Though long criticized for fostering marital instability, the migrant labor system fostered what some have termed a "patriarchal bargain" where as long as men sent home a sufficient proportion of their wages, women were willing to work for the *umuzi* and both could enjoy the heightened status of *umnumzana* and *umakoti* (Kandiyoti 1988; Moodie with Ndatshe 1994).

At democratic transition, black women gained the most in terms of formal political belonging. In addition to giving women the right to vote, women activists demanded that the new dispensation reckon with the structural gender discrimination (not just the racial and class discrimination more widely acknowledged) that had been built into the country's workings. As a result of this activism, the framers of democracy included a commitment to encouraging women's participation in government and addressing the inequalities of the past from a particularly gendered perspective, such as through reform of the Maintenance Court (Hassim 2005). Unfortunately, much of the progress towards these goals took the form of newly enshrined legal rights and very little substantive redistributive change (Hassim 2005). The experiences of women in preceding chapters have shown the challenges impoverished women face in meeting kin and cultural expectations, in many ways due to the inaccessibility of marriage and work. Women place much of the blame for their inability to belong in these spheres on the failures of men and the state.

Intimacies in an Age of Insecurity

In 2014, the group of twelve black African women, whose experiences frame this chapter, stood out from the many other women I met, first because their children shared the same father, and second because they had married the father of their children with customary *ilobolo* exchange and also though an Islamic Nikah ceremony. Though there are colloquial evaluations of the relative virtues of foreign men—Malawians are good lovers, Nigerians are rich and powerful, Tanzanians are family men—marriage between South Africans and foreigners remains uncommon for all the aforementioned reasons. Thus, I was surprised to encounter this tight knit group of transnational spouses.

When I asked the women to describe the origins of their relationship, their stories all began with an outpouring of frustration and criticism of the local men they had dated. The women spoke from their own experience in terms that mirrored the circulating tropes of the absent black father. Many

friends and sisters had children by multiple fathers who did not offer support. One woman summed it up well when she said, "I don't know what
kind of men are these [local] men. Because I don't understand how can a
man be able to take a plate of food and eat and they don't know what their
child is eating." To eat for one's self is a criticism that cuts to the heart of
moral personhood. This selfishness of men she saw as a violation of the
sanctity of fatherhood. She went on to complain that men were not only
financially absent, but though they were not working, they remained *physically* absent, as they had been during labor migration. She bemoaned the
embarrassment her daughters felt when their schoolmates teased them for
not having a father. "You can be responsible and you don't have the money."
She said, "At least he should show his children that they have a father."

Their foreign husbands' different orientation to family was a key distinction many women cited in their decision to pursue the relationship. Thuli
was one of the women who had been quite reluctant to date a foreigner, due
to the derision she felt in the community. However, her experiences with
local men gave her different terms on which to evaluate the relationship:

> We are able to stay together as a family. What I saw different about him
> from other South African man is that his children always come first. Other
> South African make their children a last priority. With him I know what-
> ever happens his children will always be his first priority.

One of the most important priorities was that foreign men chose to put
their earnings toward the payment of *inhlawulo* and *ilobolo*. While the exact
amounts of these ritual payments are negotiated between families, they are
sizeable investments, many times the monthly income of even the most successful of the foreigner husbands I knew. For example, monthly rent for a flat
for the family would cost about R4500 in 2014 (approximately $450). The *in-
hlawulo* payment for Zandi's first child was R6000 (approximately $600). This
payment had to be completed before negotiations over *ilobolo* could begin,
with the final amount totaling somewhere in the range of R50,000–R70,000
($5,000–$7,000). As scholars over time have noted, this bridewealth payment
is not unidirectional but part of a larger exchange between families that takes
place over the course of many years (Comaroff and Roberts 1981). However,
that exchange was complicated by the cultural differences between the bride
and groom's family and the lack of space and accommodation in the Point

neighborhood to enable the kind of celebratory gathering that would usually take place in the rural areas. This is all to say that a primary rationale for women choosing to marry foreigner men is that foreigner men who had the means to marry them agreed to use that money to pay *ilobolo*.

The social import of formalizing marriage for the women I know cannot be overstated (Ansell 2001; Burman and van der Werff 1993; Dlamini 1994; Shope 2006; Walker 1992; Yarbrough 2017) . Finding a man who will pay *ilobolo* is equivalent to winning the social lottery (Hunter 2006; Rice 2015). The payment of bridewealth is a signal of the social value of the woman and of the good work her family did in raising her (De Haas 1987). By getting married, women met a primary kin obligation as daughter and sister—sister because theoretically, brothers can use their sister's *ilobolo* to formalize their own marriages. Further, she ensured that her children would be a legitimate part of a lineage, thereby appeasing her ancestors. Movement into the role of married woman gave these women the status of moral adult personhood, though tempered by discrimination against their spousal choice. In doing so, it gave them access to a form of belonging that had been inaccessible in recent decades.

Foreign men's allocation of money was not simply important economically but was also critical for its indication of emotional commitment. In South Africa, two competing ideologies operate simultaneously in regard to the relationship between love and money (Thomas and Cole 2009). The first, common in the Global North, envisions love and money as existing in "hostile worlds" in which the presence of one negates the possibilities of the other (Zelizer 2005). This was in operation when Sthembile was concerned about being accused of being a prostitute for dating a foreigner. In the second, money or economic support are an important constitutive part of love. Using this orientation, South African women argue that, though they recognize *ilobola* creates obstacles for formalizing marriage, the practice is absolutely critical to the demonstration and creation of love. Unless they paid *ilobolo*, women claimed, how could they know that men truly loved them and how could they be inspired for their love to grow (Yarbrough 2018). The women I knew used this second set of logics to argue that their foreigner husbands' spending choices—on bridewealth, on food, on the children—demonstrated the greater love they had for their wives and family and brought about greater love from the women in return.

Their spouses' willingness to participate in this important social practice of *ilobola* helped to bridge differences in language and culture and enhanced the acceptance of women's extended family for these unusual unions. Sthembile's engagement story demonstrates this well. It is common practice that *ilobolo* negotiations take place over multiple days with representatives from the groom's family coming to visit and celebrate at the bride's family home to begin the process of joining the families together. From the outset, that format was not going to be feasible, and Sthembile spent considerable effort gently managing her family's expectations and guiding her father and uncle on to how to smooth the cross-cultural interactions. Sthembile's intended, Abdoul, was a Muslim man from Burundi who had an elder kinsman "uncle" also living in Durban. This uncle and an old Zulu man Abdoul had befriended, agreed to act as his representatives in the process. The groom would not usually be allowed to be present during the negotiations, but in this case he was allowed to join and act as a translator between his uncle and the rest of the party. Abdoul had very little time he could be away from work, so the negotiations had to be shortened to allow him to travel back and forth to rural Zululand from Durban in the same day.

The assembly that drove out to Sthembile's family home posed a strikingly different picture from the caravan of extended kin that would usually attend such an event.[6] Instead of multiple cars laden with family, gifts, and animals to feed the families for next few days of celebration, there was a small white pickup truck with a few boxes and a goat in the back. Abdoul and his uncle wore slim-tailored Burundian *agbada*—tunics that fell to the knee over matching pants—whose burgundy color matched the dress shirt his Zulu friend wore. Negotiations often begin with a *vulamlomo* gift (literally, to open the mouth) that is intended to set participants at ease in order to begin the process. Rather than a bottle of brandy, which is often given, Abdoul, who does not drink alcohol, presented Sthembile's mother with a china tea set ornately decorated in pink roses and rimmed in gold. Sthembile reported later that this gesture pleased her teetotaler mother immensely. There was very little back-and-forth bartering, particularly because Abdoul and Sthembile had no children together, which would have required additional discussion, and the group quickly arrived at an amicable agreement. Sthembile had counseled Abdoul not to pay too much of the *ilobolo* too early, as he initially desired, because it would be taken as resistance to ongoing relationships with her family. Instead, he made a small cash payment and gave her father a watch, her uncle a music speaker, and her mother a set of decorative canisters. There wasn't time to slaughter and roast the goat, so the group had meat that Sthembile's mother and aunt had cooked earlier, with tea, coffee, soda pop, and cakes from the local shop before the groom's group set off to return to Durban. If those who had been part of the negotiations had missed the Zulu beer, they had ample opportunity to make up for it the following day when Abdoul's goat was roasted and the neighboring community was invited to celebrate the unorthodox but joyful engagement.

Sthembile's story reveals multiple forms of accommodation Abdoul and Sthembile's family used to negotiate a ritual that both found acceptable. One can imagine many points where either party could have balked at the possibility of compromise—over the participation of the groom, over language barriers, over the absence (or presence) of alcohol, over the duration of the process. Sthembile's family could also have outright rejected the very possibility of their daughter marrying a foreigner. However, through visits to town and the couple's visits to the farm they came to know him and accept him as a thoughtful, hardworking man and a good match for their daughter. Sthembile joked that many of her family's neighbors had criticized Abdoul, but their comments quieted when they had his goat's meat in their mouths. Though their marriage came about amid growing xenophobia, Sthembile, Abdoul, and their community were able to forge a union that gained them all greater respect and belonging.

Far more than the mollifying power of meat, participating in *ilobola* transformed Abdoul, Sthembile, and Sthembile's family's position in their respective relationships. As Hunter has robustly demonstrated, paying *ilobolo* signals a man's ability to occupy a provider role, a highly valued component of Zulu masculinity that affords deep respect (2004, 2005, 2006, 2009, 2010). In terms of relational personhood, the sacrifice and persistence that paying *ilobolo* requires, particularly in the present day, is indication that a man has extended himself to include his fiancée and her family in his interdependent relationships and is prepared to take on the obligations that come with marriage (Rudwick and Posel 2015). Abdoul's payment of *ilobolo* not only legitimated him in the eyes of Sthembile, her community, and her living family, it also showed honor to her family's *amadlozi* or ancestors. Described as "shaking hands with the ancestors of the bride and her family," *ilobolo* serves to introduce the groom and his family to the bride's decedents so as to court their blessings and forestall any harms of illness or bad luck that they might inflict on the families (Rudwick and Posel 2014, 133; Ngubane 1981). Payment of *ilobolo* also marks a woman, and by extension her family, as accomplished and valued. Contemporary Zulu women view *ilobolo* as a "reward for having carried yourself well," meaning having lived a life of conduct deserving of respect (Rudwick and Posel 2014, 128). Such actions were partially viewed as the result of women's own choices but were also attributed to the efforts of her family to *khulisa* (raise or nurture) her well.

For the Muslim Sisters, the good character of their husbands was not just demonstrated through their commitment to *ilobola*, but also through their honesty. "Why Toussaint?," I asked Zandi. "Awweeeee," she giggled, "you know mens, they lie. Me, I don't like someone who thinks he is big and tells stories . . . and Toussaint don't lie. He don't lie." Another woman, Maya, regaled a story of a previous boyfriend who always left her waiting, saying, "I'm coming, I'm coming," but never turning up. She said she came to expect that nothing he said was true. When she first met her Burundian husband, he charmed her by being twenty minutes *early*.

The most critical form of honesty for all the women was fidelity. They spoke disparagingly about the proclivity of the South African men they knew to sleep with multiple women. In part, this was an issue of sexual loyalty, of no small import in a country with such a high AIDS rate. But also at stake was a division of resources. If men were with other women, it meant some of their money was going elsewhere. The women I knew were relieved to not have the conflicts that infidelity brought on. "We do fight," Maya said, "but never one day do we fight about a lady. If he is cheating (*she laughed*), he is doing it so nicely that I can't see anything, ever." More important than the act of infidelity, for Maya, was that she did not feel the effects of divided attention or resources.

As they talked about their foreign husbands' fidelity, the women made a striking cultural shift. They described their husbands' actions as embodying *inhlonipho*, or respect (Finlayson 2002; Hunter 1961; Soga 1932). This is a crucial concept of moral personhood that sits at the heart of what it means to be Zulu or Xhosa (Mayer 1972; Whooley 1975). Historically used to indicate acts of deference that upheld social hierarchies, often gendered, this precolonial concept became linked to specifically female sexual purity through Christian missionary influence (Hunter 2010). However, in our conversations, the women I knew used it to indicate a male commitment to marital *equality* in both conduct and communication. One woman, Maya, explained:

> I went with him because I saw his qualities, the way he treated me. Because in previous relationships that I was in, the people I was with, either they would cheat or did not treat me right. With him I saw that he was not the type that liked woman and he respected me. When we had a problem, he knew how to talk with me without fighting me. He knew how to humble himself and apologize.

Here, critically, it was *men* who demonstrated deference and sensitivity and, notably foreign men. In this way, women like Maya took up ideas of conduct befitting a morally upstanding Zulu or Xhosa woman and laminated them onto their foreign husbands. I see this as part of a renegotiation of marital meaning that has taken place as companionate marriage and spousal choice—important means by which women assert a modern identity—have been knit together with so-called traditional marriage forms (Burbank 1995; Davidson and Hannaford 2022; Hirsch 2003; Hirsch and Wardlow 2006; G'sell 2022; Rice 2023; Thomas and Cole 2009).

Explanations such as what I have just detailed that justify marital choice through appeals to moral ideas such as fidelity, cultural obligation, or respect were also political acts for the women I knew. These women were constantly asked to explain their justification for such a surprising marriage to a host of questioners, myself included. Thus, their answers were well-rehearsed and anticipated the accompanying judgments. When I asked Thuli how her family had responded to her relationship, she answered, "They were saying the things that most South Africans say about foreigners. That he wants to marry me because he wants to get an identity document and he wants to stay in the country, or he could just leave me, all those things." Sthembile noted that her motivations were also questioned, "When people hear you are with a foreigner they always assume you with him cause you after his money and also that you had no other choice because no other person is interested in you." Notably, this critique of the mercenary African woman is not limited to Point women's detractors, but has a long history on and off the continent (Ferguson 1999). Thus, appeals to affection and attachment become all the more important amid a milieu where arguments about the instrumentality of the marriage choice are seen to undermine emotional sincerity. In their choice of a foreign husband, women face a complicated calculus that often includes a history of failed relationships with local men, the prospects of achieving social belonging through marriage, and the economic support that came with that commitment. It is benefits such as these that allow women to endure the anticipated and surprising hardships they face due to their marital choice.

New Forms of Marginalization

By marrying a foreigner, I contend South African women gained a greater sense of belonging in the spheres of kinship and cultural expectation. However, these gains were not uncomplicated, and they came at the expense of other forms of exclusion and marginalization. As Zandi said, "When I go to any office, I have to be prepared to fight. I have to fight because I know the treatment I am going to get is not nice." The everyday forms of discrimination women faced arose from assumptions about the relationship between Islam and racial identity. All of the women I knew had converted, usually from Christianity, and wore a hijab and often long tunics when they went out in the neighborhood. Muslims in South Africa are a small minority, and Islam is racialized differently based on which Muslim groups are present in a given place. In Durban, Islam is associated with the city's large Indian population. The women I knew, all of whom were black South Africans, presented an unusual union of black bodies and Muslim dress that onlookers were at pains to comprehend.

The first assumption people made was that the women I knew were foreigners. When running errands in town they faced sneers on the sidewalk, rude shopkeepers, or taxi drivers who would not give them change. Much of the derision came from fellow South African women. "I will get in the taxi," Zodwa said, "and the women will be pulling up their face and will say to their friend in Zulu 'aren't they hot in all those clothes? Maybe that is why they are so smelly, they are always sweating.'" Zodwa had an arsenal of swift retorts she often used to demonstrate her cultural and linguistic

FIGURE 6.1A AND B The attire of Muslim Sisters as compared to their local peers. Photos by informants.

comprehension as well as her married status, "My hair is so much cleaner than in my *isicholo.*" She would reply in Zulu, speaking of the circular hat exclusively worn by married Zulu women.[6] Women expressed frustration about how, quickly after their response, such mocking would shift to nervous laughter and exclamations of *"ungumngane wami, ungusisi wami!* (you are my friend, my sister)." Zandi and Zodwa criticized what they saw as the "small mindedness" of their kinswomen, saying, "I am no more your friend than five minutes before. You need to know that I am *from here* for you to treat me better?"

A second misperception was that the women were poor and had dressed in Islamic clothes to come to the city to beg. On Fridays, there were groups of black South African women who would come to town, dressed in hijab for the occasion, to take advantage of the practice of Zakat or alms-giving to poor Muslims. Zodwa, who worked in town in a predominantly Indian neighborhood by one of the oldest mosques, hated patronizing local businesses for this reason. One day she had gone to buy lunch, and as she arrived at the counter to place her order, the Indian shopkeeper took a R2 coin out of the zakat drawer, brusquely gave it to her, and waved her away.

The insult of such assumptions was threefold. First was the presumption that their conversion to Islam was insincere. Their decisions to convert and cover themselves took place over the course of many years and serious consideration. They spent many hours a week attending madrassa classes, and Zodwa was proud to be one of the teachers. The suggestion that their conversion was careless was a mere ploy to gain resources was quite hurtful. Second was the insinuation that they were so poor that they would beg. All of the women struggled to make ends meet but found the idea of begging, and particularly begging through the deceptive appropriation of a sacred practice, to be disgraceful. The third insult was the suggestion by fellow Muslims, and particularly Indians, that they were somehow lesser than sisters in faith. There are historic separations between the Indian Muslim community and the (comparatively small) black South African Muslim community that feed into racial divides forged under white minority rule (Kaarsholm 2008). Indians and Africans were often pitted against each other to compete for very limited resources and tenuous political power, and while they also had many moments of collusion, particularly against a racist state, there are also old tensions that can be reignited at key moments.[7] A common stereotype held by Indians is that black South Africans are duplicitous and morally corrupt. Conversely, black South Africans often complain that Indians look down on them and mistreat them. That the shopkeeper Zodwa encountered assumed she was a beggar instead of a paying customer fed into these simmering resentments and deepened the insult. She felt that as a Muslim sister she should have been treated with respect, but because of her black skin she was presumed to be a deceitful African and was brushed off as an unwanted nuisance.

The particular conflation of Islam with Indian-ness in Durban also led to problems within the women's own cultural groups. Once they dispelled the assumptions that they were foreigners themselves or impersonating believers to attract resources, their decision to convert, even when sincere, attracted ridicule. Other black South Africans accused them of being disloyal to their culture and to their race by appropriating what they deemed as "Indian culture." Because of the aforementioned racial tension between Indian and black South Africans, practicing "Indian culture" was viewed as defecting and seen as implying that the women thought Zulu or Xhosa culture was not good enough for them.

In addition to the feelings of anger that these accumulated forms of discrimination produced, women married to nonnationals also spoke of a deep sense of isolation. In part, this arose from friends or kin who did not accept their marriage and broke off ties with them. At other times, this was a product of living in the Point neighborhood that, despite its density, lacked a cohesive sense of community. Women complained that they did not fully know their neighbors or have close friendships which they saw as more possible in the townships. Many of the women I knew did not work and stayed at home to care for young children. They often bemoaned what they felt were more rigid gender norms held by their husbands that discouraged their working or going out where they might interact with other men.

The social effects of this isolation were varied. At one level, it manifested as a sense of loneliness. Women complained that nobody came over to drink tea, or that they knew few people with whom they could leave their children when they went to the shops. The closeness of the group of women who attended madrassa together was an attempt to minimize these effects. At another level, it manifested as a lack of social support that left these women more vulnerable.

Though all of their husbands worked, the earnings were unreliable and there were many months when income did not cover expenses. In such moments, the economic support of kin or loans of money or food from friends and neighbors was the stuff of survival. Further, despite the positive qualities they attributed to their husbands, all of the women had experienced some form of physical violence from their husband.[8] For Zandi, who had the support of her family and the presence of Toussaint's extended kin in Durban, she could call on other family to assist her in creating a livable home situation. Alternatively, Zodwa, whose family had disowned her and who lacked affinal kin, felt disempowered by a dearth of advocates and trapped within a marriage that had not lived up to her expectations.

———

In April 2017, there was another spate of xenophobic violence in South Africa, this time accompanied by a PRO-xenophobia march. It is sadly not a phenomenon unique to South Africa, though the history of apartheid does contribute a particular flavor. As we have seen across the chapters of this book, the creation of "insiders" and "outsiders" along the lines of race, class, or geographic residence was a critical part of the functioning of the South African polity. The violence of the last two decades is not simply a moment of zealous nationalism. "The nation" has long been a body in danger of contamination by "outsiders"—he they native or foreign. Similarly, the welfare of "insiders" has been premised on the exclusion of "outsiders" who, for much of the last century, were black Africans.

The African nonnational is the present-day "outsider." Thus concerns about marriage between nonnationals and South Africans must be understood as part of a much broader resistance to mixing between ethnic groups, across races, across class that pervades South Africa and its history. This resistance is not solely an issue of xenophobia—or the construction of the stranger as a threat to society as per Fourchard and Segatti (2015). It is also part of a long discourse of antimiscegenation whereby African immigrants are understood to embody differences in culture, ethnicity, and at times race that could sully the purity of the host community. It can be understood as akin to the pervasive historic concern about interracial marriage. Also at issue is a class conflict wherein foreigners' economic ability to formalize marriages—and access their symbolic capital—has provoked intense jealousy from South African men who feel that their poverty is a reminder that they have been left out of the promises that democracy was supposed to fulfill. In many ways, the claims that foreigners have "stolen" black men's women and jobs is an accusation that the very content of citizenship has been possessed by outsiders. But what of the women they have putatively stolen?

Under democracy, black South African women have access to markers of citizenship that their mothers and grandmothers could only fight for. They can retain custody of their children, own property even in the city, take an absentee father to court. They can vote for the highest office in the country and expect that a number of their leaders will look like them. None of the women I know denied the import of the many benefits they now enjoyed. But, they often bemoaned the hardships that had accompanied them. Without access to marriage or jobs, women felt blocked in their ability to meet their obligations to their elders or their children. In short, their membership in the nation felt incomplete. In chapter 4 we saw how they performed motherhood as a means to having their claims legitimized and to garner the resources for their children. Chapter 5 showed how some women did or did not use the Maintenance Court as part of a larger effort of family making. This chapter considers marriage as another strategy to shore up belonging, only here it is marriage to a foreigner.

I have argued marriage to a foreign man became a pathway for some black African women to achieve relational citizenship. Across this book we have seen how black South African women have had to fight for the privilege of secure social reproduction. Women in other chapters found a variety of ways to make their lives more secure and eke out various forms of inclusion. However, none of these included marriage. Women in this chapter functionally lived as housewives, focused solely on the care of the house and their children, a status their foremothers only could attain in marriage to men who migrated. These women gained the respected status of *umakoti* or bride and the financial and social partnership of a husband they could build a home with. The women and their children became legitimate members of their own and their husband's lineages and, in the event that their family accepted their marriage, were able to retain close ties to their natal family. In other words, they won the lottery.

However, these marriages, which were the very condition of possibility for these women to enjoy these additional forms of belonging, also came at the price of other forms of exclusion. In exchange for some membership in some spheres, these women sacrificed ready recognition of themselves as South African and suffered accusations that their Islamic conversion was either insincere or a form of cultural defecting. These tradeoffs highlight the import of these negotiations for women like Zandi, for poor South Africans and for others across the world who are navigating what citizenship means in our global age.

CONCLUSION

IN SCENES EERILY REMINISCENT of the apartheid era, July 2021 saw South Africa's streets filled with angry crowds burning buildings and looting shops. The scale of the destruction was massive. In Durban, which sustained some of the most intense rioting, the majority of shops and warehouses were emptied. For days, bread or rice could not be purchased for any price because there was simply none to buy. The shelves were bare and the supply lines from the port had been severed, making shortages a national issue.

Photos of the mayhem reveal the disparate motivations that spurred the rioters and the sweeping impacts: a mall parking lot filled with people struggling to carry away speakers, stereos, and appliances; women and children rolling carts filled with kilo bags of food; stick-wielding protesters marching through the streets and overturning cars, bearing signs that demand "free Zuma"; a woman dropping a baby out of the window of a burning building into a crowd of outstretched hands; heavily armed South African National Defense Force soldiers patrolling in front of a block of burned-out shops, still smoking from the fires.[1] Some took to the streets, enraged by the growing schism within the African National Congress, the party of apartheid liberation. Others used the chaos as an opportunity to accumulate the big-ticket items that signaled success, but were inaccessible to the 40 percent of the population who were unemployed. Many, weary from grinding poverty and incessant hunger, stockpiled food for hungry children at home.

In one sense, the riots may seem unexpected; after all, South Africa has been widely lauded for its peaceful transition from racist rule to liberal democracy. And, indeed, the months of pandemic lockdown that preceded the unrest created exceptionally dire circumstances, especially among the poor. However, the pandemic only exacerbated a pervasive feeling that the poor, and particularly poor women, have been abandoned by the state. For the women I know, women who became citizens for the first time in 1994, this abandonment merely reinforced what they described to me as their incomplete inclusion in the national body. Though they valued their ability to vote and their rights to social protection, they interpreted their citizenship as hollow because they could not support their children.

This book has closely considered the lived experience of citizenship. Scholars often theorize the meaning of citizenship as articulated through technocratic governance or through individuals' interactions with state policy. Citizenship as lived requires a different orientation. Across these chapters, I have traced a longer history by which citizenship for black African and coloured women was co-constituted through their recurring response to and protest against their exclusion from state provisions that supported/guaranteed secure social reproduction. In other words, the meaning of citizenship did not simply arise out of terms laid down by the state. Instead, those terms were themselves in flux as they were taken up, contested, and reworked by those to whom they were expected to apply. In the case of South Africa, motherhood has long been an identity salient to political belonging—both before colonization and after. Though the content of motherhood as a political identity was, of course, quite different within precolonial African political systems verses under colonial rule, apartheid, or democracy, the assumed coherence of the status of "mother" allowed it to operate as a simultaneously forceful and malleable ground for various kinds of claims (as seen in chapter 3). Motherhood, as it has been explored in this book, serves as one among many possible examples of the interweaving of political subjectivities generated at different scales.

The particularities of the South African case have revealed more broadly the need for an alternative understanding of citizenship not as vested in individual persons but as lived out through relationships, something Nyamnjoh (2002, 2007, 2018) has also long called for. In this book, I have argued that Point women's disappointment in their experience of citizenship under democracy reflected an understanding of citizenship as relational. They measured their political belonging by the security of their social reproduction. They argued their citizenship was tenuous because it was constituted through relationships that were currently insecure—insecure because women lacked the capacity to invest in them. While prior means of social reproduction and belonging, namely, marriage and work, had never been very secure under white rule, they were at least available. Democracy neither bolstered nor unburdened these institutions, rather, they became inaccessible, a loss for which women held the state primarily responsible. Newly gained rights, while important, only afforded juro-political citizenship. They were inadequate to achieve relational citizenship. Kinshipping strategies became a way to supplement this lack—to leverage state systems to garner both support and recognition for their needs as persons embedded in webs of relationships. Despite Point women's efforts, support was unreliable and community recognition was a critical, but imperfect, substitute for state recognition. In other words, their relational citizenship remained incomplete. Kinshipping generated a greater sense of belonging and allowed them, for a time, to "get by."

Attention to how women used kinshipping to rework their relational citizenship offers another key contribution. Within the disciplines of social anthropology, sociology, or political science as well as lay ideologies, there persists an idea that modern states are, by definition, political orders without kinship. In their edited volume *Reconnecting the State and Kinship*, Thelen and Alber succinctly declare that, "the juxtaposition of kinship and the (modern) state as mutually exclusive is thus so deeply ingrained in the Western worldview and in processes of knowledge production that decoding their coproduction poses a considerable challenge" (2017, 1). This book has taken up that challenge to show not just that kinship and the state are interconnected but *how* kin and state obligations co-constitute each other. In the preceding chapters, we have seen how Point women use this intertwining to make claims on their community and to attempt to hold the state accountable to the very modern democratic principles it purports to embrace. Conversely, as is occurring across the globe, modern states that impose fiscal austerity, in fact, rely on the kinshipping labors of women to ensure social reproduction in the face of inadequate state support. I have shown that a thoroughgoing analysis of the workings of modern statehood today requires accounting for how it is generated in tandem with kinship.

It is central that this book's articulation of relational citizenship and its focus on the coproduction of the modern state and kinship arise out of the experiences of impoverished black, coloured, and Indian women in South Africa. Citizenship as it is lived is always crosscut by inequities of sexism, racism, and classism in ways not always visible when the focus is on juro-political citizenship. In South Africa, gendered expectations have been remarkably similar across race groups, wherein women held the primary responsibility for the work involved in social reproduction. However, the conditions under which they do so vary dramatically by class and race. Motherhood has long been a valorized political identity in South Africa; historically, however, state resources have overwhelmingly been funneled to white mothers, setting them up as the ur example of relational citizenship achieved. Thus, in order to raise their children, women excluded from white privilege in South Africa have for decades had to use their kinshipping labor to make up for a lack of state support. Mothering qua social reproduction is a privilege for which black African, coloured and Indian women have continuously fought. The transition to "'nonracial" democracy promised equal realization of relational citizenship. Yet, colonial and apartheid legacies coupled with political and economic restructuring has only deepened the disparities between the few whose lives are secure and the majority who must carve out lives amid constant precarity. Rather than expanding the relational citizenship available to white families to all race groups, the democratic state instead deracialized its obligation to support children as a particular category of nonlaboring citizen. Recall from chapter 4 that the state Child Support Grants (CSG) give impoverished caregivers small monthly payments to support the care of children, amounts that, while essential, are woefully inadequate. The result is that the democratic state continues to rely on the labors of black African, coloured, and Indian women to sustain themselves and their families on virtually nothing.

The state response to the COVID-19 pandemic brought these issues into even sharper focus. In April 2020, the South African government rolled out a pandemic relief package that increased the levels of all grants by R250 (roughly $17) per month for six months and created a monthly Social Relief of Distress (SRD) grant (R350/$25) for unemployed people who did not receive other forms of government assistance. Tellingly, the Child Support

Grants—the largest category of grants—were handled quite differently. Rather than every CSG increasing, every caregiver who collected a CSG received a R500($34) top-up, regardless of the number of children in their care. Further, unemployed women were deemed ineligible for an SRD *if they collected a grant for one of their children*. Thus while the caregiver top-up symbolically acknowledged that caregivers also had needs in the pandemic, the lack of a CSG grant increase materially meant that caregivers had to use "their" top-up to cover both their needs and their children's. The caregiver top-up hardly offset rising food costs resulting from the loss of school feeding schemes during school closures and left nothing for caregivers themselves.

The selective stinginess of the pandemic response reflected the long-standing ambiguous status of women caregivers in the eyes of the state. Before the pandemic, the dominant rhetoric had been that the CSG was only to support children who should not be expected work, whereas unemployed caregivers should find jobs to sustain themselves. Yet, when the state targeted the unemployed with the SRD—to date the closest it had come to implementing a basic income grant—women were deemed ineligible on the very basis of their status as poor caregivers. The lack of support within the relief package for women created a public furor. A coalition of researchers and rights organizations, unsuccessfully, petitioned for an immediate revision, calling the relief program "inequitable and punitive to women and children" (Coalition 2020). One impoverished woman articulated to a reporter what many were feeling, "The government really cast us aside as poor women with children. We deserved better. We should have also been recipients of the R350 grant because the child support grant is only meant for the children. We have been surviving from hand to mouth even before the lockdowns" (Xolo 2021). Not surprisingly, the caregiver top-ups ended in October 2020 whereas the SRD ended in April 2021. Riots erupted four months later.[2]

This book has shown that for decades many black African and coloured women have been angry and frustrated by the lack of a reliable income, a secure home, and regular meals. They are enraged that in the new South Africa, they still must fight for their basic social reproduction. The "anger of the poor can go in many directions," warned S'bu Zikode, leader of the powerful impoverished people's movement Abahlali baseMjondolo

(Xolo 2021). That was in 2008, just before a bout of xenophobic violence, and much has deteriorated since. For many women in the Point, anger and desperation fueled their dogged work to sustain themselves and their families—work that kept riots like those in 2021 at bay for so long. While they desired and expected that democracy would bring secure livelihoods backed by state investment, they did not passively await a change in policy. Instead, they forged ties, albeit sometimes tenuous ones, that maintained their lives and shored up their sense of belonging. Through kinshipping they generated recognition for their needs not as autonomous individuals but as persons embedded in webs of relationships that tethered them to family, community, cultural group, and, indeed, nation. In other words, they reworked citizenship as relational. It wasn't what they had hoped for under democracy, but it worked for a time, until it didn't.

Each of the previous chapters has detailed a different example of Point women's kinshipping labors and attempts to rework their citizenship. While women in the second decade of democracy are concerned about the content of their citizenship, the story does not begin there. The notion of relational citizenship—which brings together national belonging, a politics of interdependence, and social reproduction—was borne from years of racialized exclusion that predate the current moment. As we saw in chapters 2 and 3, for close to a century, a key marker of inclusion in the national community was state investment in social reproduction. Until the late 1980s, the most robust state support was given to white families, with coloured and Indian families receiving far less and black African families collecting a pittance. Thus when Rosemary and Rose, in chapter 3, leveraged circulating discourse about the central role of mothers in securing the national future, their claims to support from the apartheid welfare state were simultaneously efforts to rework political belonging under racist rule. They were arguments their activist foremothers had made for decades, that that needs of black and coloured mothers and children should be recognized and addressed.

The women living in the Point in 2014, from chapter 4, were the daughters and granddaughters of those who negotiated with social workers in the 1960s. They were well aware of the privileges they had won with democracy. However, jobs and spouses were far less available than they were for their foremothers, and the cost to raise children had risen considerably. The newly deracialized welfare program—a key mechanism by which relational citizenship had been provided to whites—was fraught with contradictions. On the one hand, the broad eligibility of the CSG was an attempt to redress the racial inequality previous welfare had wrought. On the other, the size of the payments were constrained by fiscal feasibility and a state ideology that generous welfare support would dampen able-bodied adults' initiative to find a job. In other words, rather than extend relational citizenship to people of all race groups, the democratic state recognized an obligation to provide a modicum of support to those who could not work because of physical ability or age. Able-bodied adults gained juro-political citizenship, but they were expected to achieve political recognition and belonging through work-membership or securing a valorized, yet unavailable, job. Point women used kinshipping to take another route to citizenship. Since the needs of children were widely viewed as the most legitimate, Point women used performances of adequate motherhood to claim support. In the face of a CSG framework that disregarded the labor of those who collected the grants, these performances of motherhood made Point women's caregiving work visible. They demanded recognition that resources did not simply transform themselves into well-cared-for children but required an important intermediary who also mattered. They were arguments that the needs of kin are intertwined and that concern for the welfare of children necessarily entailed concern for the welfare of those who cared for them. In their performances, Point women called on community members as "aunties," "uncles," and other forms of kin and patrons who, by virtue of this hailing, were obligated to provide support. The support they received, though insecure and modest, was an affirmation that Point women's needs as mothers were recognized by their community. In the absence of work-membership, Point women employed kinshipping to rework their belonging in their community and achieve a limited form of relational citizenship.

An important counterpoint to the CSG, which acknowledged at least partial state obligation to support children, was the Maintenance Court, which served to enforce the legal obligation of biological parents to also provide that support. As we saw in chapter 5, the court was another ineffective mode of political inclusion that Point women used kinshipping to rework for their benefit. Point women viewed their challenges in supporting their children as the product of both the failures of the state and the failure of fathers to meet their obligations to women and children. Point women found a ready ally in state discourse and policy in their frustration with nonsupporting men. Absent fathers were framed as irresponsible citizens contributing to the weakening of families through their economic neglect. Activists and policy makers alike cast the court as a venue for women to claim their newfound rights and to combat the gendered and economic injustices wrought by irresponsible men. On paper, the court and the policy behind it suggested state commitment to the idea that women should not have to shoulder the burdens of child-rearing alone; recognition that could enhance poor women's sense of belonging in the new nation. However, once again, the material reality was far different. For the law to have any effect on men sharing financial responsibility, women had to go to great lengths and endure emotional turmoil for what were often short-lived payments. As a result, many women's experience of the court was one of profound disappointment and alienation from their former lovers and from the state that purported to back them. Like the CSG, the state relied on women's uncompensated kinshipping labors to discipline men into paying citizens and ensure the basic needs of children were met regardless of a case's outcome.

Yet some women were able to use kinshipping to leverage the court to meet their goals of relational citizenship. Though it was mostly toothless, the threat of a court case was a powerful tool that some women used to compel their former partners to pay. In the absence of other mechanisms of social discipline such as marriage and extended family, the ability to appeal to the authority of the state to enforce obligations was an important symbolic affirmation for some women. For other women, bringing a court case was a validating and empowering process because a court officer echoed their belief that they should not be raising children unsupported. Those women who depended less acutely on the monetary success of a maintenance case were able to glean satisfaction from the case as state-backed retribution for mistreatment. Using the maintenance process in this way, these women achieved a greater feeling of membership in the new nation even if their financial status often did not change significantly.

Relational citizenship was illusory in the early 2010s for Point women because waged work, and the marriages it enabled, were also unavailable. The kinshipping strategies of most of the chapters enabled women to eke out a form of belonging and security by solidifying their relationships with their community, their former lovers, and the state. But none of these were substitutions for secure jobs and marriage. Some women worked around the obstacles to marriage to an unemployed man, as we saw in chapter 6, by marrying employed migrants from the rest of the African continent. Like the strategies detailed across the book, these efforts had uneven effects on Point women's sense of belonging. At one level, marriage to a foreigner and, for some women, conversion to Islam, marked them as outsiders subject to growing xenophobia. Viewed as foreigners themselves, cultural defectors, or insincere converts, they were no longer readily recognizable as members of the black South African community. On another level, they achieved the revered status of *umakoti*, or bride, by meeting the critical cultural expectations of bridewealth exchange. They ensured their children were part of a legitimate lineage, appeasing elders and ancestors alike and in some cases, retaining close ties to natal kin. In key ways these women achieved an idealized form of relational citizenship, living as housewives supported by working men, but this came at the cost of other forms of belonging. Taken together, these examples show the precariousness and the power of kinshipping to rework relational citizenship when other forms of belonging are structurally inaccessible.

Realizing Relational Citizenship

Point women's desires for what I have termed *relational citizenship* arose out of a very particular South African history. Yet, the ethical and political underpinnings of their claims has far-reaching applicability. I contend that a politics centered on ensuring relational citizenship forwards a larger project of embracing a shared responsibility to ensure that people can live amid relationships in ways they find meaningful and sustaining. This is a project that embraces a "politics of interdependence" that, in direct response to liberalism's presumption of individual autonomy, recognizes and embraces relationships as both undeniable and fertile sites for building desired futures (Kowalski 2022). Relational citizenship foregrounds this interdependence, highlighting that people enter into social, political, and economic life always already embedded in relationships with others. These relationships can take many forms, they can be caring, exploitative, uplifting, abusive, and so on. However, before we begin to ask questions about the livability and desirability of these relationship dynamics, questions at the heart of feminist politics, we must first acknowledge that these relationships exist for all persons.

By highlighting the ubiquity of interdependence, the concept of relational citizenship shifts dependency, a status greatly maligned by western political theory, from the purview of only select groups—the young, the old, the infirm, women, the poor, the disabled—and distributes it across all persons. This is not to erase the important differences and specific contours of people's dependent relationships as much as to say what is important are those differences and the structures that shape them, not the question of whether or not a person is dependent in the first place.[3] Indeed, as ethnographers of carework have deftly demonstrated, autonomous individuality is a highly valued illusion that requires enormous labor to sustain, labor that is frequently exploitative, destructive, and, by design, obscured (Buch 2018). It is only by acknowledging that these relationships are already in place that we can begin to ask questions about how relationships can be ordered to be mutually sustaining and just.

As has been seen across this book, relational citizenship arises as a concept from the particularly racialized and gendered experiences of black African and coloured women as mothers raising children in the new South Africa. Thus it is part of a long tradition of maternalist politics in South Africa and maternalist theory more broadly and benefits from this work while offering alternatives to their potential limitations. Relational citizenship seeks to acknowledge the value and necessity of the labor involved in sustaining relationships, labor frequently allocated to women and, in the care economy, poorer women of color. However, informed by a theory of relational personhood, relational citizenship eschews the gender essentialism that can, oftentimes unintentionally, creep in to maternalist orientations, essentialism that inadvertently reinforces patriarchal ideologies that carework *is inevitably* gendered. Instead, maintaining, sustaining, and organizing relationships is labor from which all persons benefit and that all persons can undertake in one form or another but which has historically and problematically been shifted onto women and particularly women of color. Collective investment, from the state, from communities, from aid organizations, and the like, can change the conditions under which women perform that labor and can be used to redistribute that labor more equitably (Kowalski 2022). Under a relational citizenship paradigm, this also means that women aren't asked to choose between claims for their children or claims for themselves. Rather, as the women across this book have shown, claims made in the name of relational citizenship are demands for support of both in ways that cannot be separated—support of people as interdependent.

Embedded in relational citizenship—as a theory of citizenship—is an understating that supporting relationships such that those involved can lead lives they value is a collective responsibility. One mode of support is the guarantee of the basic economic resources to ensure survival. The idea of the universal right to economic security is not new; however, we have seen a revival in the demands for and implementation of Basic Income Supports (BIS) in response to long existing precarity care crises that the COVID 19 pandemic exacerbated (Bhandary 2019; Care Collective 2020; Dawson and Fouksman 2020; Dengler and Lang 2021; Elson 2016; Matthews, Groenewald, and Moolman 2022; Sevenhuijsen et al. 2003). Such movements are all the more important in our present era of wageless life in which, globally, 58 percent of workers are employed in the informal economy (Sodergren, Karkee, and Kapsos 2023). Yet even staunch supporters of BIS, myself included, argue that economic support, while necessary, is only a first step in transformative policy making that would ensure robust relational citizenship. This requires governmental investments in quality universal health care, childcare, and education, just processes of adjudication and protection; sustainable infrastructure for housing, transport, foodways, power, and sanitation; and social protections that can help people weather the inevitable challenges and disruptions of life in ways that account for the multiple forms of discrimination that persist in our world (Hassim 2021; Hochfeld 2022; Matthews, Groenewald, and Moolman 2022). It is not insignificant that many of these are present in the UN Sustainable Development Goals for 2030—for example, no poverty; zero hunger; good health and well-being; quality education; gender equality; clean water and sanitation; affordable and clean energy; decent work and economic growth; reduced inequalities; peace, justice, and strong institutions—though this does not lessen the work to be done to realize them. My aspiration is that relational citizenship provides policy makers, activists, researchers, and street theorists another framework to use in our pursuit of collective well-being.

As Taylor Gooby notes, citizenship is both a normative and an empirical concept—enabling a description of an existing status and energizing demands about what rights and obligations national membership *should* entail (quoted in Lister 2005, 475). In a world where waged labor can no longer be taken for granted and livelihoods are increasingly insecure, relational citizenship offers an alternative formulation of what it means to belong to a political community. It imagines political configurations that ensure livelihoods that don't just enable subsistence but thicken people's embeddedness within crucial relationships of belonging on which social membership hinges. This fuller version of citizenship supports people in negotiating the terms of their interdependence—in creating a future beyond simply getting by. Realizing relational citizenship means creating a world in which our collective interdependence is recognized, supported, and provides a groundwork for a flourishing life.

GLOSSARY

*isiZulu and isiXhosa have many linguistic similarities and often use similar words and thus often cannot be definitively categorized as belonging to one or another language.

armoeder poor (white is implied) mother (Afrikaans)

amadlozi human spirits or souls, ancestors (isiZulu)

amagwinya a fried doughnut, "fat cake" (isiXhosa or isiZulu for the Afrikaans *vetkoek*)

amakholwa Christians (usually referring to black African converts), literally "believers

babamkhulu grandfather or big man (isiZulu)

baas (boss) boss or greeting of a superior (Afrikaans)

eMzanzi South Africa, literally "in the south" (isiXhosa or isiZulu)

khulisa a shortening of the verb *ukukhula* meaning to grow with a causative -isa suffix. Used to mean "to raise or nurture," usually a child (isiXhosa or isiZulu)

ilobolo bridewealth (noun form) *ukulobola (verb)* to pay bridewealth (isiXhosa or isiZulu but used among many more language groups)

inhlawulo a fine paid to a woman's family for pregnancy without *ilobolo* (isiXhosa or isiZulu) *inhlonipho*   respect or deference sometimes referred to in speech by the stem, *hlonipha* (isiXhosa or isiZulu)

isibongo   surname (isiZulu)

isicholo   *a* hat worn by married women (isiZulu)

isifebe   a sexually immoral woman, a prostitute often shortened to *febe* (isiXhosa or isiZulu)

isifazane oqomayo   a dating woman, literally "a woman who chooses" (isiZulu)

isondlo   child support/maintenance (isiXhosa or isiZulu)

shebeen   an unlicensed drinking establishment, often in a home

stokvel   rotating savings club (township vernacular from "stock fair")

swartgevaar   the threat black Africans purportedly posed to white supremacy, literally "black peril" (Afrikaans)

Togt   n. casual labor adj. casual; hired by the day (Afrikaans)

ukuhlangana   n. relationship or connection v. to join or unite (isiXhosa or isiZulu)

ukuhlobongo   to engage in penis-thigh sex (isiZulu)

ukukipita   to cohabit, literally "to keep it," a Xhosa/Zulu-ization of the English "keep"

ukuphanda   to hustle, often shortened to -*phanda* (isiXhosa or isiZulu)

umakoti   a married woman, or bride (isiZulu)

umnumzana   a male head of household (marriage implied). Can also be used as a greeting "sir" (isiXhosa or isiZulu)

umuzi   household (isiZulu)

utshwala   specifically a traditional beer of sorghum and maize meal, also used to mean alcohol in general (isiZulu)

volksmoeder   mother of the people or nation (Afrikaans)

vulamlomo   a gift to begin *ilobolo* negotiations, literally "to open the mouth" (isiXhosa or isiZulu)

NOTES

Introduction

1. The names of my interlocutors have been changed in accordance with their wishes.

2. My use of "theory from the street" rather than the more commonly used "theory from below" is inspired by Ryan Cecil Jobson's call during a 2022 panel at the American Anthropological Association conference in Seattle for anthropologists to be "relentless evangelists for ordinary people." Theory from the street shares with theory from below the commitment to take seriously the analytic work of people often excluded from places of dominant knowledge production. However, the location of "the street" evokes an urban public space and seeks to not inadvertently harden hierarchies of "above" and "below" that both orientations seek to disrupt. Julie-Anne Boudreau also uses this phrase in her work at the intersection of state policy and urban life in Mexico (2019).

3. South Africa has a highly variegated history of multiple colonialisms whose laws articulated differing forms of political belonging. Though Portuguese explorers came to South Africa in 1488, the extractive labor relations that characterize colonial rule began in 1652 when the Dutch East India Company established a small settlement at the Cape of Good Hope. From 1652 to 1910, understood as an early period of colonialism, there were bitter power disputes between the Dutch and the British. In 1910, four colonies were brought together to form the independent Union of South Africa. Described as a government of "self-rule," political decisions were made by predominantly white male landowners who implemented internal colonial-style laws that systematically separated and regulated the labor and lives of the majority population who was overwhelmingly excluded from white priveledge. Called the segregationist period, these policies further entrenched white power and economic gain and laid the foundation for apartheid. Beginning in 1948, apartheid retained and elaborated South Africa's segre-

gationist framework and hardened the legal boundaries between racial groups. While some apartheid legislation began to unravel in the late 1980s and early 1990s, it wasn't until the first democratic election of universal suffrage in 1994 that colonialism is thought to have ended in South Africa.

4. Both white and male allies were of course a crucial part of this activism, as South African historiography has effectively covered.

5. I take up Cole and Durham's suggestion that the term *regeneration*, rather than *reproduction*, signals a dynamic potential for the nature and terms of these bonds to change (Cole and Durham 2006; Kowalski 2022).

6. I am indebted to Gillian Feeley-Harnik for the terms *kinshipping* and *kinchopping* to describe the processual and contingent nature of kinship bonds.

7. My work aligns with the communitarian tradition that takes the nation-state to be one in many nested and overlapping layers of belonging. These may include space-based, local communities, ethnic or racial identity groups, or supranational groupings all of which comprise citizenship (Avineri and De-Shalit 1992; Daly 1993; Marshall 1950; Phillips 1993). Emphasizing this layering is part of a broader move in feminist scholarship to incorporate gendered and non-Western centric visions of belonging by decentering the nation-state from conversations about citizenship (e.g., Pateman 1988; Vogel 1991; Walby 1994; Yuval Davis 1999).

8. In a 2008 survey conducted by Afrobarometer, South Africans were offered a number of statements that reflected different understandings of state power. Overwhelmingly, they chose the phrase, "People are like children, the government should take care of them like a parent" (Afrobarometer 2009: 4). While this is a source of great frustration for those who emphasize a rights-based liberal democracy, scholars like Englund remind us that such kinship-based understandings can offer powerful forms of critique and claim making (2006; 2008). Further, it is not only citizens who make such claims; politicians also use the idiom of parenthood (frequently, fatherhood) and the nurturance it implies to legitimize their political roles (Schatzberg 2001).

9. This literature is vast, but some notable examples of this phenomenon are (Ciccia and Sainsbury 2018; Lister 1994; O'Connor 1996; O'Connor, Orloff, and Shaver 1999; Orloff 1993; 2009). For work discussing the dynamic nature of dependence, see Brown (1995) and Fraser and Gordon (1994). It is important to also note that there are feminist theorists of welfare in South Africa such as Shireen Hassim and Frances Lund who are highly cognizant of and attentive to the value that poor women place on their interdependent relationships and do not necessarily embrace the more extreme goals of independence promoted by some women's rights scholars.

10. Relational citizenship is a theory of citizenship as both multilayered and embodied (Yuval-Davis 1999). Key debates in citizenship studies have centered on whether citizenship is best understood as a relationship between an individual and the state (as in liberal theory) or whether it is mediated by other belongings (as in the communitarian tradition). A related debate, of particular interest to feminists, is also whether citizens should be understood as abstract, universal beings or as particularly situated. Through its emphasis on interdependencies, relational citizenship seeks to account for people not just as members of racial, gendered, or classed groups, but also the ways in which blackness becomes gendered and classed or womanhood becomes racialized

and classed, and so on, in ways that shape dilemmas of interdependence and people's response to them (Yuval-Davis and Anthias 1989; Yuval-Davis 2007).

11. In one sense this issue has been addressed by scholars who rightfully note the blurriness between ideas of productive and reproductive labor and those who theorize various forms of commodified social reproduction and, notably, the potential to refuse reproductive labor (e.g. Berg 2014). Here I join a growing number of scholars thinking through social reproduction, belonging, and obligation in a late capitalist era of wageless life (to name a few: Bhattacharya and Dale 2020; Fraser 2022; Jaffe 2020).

12. Scholars of queer kinship have long been at the forefront of theorizing the constructed nature of kinship ties, and the recent turn to a framework of "queer transculturation" is an important reminder to attend to the asymmetrical power relations present in theorizing queer kinship in the Global South for predominantly Northern readers (Mizielińska, Gabb, and Stasińska 2018). Using this framework, Yarbrough beautifully describes the relative political value of normative versus nonnormative kinship in the context of marriage in South Africa (2018).

13. TBD, 1DBN, Box 612 Gracia-Correira Protection of Children case number 33/2/4/198/63.

14. There are important gendered implications of the different moral evaluations given to earning a living versus making a living (Barchiesi 2011; Ferguson 2015; Hunter 2010; James 2014). The organization of the migrant labor economy historically excluded black African women from earning a living and made them more reliant on unwaged livelihood strategies. In contrast, black male success, as measured by the ability to marry, build and support a rural homestead, was predicated on the ability to earn a living. In the postapartheid era, waged work became ideologically tied to citizenship status.

15. In the past two decades, there has been an efflorescence of scholarship on the "crisis of social reproduction." In Africa, this scholarship centers on youth unable to transition to adulthood (see Alber, Geest, and Whyte 2008; Christiansen, Utas, and Vigh 2006; Cole and Durham 2008; Hansen 2005; Hunter 2010; Mains, Hadley, and Tessema 2013, 2007; Masquelier 2013, 2005; Mbembe 2008; Prince 2006; Roth 2008; Vasconcelos 2010; Vigh 2006; Weiss 2004). I am not just concerned with adulthood as it affects social reproduction, but social reproduction as it shapes people's notions of citizenship. I also join with Jones (2009) to emphasize that blockages should not be taken as stasis but should provoke scholars to attend to how people forge alternative means or ways to work around the blockage.

16. Examples of this explicit commitment abound in policy documents from the late 1990s. The 1994 outline for the Reconstruction and Development Programme (RDP) stated, "No political democracy can survive and flourish if the mass of our people remains in poverty, without land, without tangible prospects for a better life. Attacking poverty and deprivation must therefore be the first priority of our democratic Government" (African National Congress 1994: para. 1.2.9). The 1996 Constitution guarantees everyone the right of access to social security, "including, if they are unable to support themselves and their dependents, appropriate social assistance. The state is obliged to "take reasonable legislative and other measures, within its available resources, to achieve the progressive realisation" of this right. The Constitution also imposes a par-

ticular duty on the state to ensure that children under the age of eighteen have access to "basic nutrition, shelter, basic health care services and social services" (Republic of South Africa 1996). The 1997 White Paper for Social Welfare tied social protection to basic income: "Every South African should have a minimum income, sufficient to meet basic subsistence needs, and should not have to live below minimum acceptable standards" (Department of Welfare 1997: chap. 7, para. 27).

17. The expanded definition of unemployment includes those who are unemployed and who are available to work, whether or not they have taken active steps to find employment.

18. Though it is widely acknowledged that the high cost of bridewealth and nuptial gift exchange limited marriage to the wealthy, many black South Africans argued that doing away with or modifying the gift amounts would negatively affect the symbolic value of the exchange (Rudwick and Posel 2014 and 2015; Yarbrough 2017).

19. Though records of formal marriage rates have been gathered in South Africa for over a century, they are imprecise measures of marital status among black South Africans, for whom marriage is a multiyear process and not a single event (Breckenridge 2012; Hunter 2010). Furthermore, in more recent censuses, there is no attempt to differentiate between marital status and cohabitation, which have very different social meanings (Budlender, Chobokoane, and Simelane 2004; Hosegood, McGrath, and Moultrie 2009). Despite these limitations, researchers have found that since the 1960s there was not only an increase in the age of first marriage for black African women, but that increasing numbers will never be married in their lifetime.

20. Fertility in South Africa has also declined over the past forty years (and longer) from an estimated birth rate of over six children per black African woman in 1960 to 3.2 in 2001 (Moultrie and Dorrington 2004; Moultrie and Timæus 2003; Norling 2019; UNDESA and Gapminder 2019). Scholars attribute the recent decline to long birth intervals and high rates (by regional standards) of contraceptive use and not to HIV (Hosegood, McGrath, and Moultrie 2009).

21. Household survey data from 1995 and 2008 suggest that amid marriage decline, rates of cohabitation have trebled from about 5 percent to 15 percent (Posel and Casale 2013). Nonetheless, Posel and Casale used data from the SASAS (2005) to suggest that a majority of unmarried African men and women (64 percent of those twenty to thirty-nine years) do not view cohabitation as an acceptable alternative to marriage (Posel and Casale 2013).

22. This section title is a nod to Tessa Hochfeld's important book on the CSG, *Granting Justice*.

23. When measured by individuals, in 2018, eighteen million individuals, or 31 percent of the population, received a social grant. In terms of race, more than one-third of black African individuals (33.9 percent) received a social grant, compared to 29.9 percent coloured individuals, 12.5 percent of Indian/Asian individuals, and 7.5 percent of the white population received grants (STATSSA 2020).

24. There are a number of unintended consequences of creating welfare policies that harden the relationship between caregiving and gender. For example, entitlements directed at the male head of the household can undermine women's independent access to benefits (Sainsbury 1996). Conversely, targeting mothers directly can equally narrow

women's access to support and subject them to moral regulation (Fraser and Gordon 1994). As a grant targeting children, the CSG sought to "follow the child" into whatever caregiving arrangement they found themselves.

25. The racial inequalities in this figure are striking: 33 percent of African children have no working adult at home, while 13 percent of coloured children, 10 percent of Indian children, and 2 percent of white children live in such circumstances (Hall 2021).

26. The Lund Committee, appointed by the director-general of social welfare in 1995, was composed of overwhelmingly female activists and scholars deeply knowledgeable about the gendered and racialized nature of poverty. Across the group they also had a sophisticated gendered analysis of economic and social policies and a working knowledge of feminist social reproduction theory. The committee was mandated to evaluate the existing system of state support and to develop social assistance programs that effectively targeted children and families. However, for any proposal to be taken seriously, it had to "redistribute within the existing envelope," meaning not raise the social welfare budget (Lund 2008). In a conference in 1998, the chairwoman of the committee, Frances Lund, said, "This is an uncertain climate for social security, and there is a lack of popular and political support for the grants for women. If we devise a plan within the fiscal limits . . . we are likely to retain the existing budget for family-related social security. If not, we'll lose it" (quoted in Hassim 2003: 518).

27. Though the transformation of the SMG into the CSG had a redistributionist bent, it was redistribution among the poor and historically disenfranchised. Commenting bitterly on the painful decision to withdraw the State Maintenance Grant (SMG) from some 400,000 poor women and children, Frances Lund said, "in the case of this welfare reform, a few already poor people (mostly coloured and Indian) will get a lot less; a lot of people will get a tiny something for the first time" (quoted in Hassim 2003: 522). Notably, the decision to withdraw the SMG was not solely based on financial constraints but was also due to a concern that the SMG was problematically premised on a nuclear family model that did not fit the current South African context, if it ever did (Lund 2008).

28. In the continued public-private partnership of welfare provision in South Africa, a number of research units and advocacy organizations that contributed to creating the CSG have become independent watchdogs over the government's implementation of it and have contributed substantially to the amendments since its rollout. Organizations such as the Centre for Applied Legal Studies at the University of the Witwatersrand, the Children's Institute at the University of Cape Town, the Community Agency for Social Enquiry, the Black Sash, and the Alliance for Children's Entitlement to Social Security conduct research, identify effective practice, identify administrative incompetence, relay their findings to the general public, and provide the government with detailed recommendations for change. One of the most recent examples of their work was the Black Sash's outcry against the state's termination of the COVID-19 Social Relief of Distress (SRD) grant—the closest South Africa has come to a Basic Income Grant—in April 2021 while COVID raged.

29. As Hassim as noted, the creation of the CSG created a peculiar confluence in the postapartheid moment in which a feminist-led government agency, advised by women-

friendly social scientists and bureaucrats, was accused of being antidemocratic and antiwomen by a host of women's organizations (Hassim 2003). Newspapers reported that following the announcement of the new policy, welfare offices were "stormed by angry women," and organizations such as the Black Sash and the Community Law Center released condemning statements arguing that: "The implication of these proposals is that vulnerable and disadvantaged women and children in South Africa will bear the costs of remedying past injustices" (quoted in Hassim 2003).

30. The verb *ukuphanda* retains a great deal of ambiguity that allows the user to skirt direct moral judgment such as in this conversation: "Besishoda, yabo. So ngihamba ngiyophanda" [We were short/lacking (e.g., hungry), you see. So, I went and made things happen]. From a Zulu-English/English-Zulu dictionary, ukuphanda translates to "scratch up" or to "dig by scratching" (Doke et al. 2008: 645; Margaretten 2015: 70). However, the connotation is often associated with criminal activity. Many thanks to Molly Margaretten who helped me understand how this verb was being used.

Chapter 1

1. A 1943 survey conducted by Durban's Native Administration Department showed that the number of Africans employed by twenty-five of the city's industrial establishments, selected at random, rose from 3,904 in 1939 to 14,985 in 1943. By 1945 the total number of African males registered in employment by the Native Administration Department had reached 71,210 (TBD, 3DBN, Crime, Unauthorised Shacks, file 4. Memorandum by Mrs. Maytom February 22, 1948). This massive migration was due to a number of push/pull factors that centered on the fact that life in the rural reserves allocated to black Africans was growing increasingly unsustainable, and families there increasingly depended the wages sent home from men who migrated to work in the city. By the late 1940s, physician Sidney Kark found that 90 percent of the men between the aged of twenty and twenty five were temporarily absent from the rural area of Pholela in Natal (1950; Hunter 2010). This had profound effects on life in the reserves where, in the absence of husbands, women gained greater freedom and authority, but at the cost of greater labor burdens and the emotional stress of maintaining a long-distance marriage (Kark 1950; Moore and Vaughan 1994).

2. TBD, 1DBN, Box 608 Erasmus Protection of Children case number 33/2/4/77/63.

3. It was a persistent challenge to find longtime current or former Point residents willing to speak with me about daily life in the Point prior to the 1980s. This is likely due to the stigma and poverty associated with the neighborhood that whites felt acutely. However, other Durbanites also nostalgically reminisce about the Point as a place of carefree leisure and diversion. They characterize the Point as a child's wonderland filled with innocent amusement and, importantly, very safe. Such portrayals act as not-so-subtle racial and political critiques when people contrast these remembrances to what they see as today's dangerous environment of criminality under black majority rule. Examples can be found on the website www.fad.co.za.

4. Addington Hospital historically served the white and coloured race groups until 1995, but the Children's Hospital had a mandate to serve children of all races, a thorn in the side of the apartheid government that led to the hospital's closure in 1985 (Burns 2011). A large municipal and community task force succeeded in reviving the Chil-

dren's Hospital, and the teen sexual health drop-in center opened in 2012, while the larger outpatient facility opened during my fieldwork in 2014.

5. The most recent incarnation of this is the luxury development that was constructed at the southern tip prior to the world cup in 2010 by a Malaysian and South African development partnership. The old railway houses were converted into R4million single-family homes, and a yacht harbor was built. The five luxury high rises stand mostly empty, though some restaurants and activities such as the evening farmer's market have sprung up there.

6. In 2001, residents were given the opportunity to buy their flats under a scheme called sectional title but were not informed that under this scheme they would be responsible for an increasing monthly levy in addition to utilities, and the shared cost of building maintenance. As a result, many are heavily in debt and under the law could be evicted from their homes (Rondganger 2015).

7. In 2014, I encountered a handful of black Africans who had been allocated a government (RDP) house in the townships or outskirts of the city. While they would have preferred to live in their house, many chose to remain in the city, citing that were they to leave, they would be sitting, hungry, in an empty house far from any opportunities for money making (see Mbili 2016).

8. Original statement in isiZulu and English: Like besengishilo uma uhlala drobheni mpilo iyashesha basuke becabanga kuthi unayo imali ngoba uhlala drobheni all those things.

9. Original statement in isiZulu and English: Actually anginabo abangani. I do not believe in friends' anginabo abangani nje at all . , , ngoba ngiyazi ukuthi bu capable of.

10. A Zulu idiom captures this well: "Imiphanda ibulalwa yizakhelani," which quite literally translates to "pots are broken by neighbors" but more broadly means "the worst harm is done by one's friends" (Doke et al. 2008, 645)

11. Though there is very little written on the Point, the existing scholarship showcases the complexity and dynamism of the neighborhood. As one of the earliest sites of white settlement, academic and lay historians have long been concerned with the history of the port, the railway, and the neighborhood that grew up around them (Henderson 1904; Ingram 1899). These early sites of racial intermingling, dubbed "Bamboo Square" and "Black Belts," attracted numerous municipal attempts at racial policing in the name of slum removal (Kearney 2002; Maylam 1983; Wassermann and Kearney 2002). The neighborhood's history as a concentrated site of black African labor migration reveals the enormous labor required to create and maintain racial segregation (Kuper, Watts, and Davies 1958; Maylam 1988). The social and economic workings of the port offered key insights into the development of urban class consciousness in South Africa, cross-racial labor relations particularly between Indian and black Africans, and municipal attempts at the management of black African labor migrants and the related protests (Callebert 2012b, 2012a, 2017; Cox and Hemson 2008; Hemson 1977, 1979, 1996; Hyslop 2018; La Hausse 1988, 1990; Sadler 2002). Work on the contemporary social landscape of the Point is comparatively even more sparse. Nevertheless, it has served to illuminate the complex lived reality of groups often reviled as social problems, such sex workers, drug dealers, and street youth (Leggett 1999; Leggett and Burton 1999; Margaretten 2011, 2013, 2015; Trotter 2009, 2007).

Chapter 2

1. An excellent example of the ambiguous ends to which citizenship can be put are the water wars in which Johannesburg residents attempted to claim their rights to water and were subject to government oversight—and monetization—of their water consumption in the name of putatively ensuring their rights. This is elegantly analyzed in Von Schnitzler (2016).

2. Invocation of mothers in nationalist projects is not new nor specific to South Africa, and feminists have long warned of the potential political dangers of such discourse (Gaitskell and Unterhalter 1989; Hassim 1993; Kumar 2002; Lister 2003; Ngcobozi 2020; Plant 2010; Ruddick 1995; Scheck 2004; Van Allen 2009;).

3. Importantly, "the colony" had neither a cohesive vision nor makeup but, rather, functioned as a "bumbling plantocracy" that haphazardly enacted or revamped frequently contradictory policies (Hyslop 2008, 127). Thus, effects of policy must be understood as circumstantial and not the outcome of a well-elaborated program (Essop Sheik 2014).

4. In the Cape Colony, which contained a large number of Khoisan and imported enslaved persons, but a more equal balance of European whites to other race groups, all occupants were subject to the same Roman Dutch law as part of a larger ostensibly assimilationist and civilizing enterprise. This meant that men of all races could vote, if they had an annual income of £50 or occupied property worth £25 (Simons 1968).

5. In 1852, the European population of Natal was only 7,629 while the African population exceeded 100,000. By 1880, Europeans had increased to 25,271, black Africans to over 362,000, and there was an Indian population of 18,877. "Population," Natal Blue Books, 1852, 1880.

6. The cultural, religious, linguistic, and economic heterogeneity of the Indian community in South Africa has long been in tension with their treatment by white governments in primarily racial terms (Freund 1995). Passenger Indians persistently resisted their increasing exclusion with the notable support of Mohandas K. Gandhi (Burton et al. 2018; Essop Sheik 2005; Hughes 2007; Morrell and Hamilton 1996; Padayachee 1999).

7. This system of indirect rule, also termed the Shepstone System, was created by the infamous Theophilus Shepstone, diplomatic agent to the native population and the colony's first secretary for native affairs (see Guy 2018). Developed through a collusion of colonial administrators, anthropologists, and lawyers, it was administered by chiefs overseen by colonial officials such as Shepstone (Chanock 1989). Theoretically, Africans could petition for exemption from tribal law, however, the requirements were virtually impossible to meet.

8. The Hut Tax was a unique colonial technology developed in Natal that by the 1850s contributed more than a third of all colonial revenues (Harries 1987). The homestead head was taxed based on the number of wives' houses or "huts" he had within the homestead. Though assessed on male heads, Jeff Guy argues "it was in effect a tax on the productive capacity of married women and their children" (2014, 38).

9. Under the Native Code, if a woman and her children were deserted, it was the "natural duty" of the male household head (*umnumzana*) to support them (Chanock 2001). The law did not recognize women's adversity in desertion, only those of her male

guardian. The *umnumzana* could claim a token payment (*isondlo*) from the deserting man. This was symbolic, not reimbursement for the cost of support. For extramarital pregnancy, the *umnumzana* could claim *inhlawulo* payment for "damages" to his patriarchal authority. In the rare event that an African woman divorced and gained child custody, she could claim *isondlo*. However, the children still remained a part of their father's lineage, meaning they had spiritual obligations to his ancestors (*amadlozi*), and daughters' *lobolo* was still paid to him (Simons 1968).

10. Under the colonial common law 1896 Deserted Wives and Child Protection Acts, settler women—who achieved legal majority at twenty-one—could claim maintenance (child support) from an errant husband for themselves and their children. African women who were customarily married could not claim maintenance for themselves because such marriages were not recognized. On paper, African women could have a male custodian claim maintenance on her behalf, but this required proving the child(ren) were otherwise not being supported.

11. In the early twentieth century, high infant mortality rates prompted the creation of purportedly scientific mothercraft programs to train women in "good and proper infant care" (Davin 1997; Muirhead and Swart 2015). Strongly influenced by child welfare and health reformer Dr. Truby King in New Zealand, the mothercraft regime was laden with ideas about white middle-class superiority and women's gendered obligations, thus appealing to both British and Afrikaner concerns about preserving white supremacy (Duff 2016).

12. Whites had historically been a significant portion of the country's poor. However, through the Transvaal Indigency Commission of Enquiry of 1906 to 1908, white poverty became a unique category of intervention (Transvaal Government 1908). Unemployment was to be addressed through job creation in the mines and railroads, and moral and economic regeneration was to take place through state-based education and temporary aid.

13. In his writing, Daniël Francois Malan, one of the architects of apartheid, articulated the ideological link between white poverty and *swartgevaar* (Black Peril): "The Black Peril would not exist if it were not for a White Peril that is a hundred times greater, which undermines and destroys the black's respect for the white race" (translated from the original Afrikaans in Koorts 2013). White ascendance, and the respect that staved off black violence, was predicated on appropriate conduct.

14. In addition to undermining assumed white racial purity, there was also the nightmare that a political union that crossed racial lines could upend the white ruling class (Breckenridge 2007; Freund 1988).

15. The Durban Bantu Women's Society was part of a growing network of overtly maternalist organizations concerned with social welfare including the Amadodakazi Ase Afrika/Daughters of Africa and the Durban Bantu Child Welfare Society run by African women such as Sililo, Katie Makanya, Constance Mtimkulu, Bertha Mkhize, and Lillian Tshabalala (Du Toit 2014, 2018; Healy-Clancy 2012).

16. *Report of the Native Economic Commission* (Pretoria, 1932) in Seekings 2007, 390.

17. The Stallard report by the Transvaal Local Government Commission was chaired by Colonel C. F. Stallard, often called the Stallard Commission. Transvaal Provincial Administration (1922) Report of the Local Government Commission. T.P. 21, Pretoria.

Historians of South Africa have written extensively about the significance of the report in shaping subsequent policies of urban segregation.

18. Relationships between Indians and Africans in Durban have always been complex. Interracial intermingling is crosscut by class conflict and collusion, much of which has taken place under a white supremacist state that denied privileges to both groups. Between 1920 and 1951, Indians and Africans competed for very limited resources in terms of housing, labor, and trading space as Durban's population more than doubled and the state struggled to maintain segregation. Although disadvantaged relative to whites, many Indians held greater economic privilege or potential for economic mobility than Africans, a context that often led Africans to see Indians as "collective competitors and targets of frustration, rather than as coworkers" (Nuttall 1993, 268). Indians were the middle managers, landlords, shopkeepers, and transport system for the coloured and African populations (Vahed 1997). Thus, periods of inflation or food scarcity were often experienced in interracial terms—rising prices in Indian stores, increasing evictions by Indian landlords, Africans dodging payment, African theft of produce, and so on (Desai 1993). Though there were punctuated moments of interracial violence, notably in 1949 and 1985, there was also decades of peaceful coexistence and collaboration (Desai 1993; Edwards 1989; Freund 1995; Flint 2008; Hughes 2007; Kaarsholm 2008; Meer 1960, 1969; Padayachee 1999; Soske 2017; Thiara 1999).

19. The establishment was a five-bedroom house in Shepstone Street, likely rented from Indian landlords. An October 1908 raid found fifty-seven casks, drums, and paraffin tins in which various brews were stored (Report re: Preparation and Sale of Native Beer in Durban, May 11, 1908, quoted in La Hausse 1984, 130).

20. Scholarship on Durban's eighteen-month beerhall boycott in 1929 tends to focus on A. W. G. Champion, an organizer of the Industrial and Commercial Workers' Union (ICU), which became a popular front for organizing against the racist state (Crush and Ambler 1992; La Hausse 1984, 1988). Women were just as much a part of violent protests, wielding sticks, destroying property, and displaying their naked bottoms, much to the shock of police (Bonnin 2000; Bradford 1987; Bozzoli 1987; La Hausse 1982; Redding 1992; Rogerson 1992; Sadler 2002; Mager 2010).

21. TBD, 3 DBN 4/1/2/338 Report on the Working of the Monopoly System in Durban as Provided for Under Section 21 of the Natives (Urban Areas) Act, 21 of 1923.

22. Though race went unmentioned, both the Department of Social Welfare and the Children's Act of 1937 were the result of widespread concern about white poverty most explicitly articulated in the infamous Carnegie Commission Report on the poor white problem (Posel 2005; Du Toit 2014, 2018). Yet, in 1937 the new government was particularly sensitive to the needs of poor black Africans and slowly extended limited welfare programs to them (Seekings 2007).

23. The state went to great lengths to detail which areas of Durban counted as "rural," "as a mechanism to exclude Africans from access to child-maintenance grants" (Du Toit 2018, 987).

24. As part of their claims to inclusion, black Africans in the 1940s began to refine the definition of poverty to reflect their deprivation specifically vis-à-vis inflated living standards of mostly white "insider-citizens" (Seekings 2016). Wylie describes how the consumption of mielie meal—a staple of the black African diet—without accompany-

ing relish was seen as "living below an acceptable level of consumption" and sugar shifted from a luxury to a necessity (2001, 109).

25. Various Christian African women-led organizations emerged in the post–World War I period, such as the Bantu Women's Self-Improvement Association (1918) and the Bantu Purity League (1919), to "to keep the girls pure in the right way" amid anxiety about premarital pregnancy (Marks 1986, 228).

26. See the following on debates about the role of women in the creation of the volksmoeder image: Brink (1987, 1990); Du Toit (2003); Kruger (1991); Gaitskell and Unterhalter (1989); McClintock (1991, 1993); Vincent (1999, 2000).

27. Unlike the State Maintenance Grants, these allowances were for intact nuclear families with three or more children where one or more people were employed. Eligibility was based on a *minimum* income. The Social Security Committee recommended that urbanized Africans should receive them, even if they could not meet the minimum income, but the recommendation was not heeded.

28. Welfare in South Africa was meant to support and maintain a racial hierarchy. In 1944, the ratio of payment amounts for whites, coloureds and Indians, and black Africans was 12:6:1. In 1965 the ratio was 11:4:1; 1975, 7:3:1; 1980, 3:2:1; and 1992, 1.2:1.1:1 (Devereux 2007, 545–46).

29. The 1921 Child Protection Amendment Act created Mothers Pensions, which would later become the State Maintenance Grant to help support mothers and children who had lost their attachment to a wage-earning spouse (Mase 2013). A child with a father deemed capable of working was considered ineligible for the grant, and children had to maintain school attendance to retain eligibility. Rural black African children were excluded on the pretense that they were supported by their tribal community. In the case of urban black African children, all other avenues of support had to be exhausted before an application for a maintenance grant could be made. Despite these barriers, by the end of 1942, 13,276 whites, 5,816 coloureds, 3,034 Indians, and 190 black Africans were receiving maintenance grants (Iliffe 1987).

30. Within the Indian and coloured populations, the dramatically smaller scale of national welfare spending was partially offset by active community and religious-based private welfare organizations (Lund 1996). While often poor, these long-established urban communities had robust family and neighbor networks that offered critical important support to residents. However, the construction of new townships on the peripheries of the city and forced relocation destroyed or disrupted this important informal welfare support.

31. In the early 1950s, the Department of Social Welfare transferred welfare responsibilities for African and coloured persons to the Departments of Bantu Administration and Coloured Affairs, respectively, with the Department of Indian Affairs being formed in 1961.

32. In 1949, the Department of Social Welfare spent £9,750,000 on social assistance: £8,300,000 to whites, £800,00 to coloured and Indians, and £600,000 to Africans. Whites were 20.9 percent of the population, coloureds and Indians 10.3 percent, and Africans 68 percent (Rheinalt-Jones 1949, 416).

33. Section 10 status allowed black Africans to access houses and other social welfare in the city (Frankel 1979). It refers to section 10 of the 1945 Native (Urban Areas) Con-

solidation Act (amended in 1952, 1955, and 1957), which governs black African residence in cities. Requirements for section 10 rights were stringent and difficult for many black Africans to prove—continuous occupation in an urban area since birth or continuous lawful residence for fifteen years, continuous employment with one employer for ten years, or be nuclear family (wife, unmarried daughter, or son under eighteen) of a Section 10 status holder who lawfully entered the city. Many Africans lacked documentation of their birth, employment, and in the case of women and children, proof of lawful entry into the city. Section 10 status could also be revoked for participating in illegal economic activities (e.g., beer brewing for women).

34. For example, a survey by the Department of Economics at the University of Natal estimated that a subsistence income for a family of five in Durban was £23–£24 per month in 1959. Workers living in Cato Manor/Umkhumbane were attempting to support their families on incomes of £11–£12 per month and often had to go into cycles of debt (University of Natal 1959; Watts and Lamond 1966).

35. Phillip Mayer provides a detailed account of how these relationships worked in East London in the same time period (1961).

36. On average, social assistance to black Africans totaled 14–24 percent of the poverty datum line, whereas the totals for Indians were more frequently at par or 1.5x the datum line, 2x for coloureds and 5x for whites (Watts and Lamond 1966).

37. The 1960 Sharpeville massacre marked a turning point in state repression of antiapartheid activism. Across the 1950s, the oppressed majority engaged in numerous mass demonstrations, and state suppression had escalated, but large-scale physical violence had not taken place. In the early 1960, both the African National Congress (ANC) and the Pan African Congress (PAC) planned a nonviolent national antipass protest campaign in which protesters would leave their passes at home and submit themselves en masse for arrest so as to fill the jails and grind the economy to a halt. During the March 21 protest in the township of Sharpeville (outside of Johannesburg), the police, claiming they felt threatened by rock-throwing demonstrators, fired live bullets into the demonstrating crowds, killing sixty-nine people (including children) and injuring 180 others (Frankel 2001). News of the massacre spread quickly and ignited condemnation of the apartheid state across the country and around the world (*Time* 1960). Following March 1960, the state banned the ANC and the PAC, detained those leaders who did not flee into exile, and initiated a series of State of Emergencies during which public gatherings were banned and the police could detain people extrajudiciously. Conversely, this also marked the liberation struggle's turn to armed protest.

Chapter 3

1. This is a large and growing area of scholarship, particularly as it relates to maternal identities. For a discussion of works on the 1950s and 1960s, see Healy-Clancy (2017).

2. Motherhood discourses are flexible and capacious enough to encapsulate many different ideological projects. Gaitskell, Unterhalter, and Walker compare how discourses of motherhood in circulation amid Afrikaner vs. African nationalist groups embody very different ideas and orientations (Gaitskell and Unterhalter 1989; Walker 1995). Yet these differences in the symbolic meaning of motherhood are not solely the

result of the different lived conditions of black African and white Afrikaner women. In her analysis of motherhood discourse in the Inkatha women's brigade vs. the ANC—both populated by black African township women in the 1980s—Hassim shows how even under similar conditions maternal symbolism can also be put to various ends (Hassim 1993).

3. Feminist scholars have long debated the transformative potential of public motherhood to alter the subordination of women. Some argued that public mothers, while effective, were inherently conservative because they reproduced a sex-gender system in which women were equated with maternal caregiving and domestic responsibility (e.g., Wells 1998). Others contended that public motherhood was a radical attempt to overthrow both the gendered and racialized oppression of the apartheid state because it found its apex in the lives of black mothers (e.g., Gasa 2007; Magubane 2010). Healy-Clancy deftly traces the ways in which the meaning of public motherhood shifted in the context of precolonial, colonial, Christian-dominated, and apartheid politics (2017). I concur with her that public motherhood cannot be easily read to invoke any given gender system, but instead its multivalence needs to be translated in each interaction.

4. At one level, there were continuities around core elements in the discourses of idealized motherhood (often associated with white middle-class motherhood) from the early decades of the Union and through the 1970s (Walker 1995). At another level, it is important to recognize that motherhood as discussed and practiced differed substantially according to class, race, time period, and political orientation.

5. There is a host of care scholarship and feminist work invested in unsettling these assumptions (Abel 2000; Buch 2015; Chodorow 1978; LaChance Adams 2014; Mol, Moser, and Pols 2010; Roberts 1993; Scheper-Hughes 1992; Stevenson 2014; Tronto 1993; Ungerson 1990).

6. So-called voluntary organizations such as the Society provided the bulk of social service delivery at this time with subsidies for personnel and operating budgets coming from the national government. In Durban, the Durban Child Welfare Society provided casework for children twelve and under while the cases of older children were handled by the provincial branch of the Department of Social Welfare (Lund 2008).

7. TBD, 1DBN, Dunn Protection of Children case number 33/2/4/280/63. Christopher's birthdate is the subject of debate throughout the file as Rosemary is thought to have falsified birth records. In 1969, when, according to the birthdate on the file, Christopher would have been fifteen, he was tried for car theft as a twenty-year-old.

8. TBD, 1DBN, Dunn Protection of Children case number 33/2/4/280/63.

9. As a coloured woman, Rosemary would not legally have been able to reside in Point in the 1960s, though there were many who violated that law. The flat in this description was in the neighborhood of Jacobs, south of Point. Like the Point it was an industrial area where alcohol was readily available. The social worker noted that it was "populated by mixed non-European persons" and that "it is alleged that persons in the area engage in illicit brewing and selling of liquor," suggesting the presence of African women. Rosemary gave birth in Addington Hospital in the Point and came to Point to conduct her "business" in various forms.

10. For a discussion on how this paradigm functioned in government action around Africans, see Posel (2006).

11. Report of Committee of Inquiry into Family Allowances (1961, 14).

12. Report of Committee of Inquiry into Family Allowances (1961, 24).

13. TBD, 1DBN, Dunn Protection of Children case number 33/2/4/280/6.3.

14. Report of Committee of Inquiry into Family Allowances (1961, 23).

15. TBD, 1DBN, Dunn Protection of Children case number 33/2/4/280/63.

16. TBD, 1DBN, Dunn Protection of Children case number 33/2/4/280/63, 73.

17. TBD, 1DBN, Dunn Protection of Children case number 33/2/4/280/63.

18. TBD, 1DBN, Dunn Protection of Children case number 33/2/4/280/63.

19. Report of the Family Congress (1961, 17). Family Congress Steering Committee.

20. TBD, 1DBN, Dunn Protection of Children, unboxed, case number 33/2/4/280/63.

21. TBD, 1DBN, box 464 Amos Protection of Children case number 3/2/1/3/195 sub-file 33/2/4//308/59.

22. TBD, 1DBN, box 464 Amos Protection of Children case number 3/2/1/3/195 sub-file 33/2/4//308/59. Testimony by Mrs. Erander Smith. Children's Court trial January 17, 1960.

23. TBD, 1DBN, box 464 Amos Protection of Children case number 3/2/1/3/195 sub-file 33/2/4//308/59 Testimony by Mrs. Green. Children's Court trial March 22, 1960.

24. TBD, 1DBN, box 464 Amos Protection of Children case number 3/2/1/3/195 sub-file 33/2/4//308/59. Testimony by Mrs. Amos. Children's Court trial March 22, 1960.

25. TBD, 1DBN, box 464 Amos Protection of Children case number 3/2/1/3/195 sub-file 33/2/4//308/59 Testimony by Mrs. Green. Children's Court trial March 10, 1960.

26. TBD, 1DBN, box 464 Amos Protection of Children case number 3/2/1/3/195 sub-file 33/2/4//308/59. Testimony by Mrs. Green. Children's Court trial March 10, 1960.

27. TBD, 1DBN, box 464 Amos Protection of Children case number 3/2/1/3/195 sub-file 33/2/4//308/59. Letter from Mrs. Amos to the commissioner of Child Welfare.

28. Many of Magdalena's claims were corroborated by reports; however, the Point police did issue a statement saying she had been involved in drunken brawls and various disturbances.

29. TBD, 1DBN, box 464 Amos Protection of Children case number 3/2/1/3/195 sub-file 33/2/4//308/59. Testimony by Mrs. Green. Children's Court trial March 10, 1960, and Letter from sister at St. Martin's house to commissioner of Child Welfare October 11, 1960.

30. According to Roos, the alcohol panic was driven by Geoffrey Cronje, a University of Pretoria sociologist who trained the majority of social workers during this era. Further, studies such as that done by the Johannesburg branch of the Social Services Association found that the number of white women convicted of drunkenness in Johannesburg had increased to nearly half of all white convictions for alcohol-related offenses. This was worrisome because "a European woman under the influence of liquor solicits Natives for immoral purposes" (Johannesburg Social Services Association in Roos 2015).

31. TBD, 1DBN, box 464 Amos Protection of Children case number 3/2/1/3/195 sub-file 33/2/4//308/59, and TBD, 1DBN, Dunn Protection of Children, unboxed, case number 33/2/4/280/63.

32. TBD, 1DBN, box 464 Amos Protection of Children case number 3/2/1/3/195 sub-file 33/2/4//308/59.

33. Magdalena's letters to the commissioner of Child Welfare were extensive testimonials to her commitment to her children. In one poignant one she closed the letter saying, "I'm praying night and day for my children so that I can get them back. I can't go on any more. I'm to [sic] weak to fight against [the social worker's] scheming. I pray that God will show you we have done everything right by our children, we have sacrificed everything for them it can be proved, even the children can tell you sir." TBD, 1DBN, box 464 Amos Protection of Children case number 3/2/1/3/195 subfile 33/2/4//308/59.

34. In her letters Magdalena wields her own harsh critique of Mr. Shapero and the betrayal she feels by him, "We were praying that Mr. Shapero would hep [sic] us but instead he has done just the opposite. . . . I know Mr. Shapero called a certain person a coward for not wanting to sign his papers. What a class man to have in the department of social welfare. I think nothing of him for he isn't worth the table he writes on. He's false and couldn't even tell the truth if he tried to then he wants other people to have respect for him. I haven't any as far as he is concerned, I won't forget these 3 months of hell I'm going through because of him. Never as long as I live will I forgive him." TBD, 1DBN, box 464 Amos Protection of Children case number 3/2/1/3/195 subfile 33/2/4//308/59.

35. TBD, 1DBN, Dunn Protection of Children, unboxed, case number 33/2/4/280/63.

36. TBD, 1DBN, box 608 Simpson Protection of Children.

37. TBD, 1DBN, box 464 Amos Protection of Children case number 3/2/1/3/195 subfile 33/2/4//308/59.

38. TBD, 1DBN, Children Case Files Box 611, Mkhize, subfile 33/2/4/282/63. Report by Professional Officer of DCWS for commissioner of Child Welfare, September 24, 1963. To support her wish to disappear, Grace is a pseudonym.

39. Given his job category, it is unlikely that he was a migrant laborer.

40. TBD, 1DBN, Children Case Files Box 611, Mkhize, subfile 33/2/4/282/63. Report by Professional Officer of DCWS for commissioner of Child Welfare, September 24, 1963.

41. TBD, 1DBN, Children Case Files Box 611, Mkhize, subfile 33/2/4/282/63. Report by Professional Officer of DCWS for Commissioner of Child Welfare, September 24, 1963.

42. A survey of all the social workers employed in voluntary welfare organizations across the country in 1959 revealed that the vast majority of those employees were white and 90 percent were female (Report on a Survey of Social Workers Employed in Voluntary Welfare Organizations, Pretoria, 1962, p. 27). Such a dominance of women in social work was not new, but by the 1960s it had taken on a different class character. Previously, social welfare work was undertaken on a voluntary basis by usually wealthy white women. By the 1960s, social work was both a profession, requiring accreditation, and a job. Surveys of social workers during the 1960s suggested that they saw their work as necessary to help support their families (Kunzel 1993).

43. In McKendrick's study of Natal and Wits, social work graduates from 1955 to 1965, at the time of the study (June 1970), only 24 percent of respondents were in paid social work employment. Of the remaining 76 percent, most were not employed in social work as a result of pregnancy and child-rearing, or full-time employment out-

side the profession. Across the decade, respondents as a whole reported a total of 2890.5 months of full- and part-time employment in social work, comprising 198 different social work jobs with an average duration of 14.59 months each. Thus the total time of social work employment was 33.61 months or less than three years (McKendrick 1971).

44. Interview with Pia Kemble, a social worker at Durban Child Welfare Society in the 1970s–1990s.

45. Pia told the story of a white Point mother who she worked with intensively for years, including helping her to place her last child for adoption. She described a house visit when the two of them were hanging out the window watching the "passing parade" of people below on the often crowded Pickering street, and listening to the mother assess which men to approach as potential sex work clients. The stakes were high because rent was overdue, but the mother was also cautious about her physical vulnerability due to her pregnancy. Though the interaction was described as a lighthearted event in which they both joked about the relative value of different men, Pia also noted how witnessing the mother's decision-making brought home to her the woman's vulnerability and strength. It shifted her orientation away from what she termed a more instructional approach to one more oriented to supporting existing capacities.

46. The fact that Rosemary had only three children by age thirty-two would have likely been seen as low fertility within her race group.

47. Report of Committee of Inquiry into Family Allowances (Pretoria, 1961), 85.

48. Report of Committee of Inquiry into Family Allowances (Pretoria, 1961), 59. Between 1951 and 1960 the unemployment rate of whites (though very small) had increased from 2.8 to 3.6, while the unemployment rate for coloureds increased from 10.3 to 16.3 (Muller 1968, 19).

49. In some cases, the families of the Point women I met in 2014 had been living there for decades, and I had files of those biological mothers' interactions with child welfare. I choose not to highlight these due to concerns about confidentiality.

Chapter 4

1. Though South Africa's 1996 constitution guaranteed citizens universal socioeconomic rights to housing, health care, food, water, and social services, the state is only legally bound to provide "access" to these entitlements, not their material form. In contrast, the state has a positive legal obligation to provide for the basic needs of children, met in part through the CSG and the maintenance court.

2. Many coloured people postapartheid argue that the social, political, and racial position of their race group has changed little or downgraded posttransition. They describe an inversion of the racial hierarchy in which coloureds went from not being white enough during white minority rule to not being black enough under black majority rule. Many Indians speak in similar terms, however, their status as perpetual foreigners and the long-standing antipathy between Indian and black African race groups also shape their experience.

3. First proposed by Adrienne Rich, American feminists draw a distinction between *motherhood*, as the social, ideological construct of the maternal subject, and *mothering*, as the active, relational care work that is shaped by context (1986). An important contribution this move made possible was to eschew essentializing definitions of mother-

hood as a natural element of womanhood and, instead, to conceptualize motherhood as a dynamic social and ideological role that differs based on historic, cultural, economic, and political context (e.g., Hays 1996; Lareau 2003; Glenn, Chang, and Forcey 1994; O'Reilly 2006).

4. A Zulu term that literally translates to "in the South", eMzanzi colloquially refers to South Africa in general.

Chapter 5

1. Maintenance procedures for formerly married parents are outlined in divorce proceedings and renegotiated in divorce courts.

2. The stigma against unwed parenthood did not center on sex per se. Bearing children without *lobolo* is seen by elders as a disrespectful detaching of reproduction from its crucial role in upholding kin relations—hence *inhlawulo* addresses the "damages" wrought upon patriarchal authority (Erlank 2003, 2022; Rice 2023). Historically, vigorous, yet discreet, engagement in sex was encouraged among many black South Africans as long as it did not result in children (e.g., Mayer and Mayer 1972). Nonreproductive sexuality was historically sustained through nonpenetrative practices such as *ukuhlobongo* or "thigh sex" in isiZulu (Hunter 2010). However, missionaries condemned such practices, leading to an increase in extramarital childbearing (Delius and Glaser 2002; Glaser 2005).

3. In the case of the Black Sash, a women-led social justice organization founded in 1955, an ongoing focus of their work has been to ensure particularly black African women's access to social protection.

4. Section 27 of the Constitution of the Republic of South Africa Act 108 of 1996 provides that all citizens have the right to health care, food, water, and social security, and section 28 provides that every child has the right to family care or parental care and to basic nutrition, shelter, and basic health-care services. Both are affected by parental maintenance. South Africa ratified the United Nations Convention on the Elimination of All Forms of Discrimination against Women (1979) on December 15, 1995, and signed the Convention on the Rights of the Child on November 20, 1998. Earlier, on September 30, 1990, South Africa signed the World Declaration on the Survival, Protection, and Development of Children, which does not specifically address maintenance, but charges signatories to ensure respect for the role of the family in providing support for children.

5. As of this writing, no forms are available in any African languages, and beyond the assistance of the clerk, there is little provision for the large number of claimants who are illiterate in English or Afrikaans, or any language. Updated copies of all forms can be found at www.justice.gov.za/forms/form_mnt.htm.

6. Operation *Isondlo* (isiZulu for an alimony or maintenance payment) was a three-year project launched in December 2005 by the DOJCD to capacitate the maintenance courts. The DOJCD also launched the Maintenance Turnaround Strategy, which conducted trainings, bought cameras for the courts, and initiated EFT and mediation procedures. At writing, the South African Law Commission is still finalizing its review of the entire maintenance system. Recent legislation that has gone into effect allows the cell phone tracking of maintenance defaulters, the issuing of interim orders, and the

blacklisting of defaulters on credit websites—a ruling that attracted extensive legislative debate.

7. Named after a children's television program, Ben Tens are usually younger men who rarely contribute economically to the household, but—critical for women's self-worth—engender in their partners a sense of sexual desirability and an identity beyond that of maternal caregiver. It is a term more often used by coloured women.

8. Couples can receive mediation if they are referred to the family advocate, but such referrals are rarely made, and often men do not attend.

Chapter 6

1. RDP stands for the Reconstruction and Development Program implemented in the early years of the democracy that sought to meet the constitutional guarantee of secondary rights and to redress the long history of discriminatory policy through redistribution and public works projects. Between 1994 and 2001 over 1.1 million RDP houses were built and titles to them given to predominantly black South Africans. Critics have noted that the houses were poorly constructed, were often in undesirable locations, and in many ways resembled the mass housing projects of apartheid-era townships.

2. For comparison, in 2009 South Africa received 222,300 asylum claims as opposed to the United States, which received 47,900 the same year (UNHCR 2012).

3. The 2011 census found that 2,199,871 documented immigrants were living in South Africa with a total population that then stood at 51,770,560 (UNHCR 2012). Though an exact number of undocumented immigrants is not known, a conservative estimate is that there were 500,000 in 2011. It is likely that these numbers are higher now given the political and economic strife on the continent (Warren 2015).

4. This statistic is all the more surprising because it holds a number of variables that constitute an "immigrant advantage" constant. Budlender and Fauvelle-Aymar found that, "a foreign-born migrant with the same age, gender, and level of education, belonging to the same population group and residing in the same place as a South African, has a higher probability of being employed than a South African non-migrant. This is a very unusual finding, as in most developed countries where data are available, the rate of employment for foreign-born migrants is a lot lower than for local workers" (2012).

5. I was not present for these negotiations. The description is informed by Sthembile's retelling and photographs she showed me.

6. Zodwa and Zandi related these stories to me in a mix of Zulu and English, knowing of my understanding of both. Here, they spoke in English, though the original comment would have been made in Zulu.

7. For a sampling of some of the scholarship on this, see Bonachich (1973); Desai (1993); Edwards (1989); Edwards and Nuttall (1990); Freund (1995); Hassim (2019); Soske (2017); Thiara (1999); Vahed (1997).

8. Violence against women is widespread in South Africa and has been the subject of intensive debate, activism, and academic research. For a review of some of the policy and popular understandings of domestic violence, see Mazibuko and Umejesi (2015).

Conclusion

1. In 2021, former president Jacob Zuma was on trial by the Constitutional Court for corruption during his nine years in power. The case was viewed as a test of the rule of law in the postapartheid dispensation. When Zuma refused to give evidence, he was sentenced to a fifteen-month jail term for contempt of court. Protests began in Kwa-Zulu Natal, Zuma's political stronghold, on July 9 after Zuma turned himself over to police to serve the sentence (*Aljazeera* 2021).

2. When in the midst of the COVID-19 pandemic lockdown the SRD was extended, but the caregiver top-up was not, the women's rights organization Black Sash attempted, unsuccessfully, to secure a court interdict to halt the South African Social Security Agency from canceling the grant (Ellis 2020).

3. I want to be clear that my focus on the interdependence of all persons does not foreclose what Ingrid Robeyns terms *ethical individualism* or the valuing of the particular, situated experience of individuals (2003). Rather it pushes back against ontological individualism or the assumption that persons are atomistic individuals who exist independent from the actions and needs of others. I concur with Shireen Hassim that ethical individualism is essential for a feminist project of social justice (Hassim 2008).

REFERENCES

Adhikari, Mohamed. 2006. "Hope, Fear, Shame, Frustration: Continuity and Change in the Expression of Coloured Identity in White Supremacist South Africa, 1910–1994." *Journal of Southern African Studies* 32 (3): 467–87.

African National Congress. 1943. "The Atlantic Charter from the African's Point of View." Liberty Printers. Accessed August 21, 2023: www.marxists.org/subject/africa/anc/1943/claims.htm.

———. 1994. *Reconstruction and Development Programme*. Johannesburg: African National Congress.

———. 2009. *Working Together We Can Do More*. Election Manifesto Policy Framework. Johannesburg: African National Congress.

Afrobarometer. 2009. "Are Democratic Citizens Emerging in Africa? Evidence from the Afrobarometer." In *Afrobarometer Briefing Paper 70*. Pretoria: Institute for Democracy in South Africa. www.afrobarometer.org/wp-content/uploads/2022/02/AfrobriefNo70.pdf.

Agarwal, B., J. Humphries, and I. Robeyns, eds. 2006. *Capabilities, Freedom, and Equality: Amartya Sen's Work from a Gender Perspective*. New Delhi: Oxford University Press.

Agüero, Jorge M., Michael R. Carter, and Ingrid Woolard. 2009. "The Impact of Unconditional Cash Transfers on Nutrition: The South African Child Support Grant." In *Southern Africa Labour and Development Research Unit Working Paper Number 06/08*. Cape Town: SALDRU, University of Cape Town.

Alber, Erdmute, Sjaak van der Geest, and Susan Reynolds Whyte. 2008. *Generations in Africa: Connections and Conflicts*. Berlin: LIT Verlag Münster.

Alexander, M. Jacqui. 1994. "Not Just (Any)Body Can Be a Citizen: The Politics of Law, Sexuality, and Postcoloniality in Trinidad and Tobago and the Bahamas." *Feminist Review* 48: 5–23.

Aljazeera. 2021. "Violence Erupts over Jailing of Former South Africa Leader Zuma," July 10, 2021, sec. News. www.aljazeera.com/news/2021/7/10/violence-erupts-jailing -south-africa-jacob-zuma.

Amit, Roni, and Norma Kriger. 2014. "Making Migrants 'Il-Legible': The Policies and Practices of Documentation in Post-Apartheid South Africa." *Kronos* 40, no. 1: 269–90.

Ansell, Nicola. 2001. "'Because It's Our Culture!' (Re)Negotiating the Meaning of 'Lobola' in Southern African Secondary Schools." *Journal of Southern African Studies* 27, no. 4: 697–716. https://doi.org/10.2307/823409.

Anthias, Floya, and Nira Yuval-Davis. 1993. *Racialized Boundaries: Race, Nation, Gender, Colour, and Class and the Anti-Racist Struggle*. London: Routledge.

Armstrong, Alice. 1994. "School and Sadza: Custody and the Best Interests of the Child in Zimbabwe Special Issue: Part Two: The Best Interests of the Child." *International Journal of Law and the Family* 8, no. 2: 151–90.

Armstrong, Melissa Diane. 2020. *An Ambulance on Safari: The ANC and the Making of a Health Department in Exile*. Montreal: McGill-Queen's University Press.

Ashforth, Adam. 1990. *The Politics of Official Discourse in Twentieth-Century South Africa*. Oxford: Oxford University Press.

——. 1999. "Weighing Manhood in Soweto." *CODESIRA Bulletin* 3 and 4: 51–58.

——. 2005. *Witchcraft, Violence, and Democracy in South Africa*. Chicago: University of Chicago Press. https://press.uchicago.edu/ucp/books/book/chicago/W/ bo3534802.html.

Atkins, Keletso E. 1993. *The Moon Is Dead! Give Us Our Money!: The Cultural Origins of an African Work Ethic, Natal, South Africa, 1843–1900*. Portsmouth, NH: Heinemann.

Austin, J. L. 2018 [1962]. *How to Do Things with Words*. Edited by J. O. Urmson. Eastford, CT: Martino Fine Books.

Avineri, Shlomo, and Avner de-Shalit, eds. 1992. *Communitarianism and Individualism*. Oxford: Oxford University Press.

Backer, David I., and Kate Cairns. 2021. "Social Reproduction Theory Revisited." *British Journal of Sociology of Education* 42, no. 7: 1086–104. https://doi.org/10.1080/0142 5692.2021.1953962.

Badassy, Prinisha. 2011. "A Severed Umbilicus: Infanticide and the Concealment of Birth in Natal, 1860–1935." PhD diss., University of KwaZulu-Natal.

Bahri, G. 2008. "Ensuring Personal Financial Wellness: A Range of Intervention Measures and the Role of Voluntary Approaches." In *Employee Financial Wellness: A Corporate Social Responsibility*, edited by Elsa Crous. Pretoria: GTZ, Center for Cooperation with the Private Sector.

Balibar, Etienne. 1990. "Paradoxes of Universality." In *Anatomy of Racism*, edited by David Goldberg, 283–94. Minneapolis: University of Minnesota Press.

Bannatyne v Bannatyne. 2002. J. Mokgoro. Commission for Gender Equality as Amicus Curiae. Constitutional Court of South Africa.

Barca, Stefania. 2020. *Forces of Reproduction: Notes for a Counter-Hegemonic Anthropocene*. Cambridge: Cambridge University Press.

Barchiesi, Franco. 2008. "Wage Labor, Precarious Employment, and Social Inclusion in the Making of South Africa's Postapartheid Transition." *African Studies Review* 51, no. 2: 119–42.

———. 2011. *Precarious Liberation Workers, the State, and Contested Social Citizenship in Postapartheid South Africa.* Global Modernity. Albany: Scottsville, South Africa: State University of New York Press; Scottsville, South Africa: University of KwaZulu-Natal Press.

———. 2016. "Work in the Constitution of the Human: Twentieth-Century South African Entanglements of Welfare, Blackness, and Political Economy." *South Atlantic Quarterly* 115, no. 1: 149–74. https://doi.org/10.1215/00382876-3424797.

Barnes, Sandra T. 1986. *Patrons and Power: Creating a Political Community in Metropolitan Lagos.* 2nd ed. Manchester: Manchester University Press.

Bauman, Richard. 1996. "Transformations of the Word in the Production of Mexican Festival Drama." In *Natural Histories of Discourse,* edited by Michael Silverstein and Greg Urban, 301–28. Chicago: University of Chicago Press.

Bayart, Jean-François. 1993. *The State in Africa: The Politics of the Belly.* London: Longman.

Bayart, Jean-François, and Stephen Ellis. 2000. "Africa in the World: A History of Extraversion." *African Affairs* 99, no. 395: 217–67.

Bear, Laura, Karen Ho, Anna Lowenhaupt Tsing, and Sylvia Yanagisako. 2015. "Gens: A Feminist Manifesto for the Study of Capitalism." Society for Cultural Anthropology. *Theorizing the Contemporary* (blog). March 30, 2015. https://culanth.org/fieldsights/gens-a-feminist-manifesto-for-the-study-of-capitalism.

Berg, Heather. 2014. "An Honest Day's Wage for a Dishonest Day's Work: (Re)Productivism and Refusal." *Women's Studies Quarterly* 42, no. 1–2: 161–77.

Berger, D. 1983. "White Poverty and Government Policy in South Africa, 1892–1934." PhD diss., Department of History, Temple University.

Bezanson, Kate. 2006. *Gender, the State, and Social Reproduction: Household Insecurity in Neo-Liberal Times.* Toronto: University of Toronto Press.

Bezuidenhout, Andries, and Khayaat Fakier. 2006. "Maria's Burden: Contract Cleaning and the Crisis of Social Reproduction in Post-Apartheid South Africa." *Antipode* 38, no. 3: 462–85. https://doi.org/10.1111/j.0066-4812.2006.00590.x.

Bhandary, Asha. 2019. *Freedom to Care: Liberalism, Dependency Care, and Culture.* New York: Routledge.

Bhattacharya, Gargi. 2018. *Rethinking Racial Capitalism: Questions of Reproduction and Survival.* Lanham, MD: Rowman and Littlefield.

Bhattacharya, Tithi. 2017. *Social Reproduction Theory: Remapping Class, Recentering Oppression.* London: Pluto Press.

Bhattacharya, Tithi, and Gareth Dale. 2020. "Covid Capitalism: General Tendencies, Possible 'Leaps.'" *Spectre Journal,* no. 23. https://spectrejournal.com/covid-capitalism/.

Bhorat, Haroon. 1995. "The South African Social Safety Net: Past, Present and Future." *Development Southern Africa* 12, no. 4: 595–604. https://doi.org/10.1080/03768359508439841.

Bonachich, Edna. 1973. "A Theory of Middleman Minorities." *American Sociological Review* 38, no. 5: 583–94.

Bonnin, Debby. 2000. "Claiming Spaces, Changing Places: Political Violence and Women's Protests in KwaZulu-Natal." *Journal of Southern African Studies* 26, no. 2: 301–16. https://doi.org/10.2307/2637496.

Boris, Eileen. 1993. "The Power of Motherhood: Black and White Activist Women Redefine the 'Political.'" In *Mothers of a New World: Maternalist Politics and the Origins of Welfare States*, edited by S. Koven and S. Michel. New York, Routledge.

Bose, Sugata. 2017. *The Nation as Mother and Other Visions of Nationhood.* New York: Penguin Random House.

Boudreau, Julie-Anne. 2019. "State Theory from the Street Altar: The Muscles, the Saint, and the Amparo." *International Journal of Urban and Regional Research* 43, no. 3: 405–22. https://doi.org/10.1111/1468-2427.12694.

Bozzoli, Belinda. 1991. *Women of Phokeng.* Johannesburg: Ravan Press.

Bozzoli, Belinda, ed. 1987. *Class, Community, and Conflict: South African Perspectives.* Reissue ed. Johannesburg: Ravan Press of South Africa.

Brada, Betsey Behr. 2013. "How to Do Things to Children with Words: Language, Ritual, and Apocalypse in Pediatric HIV Treatment in Botswana." *American Ethnologist* 40, no. 3: 437–51.

Bradford, Helen. 1987. "'We Are Now the Men': Women's Beer Protests in the Natal Countryside, 1929." In *Class, Community, and Conflict: South African Perspectives*, edited by Belinda Bozzoli. Athens: University of Ohio Press.

Bratton, Michael, and Nicolas van de Walle. 1997. *Democratic Experiments in Africa.* Cambridge: Cambridge University Press.

Breckenridge, Keith. 2007. "Fighting for a White South Africa : White Working-Class Racism and the 1922 Rand Revolt." *South African Historical Journal* 57, no. 1: 228–43.

———. 2012. "No Will to Know: The Rise and Fall of African Civil Registration in 20th Century South Africa." In *Registration and Recognition: Documenting the Person in History*, edited by Keith Breckenridge and Simon Szreter. Oxford: Oxford University Press.

Briggs, Charles. 2007. "Mediating Infanticide: Theorizing Relations between Narrative and Violence." *Cultural Anthropology* 22, no. 3: 315–56.

Brink, Elsabe. 1987. "Maar 'n Klomp 'Factory' Meide: Afrikaner Family and Community on the Witwatersrand during the 1920s." In *Class, Community and Conflict: South African Perspectives*, edited by Belinda Bozzoli, reissue ed., 177–208. Johannesburg: Ravan Press.

———. 1990. "Man-Made Women: Gender, Class, and the Ideology of the Volksmoeder." In *Women and Gender in Southern Africa to 1945*, edited by Cherryl Walker, 273–92. Cape Town: D. Philip; London: J. Currey.

Broughton, Tania. 2012. "Delay in Transfer of Point 'Eyesore,'" April 9, 2012. www.iol.co.za/mercury/delay-in-transfer-of-point-eyesore-1.1271929?ot=inmsa.ArticlePrintPageLayout.ot.

Brown, Wendy. 1995. *States of Injury: Power and Freedom in Late Modernity.* Princeton, NJ: Princeton University Press.

Brummer, F. 1964. *The Structure and Policy of Welfare Services in South Africa with Particular Reference to the Role of the State.* Pretoria: Government Printer.

Buch, Elana. 2015. "Anthropology of Aging and Care." *Annual Review of Anthropology* 44: 277–93.

———. 2018. *Inequalities of Aging: Paradoxes of Independence in American Home Care.* New York: New York University Press.

Budlender, Debbie. 2005. "Women and Poverty." *Agenda: Empowering Women for Gender Equity* 19, no. 64: 30–36.

Budlender D., N. Chobokoane, and S. Simelane. 2004. "Marriage Patterns in South Africa: Methodological and Substantive Issues." *Southern African Journal of Demography* 9, no. 1: 1–26.

Budlender, D., and C. Fauvelle-Aymar. 2012. MiWORC Policy Brief 2. Migration and Employment in South Africa Statistical and Econometric Analyses of Internal and International Migrants in Statistics South Africa's Labour Market Data. Johannesburg: African Centre for Migration and Society, University of the Witwatersrand.

Budlender, Debbie, and Francie Lund. 2011. "South Africa: A Legacy of Family Disruption." *Development and Change* 42, no. 4: 925–46.

Budlender, Debbie, and Bhekinkosi Moyo, eds. 2004. *What about the Children? The Silent Voices in Maintenance.* Braamfontein, South Africa: Tshwaranang Legal Advocacy Centre.

Burbank, Victoria Katherine. 1995. "Passion as Politics: Romantic Love in an Australian Aboriginal Community." In *Romantic Passion: A Universal Experience?*, edited by William R. Jankowiak. New York: Columbia University Press.

Burman, Sandra, and Shirley Berger. 1988a. "When Family Support Fails: The Problems of Maintenance Payments in Apartheid South Africa: Part I." *South African Journal on Human Rights* 4: 196–206.

———. 1988b. "When Family Support Fails: The Problems of Maintenance Payments in Apartheid South Africa: Part II." *South African Journal on Human Rights* 4: 334–54.

Burman, Sandra, and Nicolette van der Werff. 1993. "Rethinking Customary Law on Bridewealth." *Social Dynamics* 19, no. 2: 111–27. https://doi.org/10.1080/025339593084 58554.

Burns, Catherine. 1995. "Reproductive Labors: The Politics of Women's Health in South Africa, 1900–1960." PhD diss., Northwestern University.

———. 2011. "The Children's Hospital in Durban." Paper presented at WISER, July 24.

Burton, Antoinette, Faisal Devji, Mrinalini Sinha, Jon Soske, Ashwin Desai, and Goolam Vahed. 2018. "The South African Gandhi: Stretcher-Bearer of Empire." *Journal of Natal and Zulu History* 32, no. 1: 100–118.

Butler, Judith. 1990. *Gender Trouble.* New York: Routledge.

Callebert, Ralph. 2012a. "Cleaning the Wharves: Pilferage, Bribery, and Social Connections on the Durban Docks in the 1950s." *Canadian Journal of African Studies/La Revue Canadienne des Études Africaines* 46, no. 1: 23–38.

———. 2012b. "Working Class Action and Informal Trade on the Durban Docks, 1930s–1950s." *Journal of Southern African Studies* 38, no. 4: 847–61.

———. 2017. *On Durban's Docks: Zulu Workers, Rural Households, Global Labor.* Rochester, NY: University of Rochester Press.

Callinicos, Luli. 2007. "Testimonies and Transitions: Women Negotiating the Rural and Urban in the Mid-20th Century." In *Women in South African History: Basus'iimbokodo, bawel'imilambo/They Remove Boulders and Cross Rivers*, edited by Nomboniso Gasa. Cape Town: HSRC Press.

Cameron, Deborah, and Don Kulick. 2008. *Language and Sexuality*. 6th printing. Cambridge: Cambridge University Press.

Care Collective. 2020. *Care Manifesto: The Politics of Interdependence*. New York: Verso.

Carpenter, Faedra Chatard. 2006. "'(L)activists and Lattes': Breastfeeding Advocacy as Domestic Performance." *Women and Performance* 16, no. 3: 347–67.

Carr, E. Summerson. 2009. "Anticipating and Inhabiting Institutional Identities." *American Ethnologist* 36, no. 1: 317–36.

———. 2011. *Scripting Addiction: The Politics of Therapeutic Talk and American Sobriety*. Princeton, NJ: Princeton University Press.

Carsten, Janet. 2004. *After Kinship*. Cambridge: Cambridge University Press.

Chabal, Patrick, and Jean-Pascal Daloz. 1999. *Africa Works: Disorder as Political Instrument*. London: International African Institute; Bloomington: Indiana University Press.

Chance, Kerry Ryan. 2018. *Living Politics in South Africa's Urban Shacklands*. Chicago: University of Chicago Press. https://press.uchicago.edu/ucp/books/book/chicago/L /bo27315111.html.

Chanock, Martin. 1989. "Neither Customary Nor Legal: African Customary Law in an Era of Family Law Reform." *International Journal of Law, Policy, and the Family* 3, no. 1: 72–88. https://doi.org/10.1093/lawfam/3.1.72.

———. 2001. *The Making of South African Legal Culture, 1902–1936: Fear, Favour, and Prejudice*. Cambridge: Cambridge University Press.

Chari, S. 2006. "Life Histories of Race and Space in the Making of Wentworth and Merebank, South Durban." *African Studies* 65, no. 1: 105–30.

Chauke, Polite, and Grace Khunou. 2014. "Shaming Fathers into Providers: Child Support and Fatherhood in the South African Media." *Open Family Studies Journal* 6, no. 1. https://benthamopen.com/ABSTRACT/TOFAMSJ-6-18.

"Child Support Grant." 2023. The knowledge-sharing platform on social protection. Social Protection. 2023. https://socialprotection.org/discover/programmes/child-support-grant-csg.

Chisholm, Linda. 1990. "Class, Colour, and Gender in Child Welfare in South Africa, 1902–1918." *South African Historical Journal* 23: 100–121.

Chodorow, Nancy. 1978. *The Reproduction of Mothering: Psychoanalysis and the Sociology of Gender*. Berkeley: University of California Press.

Christiansen, Catrine, Mats Utas, and Henrik E. Vigh. 2006. "Youth(e)scapes: Introduction." In *Navigating Youth, Generating Adulthood: Social Becoming in an African Context*, edited by Catrine Christiansen, Mats Utas, and Henrik E. Vigh. Uppsala, Sweden: Nordiska Afrikainstitutet.

Ciccia, Rossella, and Diane Sainsbury. 2018. "Gendering Welfare State Analysis: Tensions between Care and Paid Work." *European Journal of Politics and Gender* 1, no. 1–2: 93–109. https://doi.org/10.1332/251510818X15272520831102.

Clark, Brigitte. 1999. "An Analysis of the Effects of Marriage, Divorce, and Death on the

Child Maintenance Obligation in South African Law with Some Comparative Perspectives." PhD diss., Rhodes University.

———. 2005. "The South African Child's Right to Maintenance—A Constitutionally Enforceable Socio-Economic Right?" Paper presented at the 4th World Congress on Family Law and Children's Rights. Cape Town, South Africa, March 20–23. www.childjustice.org/docs/clark2005.pdf.

Clark, S., and D. Hamplová. 2013. "Single Motherhood and Child Mortality in Sub-Saharan Africa: A Life Course Perspective." *Demography* 50, no. 5: 1521–49.

Clarke, Adele. 2018. "Introducing Making Kin Not Population." In *Making Kin Not Population: Reconceiving Generations*, edited by Adele Clarke and Donna Haraway, 41–66. Chicago: Prickly Paradigm Press. https://press.uchicago.edu/ucp/books/book/distributed/M/bo28583407.html.

Clowes, L. 1994. "Making It Work: Aspects of Marriage, Motherhood, and Money-Earning among White South African Women, 1960–1990." PhD diss., University of Cape Town.

Coalition. 2020. "Submission to Ministers-of-Finance-Social-Development-and-Women-27-April-2020_0.Pdf." www.iej.org.za/wp-content/uploads/2020/04/Submission-to-Ministers-of-Finance-Social-Development-and-Women-27-April-2020_0.pdf.

Cobley, Alan G. 1997. *The Rules of the Game: Struggles in Black Recreation and Social Welfare Policy in South Africa*. Westport, CT: Praeger.

Cock, Jacklyn. 1989. *Maids and Madams: Domestic Workers under Apartheid*. London: Women's Press.

Coe, Cati. 2017. "Returning Home: The Retirement Strategies of Aging Ghanaian Care Workers." In *Transnational Aging and Reconfigurations of Kin Work*, edited by Cati Coe and Parin Dossa, 141–58. New Brunswick, NJ: Rutgers University Press. http://www.jstor.org/stable/j.ctt1mtz5qv.10.

———. 2019. *The New American Servitude: Political Belonging among African Immigrant Home Care Workers*. New York: New York University Press. https://nyupress.org/9781479808830/the-new-american-servitude.

Cole, Jennifer. 2004. "Fresh Contact in Tamatave, Madagascar: Sex, Money, and Intergenerational Transformation." *American Ethnologist* 31, no. 4: 573–88.

———. 2009. "Love, Money, and Economies of Intimacy in Tamatave, Madagascar." In *Love in Africa*, edited by Jennifer Cole and Lynn M. Thomas, 109–34. Chicago: University of Chicago Press. www.degruyter.com/document/doi/10.7208/9780226113555-007/html.

———. 2014a. "Producing Value among Malagasy Marriage Migrants in France: Managing Horizons of Expectation." *Current Anthropology* 55 (S9): S85–S94.

———. 2014b. "The *Telephone Malgache*: Transnational Gossip and Social Transformation among Malagasy Marriage Migrants in France." *American Ethnologist* 41, no. 2: 276–89.

———. 2014c. "Working Mis/Understandings: The Tangled Relationship between Kinship, Franco-Malagasy Binational Marriages, and the French State." *Cultural Anthropology* 29, no. 3: 527–51.

Cole, Jennifer, and Deborah Durham. 2006. "Age, Regeneration, and the Intimate Politics of Globalization." In *Generations and Globalization: Youth, Age, and Family in the New World Economy*, edited by Jennifer Cole and Deborah Durham, illustrated ed., 1–29. Bloomington: Indiana University Press.

Cole, Jennifer, and Christian Groes. 2016. *Affective Circuits: African Migrations to Europe and the Pursuit of Social Regeneration*. Chicago: University of Chicago Press.

Colen, Shelee. 1995. "'Like a Mother to Them': Stratified Reproduction and West Indian Childcare Workers and Employers in New York." In *Conceiving the New World Order: The Global Politics of Reproduction*, edited by Faye D. Ginsburg and Rayna Rapp, 78–102. Berkeley: University of California Press.

Collins, P. H. 1994. "Shifting the Center: Race, Class, and Feminist Theorizing about Motherhood." In *Representations of Motherhood*, edited by D. Bassing, M. Honey, and M. M. Kaplan, 56–74. New Haven, CT: Yale University Press.

Committee of Inquiry into Family Allowances. 1961. *Report of Committee of Inquiry into Family Allowances*. Pretoria: Government Printer.

Committee on Socio-Economic Surveys for Bantu Housing Research. 1960. *A Survey of Rent-Paying Capacity of Urban Natives in South Africa*. Pretoria: South African Council for Scientific and Industrial Research.

Community Agency for Social Enquiry (CASE). 2012. "An Assessment of Probono.org's Maintenance Project at Four Courts in Gauteng." March. Unpublished report.

Comaroff, John L., and Simon Roberts. 1981. *Rules and Processes: The Cultural Logic of Dispute in an African Context*. Chicago: University of Chicago Press.

Constable, Nicole. 2003. *Romance of a Global Stage: Pen Pals, Virtual Ethnography, and "Mail Order" Marriages*. Berkeley: University of California Press.

———. 2009. "The Commodification of Intimacy: Marriage, Sex, and Reproductive Labor." *Annual Review of Anthropology* 38, no. 1: 49–64. https://doi.org/10.1146/annurev.anthro.37.081407.085133.

Constant-Martin. 2001."Whats' in the Name Coloured?" In *Social Identities in the New South Africa: Cape Town After Apartheid*, vol. 1, edited by Abebe Zegeye. Cape Town: Kwela Books.

Cook, P.A.W. 1931. *Social Organisation and Ceremonial Institutions of the Bomvana*. Cape Town: Juta.

Cooper, Frederick. 1996. *Decolonization and African Society: The Labor Question in French and British Africa*. Cambridge: Cambridge University Press.

Corrigan, Terence. 2023. "Hard and Politically Unpopular Decisions Are Required to Fix Local Government." *Daily Maverick*, February 27, 2023, sec. OPINIONISTA. www.dailymaverick.co.za/opinionista/2023-02-27-hard-and-politically-unpopular-decisions-are-required-to-fix-local-government/.

Coutts, Tamazin L. 2014. "A Critical Analysis of the Implementation of the Maintenance Act 99 of 1998: Difficulties Experienced by the Unrepresented Public in the Maintenance Court as a Result of the Poor Implementation of the Act." LLM, University of KwaZulu-Natal. www.couttsattorneys.co.za/docs/Dissertation%20Submission%2013.03.14.pdf.

Cox, Kevin R., and David Hemson. 2008. "Mamdani and the Politics of Migrant Labor in South Africa: Durban Dockworkers and the Difference That Geography Makes." *Political Geography* 27, no. 2: 194–212. https://doi.org/10.1016/j.polgeo.2007.08.002.

Cruikshank, Barbara. 1999. *The Will to Empower: Democratic Citizens and Other Subjects*. Ithaca, NY: Cornell University Press.

Crush, Jonathan, and Charles Ambler, eds. 1992. *Liquor and Labor in Southern Africa*. Athens: Ohio University Press. www.ohioswallow.com/book/Liquor+and+Labor+in+Southern+Africa.

Daly, Markate, ed. 1993. *Communitarianism: A New Public Ethics*. New York: Wadsworth.

Davie, Dorothy Grace. 2005. "Poverty Knowledge in South Africa: The Everyday Life of Social Science Expertise in the Twentieth Century." PhD diss., University of Michigan.

Davies, Robert H. 1979. *Capital, State, and White Labour in South Africa, 1900–1960: An Historical Materialist Analysis of Class Formation and Class Relations*. Atlantic Highlands, NJ: Humanities Press.

Davin, Anna. 1997. "Imperialism and Motherhood." In *Tensions of Empire: Colonial Cultures in a Bourgeois World*, edited by Frederick Cooper and Ann Laura Stoler, 87–151. Berkeley: University of California Press. www.myilibrary.com?id=331138.

Dawson, Hannah J., and Elizaveta Fouksman. 2020a. "Labour, Laziness, and Distribution: Work Imaginaries among the South African Unemployed." *Africa* 90, no. 2: 229–51.

———. 2020b. "Why South Africa Needs to Ensure Income Security beyond the Pandemic." *The Conversation*, April 30, 2020. http://theconversation.com/why-south-africa-needs-to-ensure-income-security-beyond-the-pandemic-137551.

Dawson, Hannah Joy. 2023. "Father-Child (Dis)Connections: Expectations and Practices of Young Un(Der)Employed Fathers in Johannesburg." *Men and Masculinities* 26, no. 2: 1–18. https://doi.org/10.1177/1097184X231153170.

De Haas, M. 1987. "Is There Anything More to Say about Ilobolo?" *African Studies* 46, no. 1: 33–55.

Decoteau, Claire Laurier. 2013. "The Crisis of Liberation: Masculinity, Neoliberalism, and HIV/AIDS in Postapartheid South Africa." *Men and Masculinities* 16, no. 2 (2): 139–59. https://doi.org/10.1177/1097184X13488865.

De Jong, Madelene. 2009. "Ten-Year Anniversary of the Maintenance Act 99 of 1998—A Time to Reflect on Improvements, Shortcomings, and the Way Forward." *South African Law Journal* 126, no. 3: 590–614

Delius, Peter, and Clive Glaser. 2002. "Sexual Socialisation in South Africa: A Historical Perspective." *African Studies* 61: 27–54.

Dengler, Corinna, and Miriam Lang. 2022. "Commoning Care: Feminist Degrowth Visions for a Socio-Ecological Transformation." *Feminist Economics* 28, no. 1: 1–28.

Department of Justice and Constitutional Development. 2003. "Access to Maintenance for Women and Children." Presentation to Select Committee on Security and Constitutional Affairs, June 10, 2003. Parliamentary Monitoring Group. www.pmg.org.za/minutes/20030609-maintenance-courts-briefing.

Department of Social Development (DSD). 2006. *Strategic Plan 2006/7–2009/10*. Pretoria RP 22/2006. Pretoria: Government Printer.

———. 2012. "White Paper on Families in South Africa." White Paper. Republic of

South Africa, Pretoria: Department of Social Development. www.dsd.gov.za/index
.php?option=com_docman&task=cat_view&gid=33&Itemid=39.

Department of Social Development (DSD), South Africa Social Security Agency
(SASSA), and United Nations Children's Fund (UNICEF). 2012. *The South African
Child Support Grant Impact Assessment: Evidence from a Survey of Children, Ado-
lescents, and Their Households.* Pretoria: UNICEF South Africa.

Department of Social Welfare and Pensions. 1962. "Report on a Survey of Social Workers Employed by Voluntary Welfare Organizations," 5. Research and Information.
Pretoria, South Africa.

Department of Welfare. 1997. "White Paper for Social Welfare." Republic of South
Africa, Pretoria: Department of Welfare. www.dsd.gov.za/index.php?option=com_
docman&task=doc_download&gid=46&Itemid=39.

Derrida, Jacques. 1995 [1972]. "Signature Event Context." In *Limited Inc., 1–23.* Evanston, IL: Northwestern University Press.

Desai, Ashwin G. 1993. "A Context for Violence: Social and Historical Underpinnings
of Indo-African Violence in a South African Community." PhD diss., Michigan
State University. www.proquest.com/docview/304092792/abstract/ED4B56072DC5
4813PQ/1.

Devereux, Stephen. 2007. "Social Pensions in Southern Africa in the Twentieth Century." *Journal of Southern African Studies* 33, no. 3: 539–60.

Dlamini, C. R. M. 1994. *The Juridical Analysis and Critical Evaluation of Ilobolo in a
Changing Zulu Society.* Co-operative Research Programme on Marriage and Family
Life. Pretoria.

Doke, C. M., D. M. Malcom, J. M. A. Sikhkana, and B. W. Vilakazi. 2008. *English/Zulu
isiZulu English Dictionary.* Johannesburg: Witwatersrand University Press.

Donzelot, Jacques. 1979. *The Policing of Families.* New York: Pantheon Books.

Dossa, Parin, and Cati Coe. 2017. "Introduction: Transnational Aging and Reconfigurations of Kin Work." In *Transnational Aging and Reconfigurations of Kin Work,*
edited by Parin Dossa and Cati Coe, 1–22. New Brunswick, NJ: Rutgers University
Press. www.jstor.org/stable/j.ctt1mtz5qv.3.

Dubbeld, Bernard. 2013. "How Social Security Becomes Social Insecurity: Unsettled
Households, Crisis Talk, and the Value of Grants in a KwaZulu-Natal Village." *Acta
Juridica,* 197.

Dubow, Saul. 1995. *Scientific Racism in Modern South Africa.* Cambridge: Cambridge
University Press.

Dubow, Saul, and Alan Jeeves, eds. 2005. *South Africa's 1940s: Worlds of Possibilities.*
Cape Town: Double Storey.

Duff, S. E. 2015. *Changing Childhoods in the Cape Colony Dutch Reformed Church
Evangelicalism and Colonial Childhood, 1860–1895.* London: Palgrave Macmillan.

———. 2016. "Babies of the Empire: Science, Nation, and Truby King's Mothercraft in
Early Twentieth-Century South Africa." In *Children, Childhood, and Youth in the
British World,* edited by Shirleene Robinson and Simon Sleight, 59–73. London:
Palgrave Macmillan UK. https://doi.org/10.1007/978-1-137-48941-8_4.

Du Toit, Andries, and David Neves. 2014. "The Government of Poverty and the Arts of
Survival: Mobile and Recombinant Strategies at the Margins of the South African

Economy." *Journal of Peasant Studies* 41, no. 5: 833–53. https://doi.org/10.1080/03066 150.2014.894910.

Du Toit, Marijke. 1992. "Dangerous Motherhood: Maternity Care and the Construction of Afrikaner Identity, 1904–1939." In *Women and Children First: International Maternal and Infant Welfare, 1870–1945*, edited by Valerie Fildes, Lara Marks, and Hilary Marland, 203–29. New Yok: Routledge.

———. 1996. "Women, Welfare and the Nurturing of Afrikaner Nationalism a Social History of the Afrikaanse Christelike Vroue Vereniging, c. 1870–1939." PhD diss., University of Cape Town.

———. 2003. "The Domesticity of Afrikaner Nationalism: Volksmoeders and the ACVV, 1904–1929." *Journal of Southern African Studies* 29, no. 1: 155–76.

———. 2014. "'Anginayo Ngisho Indibilishi!' (I Don't Have a Penny!): The Gender Politics of 'Native Welfare' in Durban, 1930–1939." *South African Historical Journal* 66, no. 2: 291–319. https://doi.org/10.1080/02582473.2014.918169.

———. 2018. "Mothers' Pensions and the 'Civilised' Black Poor: The Racialised Provision of Child Maintenance Grants in South Africa, 1921–1940." *Journal of Southern African Studies* 44, no. 6: 973–89. https://doi.org/10.1080/03057070.2018.1548679.

Eberstadt, Nicholas. 1995. *The Tyranny of Numbers: Mismeasurement and Misrule.* Washington, DC: Aei Press.

Edwards, Iain Lulach. 1989. "Mkhumbane Our Home: African Shantytown Society in Cato Manor Farm, 1946–1960." PhD diss., University of Natal. https://researchspace .ukzn.ac.za/handle/10413/5591.

Edwards, Iain, and Timothy Andrew Nuttall. 1990. "Seizing the Moment: The January 1949 Riots, Proletarian Populism, and the Structure of African Urban Life in Durban during the Late 1940s." In *History Workshop.* Johannesburg: University of Witwatersrand.

Ekwensi, Cyprian. 1987 [1961]. *Jagua Nana.* Oxford,: Heinemann International.

Ellis, Estelle. 2020. "High Court Throws Out Black Sash Bid to Extend R500 Caregiver Grant." *Daily Maverick*, November 1, 2020, sec. Maverick Citizen. www. dailymaverick.co.za/article/2020-11-01-high-court-throws-out-black-sash-bid-to -extend-r500-caregiver-grant/.

Elson, D. 2016. "Plan F: Feminist Plan for a Caring and Sustainable Economy." *Globalizations* 13, no. 6: 919–21.

Englund, Harri. 2006. *Prisoners of Freedom: Human Rights and the African Poor.* Berkeley: University of California Press.

———. 2008. "Extreme Poverty and Existential Obligations: Beyond Morality in the Anthropology of Africa." *Social Analysis* 52, no. 3): 33–50.

Englund, Harri, and Francis Nyamnjoh, eds. 2004. *Rights and the Politics of Recognition in Africa.* Postcolonial Encounters. London: Zed Books.

Erasmus, Z., ed. 2001. *Coloured by History, Shaped by Place: New Perspectives on Coloured Identities in Cape Town.* Cape Town: Kwela Books.

Erlank, Natasha. 2003. "Gendering Commonality: African Men and the 1883 Commission on Native Law and Custom." *Journal of Southern African Studies* 29, no. 4: 937–53.

———. 2022. *Convening Black Intimacy: Christianity, Gender, and Tradition in Early Twentieth-Century South Africa.* Athens: Ohio University Press.

Essop Sheik, Nafisa. 2005. "Labouring under the Law: Gender and the Legal Administration of Indian Immigrants under Indenture in Colonial Natal, 1860–1907." Master's thesis, University of KwaZulu-Natal.

———. 2014. "African Marriage Regulation and the Remaking of Gendered Authority
in Colonial Natal, 1843–1875." *African Studies Review* 57, no. 2: 73–92.

Faier, Lieba. 2009. *Intimate Encounters: Filipina Women and the Remaking of Rural
Japan*. Berkeley: University of California Press.

Fakier, Khayaat, and Jacklyn Cock. 2009. "A Gendered Analysis of the Crisis of Social
Reproduction in Contemporary South Africa." *International Feminist Journal of
Politics* 11, no. 3: 353–71. https://doi.org/10.1080/14616740903017679.

Family Congress Steering Committee. 1961. *Report of the Family Congress*. Pretoria:
University of Pretoria, April 4–7.

Feldman, Ilana. 2007. "Difficult Distinctions: Refugee Law, Humanitarian Practice,
and Political Identification in Gaza." *Cultural Anthropology* 22, no. 1: 129–69. https:
//doi.org/10.1525/can.2007.22.1.129.

Feldman, Ilana, and Miriam Iris Ticktin. 2010. *In the Name of Humanity: The Government of Threat and Care*. Durham, NC: Duke University Press.

Feldman-Savelsberg, Pamela. 2016. *Mothers on the Move: Reproducing Belonging between Africa and Europe*. Chicago: University of Chicago Press.

Ferguson, James. 1999. *Expectations of Modernity: Myths and Meanings of Urban Life
on the Zambian Copperbelt*. Berkeley: University of California Press.

———. 2007. "Formalities of Poverty: Thinking about Social Assistance in Neoliberal
South Africa." *African Studies Review* 50, no. 2: 71–86. https://doi.org/10.1353/arw
.2007.0092.

———. 2013. "Declarations of Dependence: Labour, Personhood, and Welfare in Southern Africa." *Journal of the Royal Anthropological Institute* 19, no. 2: 223–42.

———. 2015. *Give a Man a Fish: Reflections on the New Politics of Distribution*. Durham,
NC: Duke University Press.

Finlayson, R. 2002. "Women's Language of Respect: Isihlonipho Sabafazi." In *Language in South Africa*, edited by Rajend Mesthrie. Cambridge: Cambridge University Press.

Fjeldstad, Odd-Helge . 2003. "What Has Trust Got to Do with It? Non-Payment of Service Charges in Local Authorities in South Africa." Working Paper 2003: 12. Bergen,
Norway: Chr. Michelsen Institute. www.cmi.no/publications/file/1686-what-has
-trust-got-to-do-with-it.pdf.

Flint, Karen E. 2008. *Healing Traditions: African Medicine, Cultural Exchange, and
Competition in South Africa, 1820–1948*. Athens: Ohio University Press.

Fortes, Meyer. 1949. *The Web of Kinship among the Tallensi*. London: Oxford University
Press.

———. 1969. *Kinship and the Social Order: The Legacy of Lewis Henry Morgan*. Chicago:
Aldine. www.routledge.com/Kinship-and-the-Social-Order-The-Legacy-of-Lewis
-Henry-Morgan/Fortes/p/book/9780415866521.

———. 1987. "The Concept of the Person." In *Religion, Morality, and the Person: Essays
on Tallensi Religion*, 249–86. Cambridge: Cambridge University Press.

Fourchard, L., and A. Segatti. 2015. "Introduction of Xenophobia and Citizenship: The

Everyday Politics of Exclusion and Inclusion in Africa." *Africa* 85, no. 1: 2–12.

Fourie, Bronwyn. 2012. "Point Area at Grimy Standstill—KwaZulu-Natal | IOL News | IOL.Co.Za." June 18, 2012. www.iol.co.za/news/south-africa/kwazulu-natal/point -area-at-grimy-standstill-1.1321156#.UuIwmfb8JZo.

Frankel, Philip. 1979. "The Politics of Passes: Control and Change in South Africa." *Journal of Modern African Studies* 17, no. 2: 199–217. https://doi.org/10.1017/ S0022278X00005413.

———. 2001. *An Ordinary Atrocity: Sharpeville and Its Massacre.* New Haven, CT: Yale University Press.

Franklin, Sarah B., and Susan McKinnon, eds. 2001. *Relative Values: Reconfiguring Kinship Studies.* Durham, NC: Duke University Press.

Fraser, Nancy. 1989. *Unruly Practices: Power, Discourse, and Gender in Contemporary Social Theory.* Minneapolis: University of Minnesota Press.

———. 1996. *Justice Interruptus: Critical Reflections on the "Postsocialist" Condition.* New York: Routledge.

———. 2000. "Rethinking Recognition." *New Left Review* 3 (May/June): 107–25.

———. 2016. "Contradictions of Capital and Care." *New Left Review* 2, no. 100: 99–117.

———. 2022. *Cannibal Capitalism: How Our System Is Devouring Democracy, Care, and the Planet and What We Can Do about It.* New York: Verso.

Fraser, Nancy, and Linda Gordon. 1994. "A Genealogy of Dependency: Tracing a Keyword of the U.S. Welfare State." *Signs* 19, no. 2: 309–36.

Freed, Louis Franklin. 1949. *The Problem of European Prostitution in Johannesburg: A Sociological Survey.* Cape Town, South Africa: Juta.

Freeman, Caren. 2011. *Making and Faking Kinship: Marriage and Labor Migration between China and South Korea.* Ithaca, NY: Cornell University Press.

Fresnoza-Flot, Asuncion. 2017. Gender- and Social Class–Based Transnationalism of Migrant Filipinas in Binational Unions. *Journal of Ethnic and Migration Studies* 43, no. 6: 885–90.

Freund, Bill. 1988. *The African Worker.* Cambridge: Cambridge University Press.

———. 1992. "The Poor Whites: A Social Force and a Social Problem in South African History." In *White but Poor: Essays on the History of Poor Whites in Southern Africa, 1880–1940,* edited by Robert Morrell. Pretoria: University of South Africa.

———. 1995. *Insiders and Outsiders: The Indian Working Class of Durban, 1910–1990.* Social History of Africa. Portsmouth, NH: Heinemann; London: James Currey.

Gage A. J. 1997. "Familial and Socioeconomic Influences on Children's Well-Being: An Examination of Preschool Children in Kenya." *Social Science and Medicine* 45, no. 12: 1811–28.

Gaitskell, Deborah. 1982. "Wailing for Purity: Prayer Unions, African Mothers, and Adolescent Daughters, 1912–1940." In *Industrialisation and Social Change in South Africa: African Class Formation, Culture, and Consciousness, 1870–1930,* edited by Shula Marks and Richard Rathbone, 338–57. London: Longman.

———. 1983. "Housewives, Maids, or Mothers: Some Contradictions of Domesticity for Christian Women in Johannesburg, 1903–39." *Journal of African History* 24, no. 2: 241–56.

Gaitskell, Deborah, and Elaine Unterhalter. 1989. "Mothers of the Nation: A Comparative Analysis of Nation, Race, and Motherhood in Afrikaner Nationalism and the African National Congress." In *Woman-Nation-State*, edited by Nira Yuval-Davis, Floya Anthias, and Jo Campling, 58–78. London: Palgrave Macmillan UK.

Gal, Susan. 1991. "Between Speech and Silence: The Problematics of Research on Language and Gender." In *Gender at the Crossroads of Knowledge: Feminist Anthropology in the Postmodern Era*, edited by Michaela Di Leonardo, 175–203. Berkeley: University of California Press

Garcia, Angela. 2010. *The Pastoral Clinic: Addiction and Dispossession along the Rio Grande*. Berkeley: University of California Press.

Garey, Anita Ilta, and Nicholas W. Townsend. 1996. "Kinship, Courtship, and Child Maintenance Law in Botswana." *Journal of Family and Economic Issues* 17, no. 2: 189–203.

Gasa, Nomboniso. 2007. "Feminisms, Motherisms, Patriarchies, and Women's Voices in the 1950s." In *Women in South African History: "Basus'iimbokodo, Bawel'imilambo"/They Remove Boulders and Cross Rivers*, edited by Nomboniso Gasa, 207–29. Cape Town: HSRC Press.

Gelb, Stephen. 2008. "Behind Xenophobia in South Africa: Poverty or Inequality?" In *Go Home or Die Here: Violence, Xenophobia, and the Reinvention of Difference in South Africa*, edited by Shireen Hassim, Tawana Kupe, and Eric Worby. Johannesburg: Wits University Press.

Ginsburg, F. D., and R. Rapp. 1995. *Conceiving the New World Order: The Global Politics of Reproduction*. Berkeley: University of California Press.

Ginsburg, Rebecca. 2011. *At Home with Apartheid: The Hidden Landscapes of Domestic Service in Johannesburg*. Charlottesville: University of Virginia Press. http://site.ebrary.com/lib/alltitles/docDetail.action?docID=10554884.

Glaser, Clive. 2005. "Managing the Sexuality of the Urban Youth: Johannesburg, 1920s–1960s." *International Journal of African Historical Studies* 38, no. 2: 322.

Glenn, Evelyn Nakano. 1992. "From Servitude to Service Work: Historical Continuities in the Racial Division of Paid Reproductive Labor." *Signs* 18, no. 1: 1–43.

Glenn, Evelyn Nakano, Grace Chang, and Linda Rennie Forcey. 1994. *Mothering: Ideology, Experience, and Agency*. New York: Routledge.

Gluckman, Max. 1965. *Ideas in Barotse Jurisprudence*. New Haven, CT: Yale University Press.

Goffman, Erving. 1959. *The Presentation of Self in Everyday Life*. Garden City, NY: Anchor.

———. 1981. *Forms of Talk*. Philadelphia: University of Pennsylvania Press.

Goldblatt, Beth. 2006. Gender and Social Assistance in the First Decade of Democracy: A Case Study of South Africa's Child Support Grant. *Politikon: South African Journal of Political Studies* 32, no. 2:239–57.

Goodfellow, D. M. 1939. *Principles of Economic Sociology: The Economics of Primitive Life as Illustrated from the Bantu Peoples of South and East Africa*. London: George Routledge.

Gordon, Linda. 1988. *Heroes of Their Own Lives: The Politics and History of Family Violence; Boston, 1880–1960*. Urbana: University of Illinois Press.

———. 1990. *Women, the State, and Welfare*. Madison: University of Wisconsin Press.

———. 1994. *Pitied but Not Entitled: Single Mothers and the History of Welfare, 1890–1935.* New York: Free Press.

Granlund, Stefan, and Tessa Hochfeld. 2020. "'That Child Support Grant Gives Me Powers'—Exploring Social and Relational Aspects of Cash Transfers in South Africa in Times of Livelihood Change." *Journal of Development Studies* 56, no. 6: 1230–44. https://doi.org/10.1080/00220388.2019.1650170.

Grant, M. J., and Hallman, K. K. 2008. "Pregnancy-Related School Dropout and Prior School Performance in KwaZulu-Natal, South Africa." *Studies in Family Planning* 39, no. 4: 369–82.

Grinspun, A. 2016. "No Small Change: The Multiple Impacts of the Child Support Grant on Child and Adolescent Well-Being." In *South African Child Gauge 2016,* edited by Delany A., S. Jehoma, and L. Lake. Cape Town: Children's Institute, University of Cape Town.

G'sell, Brady. 2020. "Multiple Maternities: Performative Motherhood and Support Seeking in South Africa." *Signs: Journal of Women in Culture and Society* 46, no. 1: 3–29. https://doi.org/10.1086/709217.

———. 2022. "'What Is Wrong with These Mens?': Marriage Rejection and Foreign Love in South Africa." In *Opting Out: Women Messing with Marriage around the World,* edited by Joanna Davidson and Dinah Hannaford. New Brunswick, NJ: Rutgers University Press.

———. 2024. "Diffuse and Enduring Disappointment: Considering kinship in South Africa and beyond." In *Difficult Attachments: Anxieties of Kinship and Care,* edited by Kathryn E. Goldfarb and Sandra Bamford. New Brunswick, NJ: Rutgers University Press.

Gumperz, John J. 1982. *Discourse Strategies.* New York: Cambridge University Press.

Guy, Jeff. 1990. "Gender Oppression in Southern Africa's Precapitalist Societies." In *Women and Gender in Southern Africa to 1945,* edited by Cheryl Walker. Cape Town: David Philip.

———. 2014. "Colonial Transformations and the Home." In *Ekhaya: The Politics of Home in KwaZulu-Natal,* edited by Meghan Healy-Clancy and Jason Hickel, 23–47. Pietermaritzburg, South Africa: University of KwaZulu-Natal Press.

———. 2018. "An Accommodation of Patriarchs: Theophilus Shepstone and the Foundations of the System of Native Administration in Natal." *Journal of Natal and Zulu History* 32, no. 1: 81–99. https://doi.org/10.1080/02590123.2018.1473996.

Guyer, Jane L. 1993. "Wealth in People and Self-Realization Africa." *Man* 28, no. 2: 243–65.

———. 1994. "Lineal Identities and Lateral Networks: The Logic of Polyandrous Motherhood." In *Nuptiality in Sub-Saharan Africa: Contemporary Anthropological and Demographic Perspectives,* edited by Caroline Bledsoe and Gilles Pison. Oxford: Clarendon Press.

———. 2004. *Marginal Gains: Monetary Transactions in Atlantic Africa.* Chicago: University of Chicago Press.

Guyer, Jane L., and Samuel M. Eno Belinga. 1995. "Wealth in People as Wealth in Knowledge: Accumulation and Composition in Equatorial Africa." *Journal of African History* 36, no. 1: 91–120.

Haarmann, Dirk. 1998. "From State Maintenance Grants to a New Child Support System: Building a Policy for Poverty Alleviation with Special Reference to the Financial, Social, and Developmental Impacts." PhD diss., University of the Western Cape.

Hall, C. 1979. "The Early Formation of Victorian Domestic Ideology." in *Fit Work for Women*, edited by S. Burman. New York: St. Martin's Press.

Hall, Katharine. 2021. "Income Poverty, Unemployment, and Social Grants." In *South African Child Gauge 2019*, edited by M. Shung-King, L. Lake, D. Sanders, and M. Hendricks, 7. Cape Town: Children's Institute, University of Cape Town.

Hall, Katharine, Helen Meintjes, and Winnie Sambu. 2014. "Demography of South Africa's Children." In *South African Child Gauge 2014*, edited by S. Mathews, L. Jamieson, L. Lake, and C. Smith. Cape Town: Children's Institute, University of Cape Town.

Hall, Katharine, and Dorrit Posel. 2012. "Inequalities in Children's Household Contexts: Place, Parental Presence, and Migration." In *South African Child Gauge 2012*, edited by Katharine Hall, I. Woolard, L. Lake, and C. Smith. Cape Town: Children's Institute, University of Cape Town.

Han, Clara. 2012. *Life in Debt: Times of Care and Violence in Neoliberal Chile.* Berkeley: University of California Press.

Hannaford, Dinah. 2017. *Marriage without Borders: Transnational Spouses in Neoliberal Senegal.* Philadelphia: University of Pennsylvania Press.

Hansen, Karen Tranberg. 2005. "Getting Stuck in the Compound: Some Odds against Social Adulthood in Lusaka, Zambia." *Africa Today* 51, no. 4: 3–16.

Hart, Keith. 2007. "Bureaucratic Form and the Informal Economy." In *Linking the Formal and Informal Economy: Concepts and Policies*, edited by Basudeb Guha-Khasnobis, Ravi Kanbur, and Elinor Ostrom. New York: Oxford University Press.

Hartman, Saidiya. 2021. *Wayward Lives, Beautiful Experiments: Intimate Histories of Riotous Black Girls, Troublesome Women, and Queer Radicals.* London: Serpent's Tail.

Harwood-Lejeune, A. 2000. "Rising Age at Marriage and Fertility in Southern and Eastern Africa." *European Journal of Population* 17, no. 3: 261–80.

Hassim, Shireen. 1993. "Family, Motherhood, and Zulu Nationalism: The Politics of the Inkatha Women's Brigade." *Feminist Review*, no. 43: 1–25.

———. 1999. "From Presence to Power: Women's Citizenship in a New Democracy." *Agenda*, no. 40 (Citizenship): 6–17.

———. 2003. "The Gender Pact and Democratic Consolidation: Institutionalizing Gender Equality in the South African State." *Feminist Studies* 29, no. 3: 504–28.

———. 2005. "Turning Gender Rights into Entitlements: Women and Welfare Provision in Postapartheid South Africa." *Social Research* 72, no. 3: 621–46.

———. 2006. *Women's Organizations and Democracy in South Africa: Contesting Authority.* Madison: University of Wisconsin Press.

———. 2008. "Social Justice, Care, and Developmental Welfare in South Africa: A Capabilities Perspective." *Social Dynamics* 34, no. 2: 104–18. https://doi.org/10.1080/02533950802278448.

———. 2009. "Framing Essay." *Social Dynamics* 35, no. 2: 348–54. https://doi.org/10.1080/02533950903076444.

———. 2014. "Texts and Tests of Equality: The Women's Charters and the Demand for Equality in South African Political History." *Agenda* 28, no. 2: 7–18. https://doi.org/10.1080/10130950.2014.929360.

———. 2019. *Voices of Liberation: Fatima Meer.* Cape Town: HSRC Press.

———. 2021. "Why Care?" *Transformation: Critical Perspectives on Southern Africa* 107: 53–66.

Hays, Sharon. 1996. *The Cultural Contradictions of Motherhood.* New Haven, CT: Yale University Press.

Healy-Clancy, Meghan. 2012. "Women and the Problem of Family in Early African Nationalist History and Historiography." *South African Historical Journal* 64, no. 3: 450–71. https://doi.org/10.1080/02582473.2012.667830.

———. 2017. "The Family Politics of the Federation of South African Women: A History of Public Motherhood in Women's Antiracist Activism; Winner of the 2017 Catharine Stimpson Prize for Outstanding Feminist Scholarship." *Signs: Journal of Women in Culture and Society* 42, no. 4: 843–66.

Hemson, David. 1977. "Dock Workers, Labour Circulation, and Class Struggles in Durban, 1940–59." *Journal of Southern African Studies* 4, no. 1: 88–124.

———. 1979. "Class Consciousness and Migrant Workers: Dock Workers of Durban." PhD thesis, University of Warwick.

———. 1996. "In the Eye of the Storm: Dock-Workers in Durban." In *The People's City: African Life in Twentieth-Century Durban,* edited by Paul Maylam and Iain Edwards, 145–73. Pietermaritzburg: University of Natal Press.

Henderson, W. P. M. 1904. *Durban: Fifty Years' Municipal History.* Durban: Robinson.

Higginbotham, Evelyn Brooks. 1994. *Righteous Discontent: The Women's Movement in the Black Baptist Church, 1880–1920.* Cambridge, MA: Harvard University Press.

Hirsch, Jennifer, and Holly Wardlow, eds. 2006. *Modern Loves: The Anthropology of Romantic Love and Companionate Marriage.* Ann Arbor: University of Michigan Press.

"History of Women's Struggle in South Africa." n.d. South African History Online. Accessed July 22, 2023. www.sahistory.org.za/article/history-womens-struggle-south-africa.

Hochfeld, Tessa. 2022. *Granting Justice: Cash, Care, and the Child Support Grant.* Cape Town: HSRC Press.

Hodgson, Dorothy L., and Sheryl McCurdy. 1996. "Wayward Wives, Misfit Mothers, and Disobedient Daughters: 'Wicked' Women and the Reconfiguration of Gender in Africa." *Canadian Journal of African Studies / Revue Canadienne des Études Africaines* 30, no. 1: 1–9. https://doi.org/10.2307/486037.

Hofmeyr, I. 1987. "Building a Nation from Words: Afrikaans Language, Literature, and Ethnic Identity, 1902–1924." In *The Politics of Race, Class, and Nationalism in Twentieth Century South Africa,* edited by S. Marks and S. Trapido, 113–14. London: Longman.

Holston, James. 2009. "Insurgent Citizenship in an Era of Global Urban Peripheries." *City and Society* 21, no. 2: 245–67. https://doi.org/10.1111/j.1548-744X.2009.01024.x.

Hosegood, V., N. McGrath, and T. Moultrie. 2009. "Dispensing with Marriage: Marital and Partnership Trends in Rural KwaZulu-Natal, South Africa, 2000–2006." *Demographic Research* 20: 279–312.

Howell, Signe. 2003. "Kinning: The Creation of Life Trajectories in Transnational Adoptive Families." *Journal of the Royal Anthropological Institute* 9, no. 3: 465–84.

Hughes, Heather. 2007. "The Coolies Will Elbow Us Out of the Country: African Reactions to Indian Immigration in the Colony of Natal, South Africa." *Labour History Review* 72, no. 2: 155–68. https://doi.org/10.1179/174581807X224588.

Hunt, N. 1999. *A Colonial Lexicon: Of Birth Ritual, Medicalization, and Mobility in the Congo*. Durham, NC: Duke University Press.

Hunter, Mark. 2002. "The Materiality of Everyday Sex: Thinking beyond 'Prostitution.'" *African Studies* 61, no. 1: 99–120. https://doi.org/10.1080/00020180220140091.

———. 2004. "Masculinities, Multiple-Sexual-Partners, and AIDS: The Making and Unmaking of Isoka in KwaZulu-Natal." *Transformation: Critical Perspectives on Southern Africa* 54, no. 1: 123–53. https://doi.org/10.1353/trn.2004.0019.

———. 2005. "Cultural Politics and Masculinities: Multiple Partners in Historical Perspective in KwaZulu-Natal." *Culture, Health, and Sexuality* 7, no. 4: 389–403.

———. 2006. "Fathers without Amandla: Zulu-Speaking Men and Fatherhood." In *Baba: Men and Fatherhood in South Africa*, edited by Linda M. Richter and Robert Morrell. Cape Town: Human Sciences Research Council Press.

———. 2009. "Providing Love: Sex and Exchange in Twentieth-Century South Africa." In *Love in Africa*, edited by Jennifer Cole and Lynn M. Thomas. Chicago: University of Chicago Press.

———. 2010. *Love in the Time of AIDS: Inequality, Gender, and Rights in South Africa*. Bloomington: Indiana University Press.

———. 2011. "Beneath the 'Zunami': Jacob Zuma and the Gendered Politics of Social Reproduction in South Africa." *Antipode*, February, 1–25. https://doi.org/10.1111/j.1467-8330.2010.00847.x.

———. 2015. "The Intimate Politics of the Education Market: High-Stakes Schooling and the Making of Kinship in Umlazi Township, South Africa." *Journal of Southern African Studies* 41, no. 6: 1279–1300. https://doi.org/10.1080/03057070.2015.1108545.

Hunter, Monica Wilson. 1961 [1936]. *Reaction to Conquest*. 2nd ed. London: Oxford University Press.

Hutchinson, Sharon Elaine. 1996. *Nuer Dilemmas: Coping with Money, War, and the State*. Berkeley: University of California Press.

Hyslop, J. 2000. "Why Did Apartheid's Supporters Capitulate? 'Whiteness,' Class, and Consumption in Urban South Africa, 1985–1995." *Society in Transition* 3, no. 1: 36–44.

———. 2008. "Gandhi, Mandela, and the African Modern." In *Johannesburg: The Elusive Metropolis*, edited by Sarah Nuttall and Achille Mbembe. Illustrated ed., 119–36. Durham, NC: Duke University Press Books.

———. 2018. "The Politics of Disembarkation: Empire, Shipping, and Labor in the Port of Durban, 1897–1947." *International Labor and Working-Class History* (May). https://doi.org/10.1017/S0147547917000254.

Ikuomola, A. D. 2015. "An Exploration of Life Experiences of Left Behind Wives in Edo State, Nigeria." *Journal of Comparative Research in Anthropology and Sociology* 6, no. 1: 289–307.

Iliffe, John. 1987. *The African Poor: A History*. Cambridge: Cambridge University Press.

Ingram, Joseph Forsyth. 1899. "The Story of an African Seaport, Being the History of the Port and Borough of Durban, the Seaport of Natal." www.lib.umich.edu/articles/details/FETCH-.

Irvine, Judith T. 1982. "Language and Affect: Some Cross-Cultural Issues." In *Contemporary Perceptions of Language: Interdisciplinary Dimensions*, edited by H. Byrnes, 31–47. Washington, DC: Georgetown University Press.

Irvine, Judith T., and Susan Gal. 2000. "Language Ideology and Linguistic Differentiation." In *Regimes of Language: Ideologies, Polities, and Identities*, edited by Paul Kroskrity, 35–84. Santa Fe, NM: School of American Research Press.

Isaacman, Allen. 1995. *Cotton Is the Mother of Poverty: Peasants, Work, and Rural Struggle in Colonial Mozambique, 1938–1961*. Portsmouth, NH: Heinemann.

Jackson, John L. 2005. *Real Black: Adventures in Racial Sincerity*. Chicago: University of Chicago Press.

Jackson, Michael, and Ivan Karp. 1990. *Personhood and Agency*. Washington, DC: Smithsonian Institution Press.

Jaffe, Aaron. 2020. *Social Reproduction Theory and the Socialist Horizon: Work, Power, and Political Strategy*. London: Pluto Press.

James, Deborah. 2014. *Money from Nothing: Indebtedness and Aspiration in South Africa*. Stanford, CA: Stanford University Press.

Jewkes, Rachel, and Robert Morrell. 2011. "Sexuality and the Limits of Agency among South African Teenage Women: Theorising Femininities and Their Connections to HIV Risk Practices." *Social Science and Medicine* 74, no. 11: 1729–37.

Jewkes, Rachel, Robert Morrell, Yandisa Sikweyiya, Kristin Dunkle, and Loveday Penn-Kekana. 2012. "Men, Prostitution, and the Provider Role: Understanding the Intersections of Economic Exchange, Sex, Crime, and Violence in South Africa." *PLoS ONE* 7, no. 7: e40821. https://doi.org/10.1371/journal.pone.0040821.

Johnson-Hanks, Jennifer. 2005. "When the Future Decides: Uncertainty and Intentional Action in Contemporary Cameroon." *Current Anthropology* 46, no. 3: 363–85.

Jones, Jeremy. 2009. " 'It's not normal, but its common': Elopement Marriage and the Mediated Recognition of Youth Identity in Harare, Zimbabwe." In Les nouvelles frontières de la Recherche sur l'enfance et la jeunesse en Afrique / New frontiers of child and youth research in Africa 1, no. 32. *CODESRIA*.

Kaarsholm, Preben. 2008. "Migration, Islam, and Identity Strategies in KwaZulu-Natal: Notes on the Making of Indians and Africans." Occasional Paper 13. Kolkata: Institute of Development Studies Kolkata. http://idsk.edu.in/wp-content/uploads/2015/07/OP-13.pdf.

Kandaswamy, Priya. 2021. *Domestic Contradictions: Race and Gendered Citizenship from Reconstruction to Welfare Reform*. Durham, NC: Duke University Press.

Kandiyoti, Deniz. 1988. "Bargaining with Patriarchy." *Gender and Society*. 2, no. 3: 274–90.

Kark, Sidney. 1950. "The Influence of Urban-Rural Migration on Bantu Health and Disease." *Leech* 21, no. 1: 23–37.

Kaseke, Edwin. 2002. "Zimbabwe." In *The State of Social Welfare: The Twentieth Century in Cross-National Review*, edited by John Dixon and Robert P. Scheurell. Westport, CT: Praeger.

Keane, Webb. 2007. *Christian Moderns: Freedom and Fetish in the Mission Encounter.* Berkeley: University of California Press.

Kearney, Brian. 2002. "Bamboo Square: A Documentary Narrative of the 'Indian and Native Cantonment' at the Point, 1873 to 1903." *Journal of Natal and Zulu History* 20, no. 1: 29–63. https://doi.org/10.1080/02590123.2002.11964117.

Khan, Sultan. 2012. "Changing Family Forms, Patterns, and Emerging Challenges within the South African Indian Diaspora." *Journal of Comparative Family Studies* 43, no. 1:133–50.

Khumalo, Bongani. 20002. "Restoring Respect for Family." *Saturday Star*, April 13.

Khunou, Grace. 2012. "Money and Gender Relations in the South African Maintenance System." *South African Review of Sociology* 43, no. 1: 4–22.

Klausen, Susanne. 1997. "'For the Sake of the Race': Eugenic Discourses of Feeblemindedness and Motherhood in the South African Medical Record, 1903–1926." *Journal of Southern African Studies* 23, no. 1: 27–50. https://doi.org/10.1080/03057079708708521.

Knijn, T, and L. Patel. 2018. "Family Life and Family Policy in South Africa: Responding to Past Legacies, New Opportunities, and Challenges." In *Family Life and Family Policy in South Africa: Dealing with the Legacy of Apartheid and Responding to New Opportunities and Challenges*, edited by T. Rostgaard and E. B. Eydal. Cheltenham: Edward Elgar Publishing.

Koorts, Lindie. 2013. "'The Black Peril Would Not Exist If It Were Not for a White Peril That Is a Hundred Times Greater': D. F. Malan's Fluidity on Poor Whiteism and Race in the Pre-Apartheid Era, 1912–1939." *South African Historical Journal* 65, no. 4: 555–76. https://doi.org/10.1080/02582473.2013.858764.

Kopytoff, Igor, and Suzanne Miers. 1977. "African 'Slavery' as an Institution of Marginality." In *Slavery in Africa: Historical and Anthropological Perspectives*, edited by Suzanne Miers and Igor Kopytoff. Madison: University of Wisconsin Press.

Kovacs, R., C. Ndashe, and J. Williams. 2013. "Twelve Years Later: How the Recognition of Customary Marriages Act of 1998 Is Failing Women in South Africa." In *Marriage, Land, and Custom: Essays on Law and Social Change in South Africa*. Cape Town: Juta.

Koven, S., and S. Michel. 1990. "Womanly Duties: Maternalist Politics and the Origins of the Welfare States in France, Germany, Great Britain, and the United States, 1880–1920." *American Historical Review* 95: 1076–108.

Kowalski, Julia. 2022. *Counseling Women: Kinship against Violence in India.* Philadelphia: University of Pennsylvania Press.

Krige, Eileen. 1936. "Changing Conditions in Marital Relations and Parental Duties among Urbanized Natives." *Africa* 9, no. 1: 1–23.

———. 1950. *The Social System of the Zulus.* Pietermaritzburg: Shuter and Shooter.

Kunzel, Regina G. 1993. *Fallen Women, Problem Girls: Unmarried Mothers and the Professionalization of Social Work, 1890–1945.* Yale Historical Publications. New Haven, CT: Yale University Press.

Kruger, L. 1991. "Gender, Community, and Identity: Women and Afrikaner Nationalism in the Volksmoeder Discourse of Die Boerevrou, 1919–1931." Master's thesis, University of Cape Town.

Kuper, H. 1960. *Indian People in Natal.* Durban: University of Natal Press.

Kuper, Leo, Hilstan Watts, and Ronald Davies. 1958. *Durban: A Study in Racial Ecology*. London, J. Cape; New York: Columbia University Press.

LaChance Adams, Sarah. 2014. *Mad Mothers, Bad Mothers, and What a "Good" Mother Would Do: The Ethics of Ambivalence*. New York: Columbia University Press.

La Hausse, Paul. 1982. "Drinking in a Cage: The Durban System and the 1929 Beer Hall Riots." *Africa Perspective* 20: 63–75.

———. 1984. "The Struggle for the City: Alcohol, the Ematsheni, and Popular Culture in Durban, 1902–1936." Master's thesis, University of Cape Town.

———. 1988. *Brewers, Beerhalls, and Boycotts: A History of Liquor in South Africa*. Johannesburg: Ravan Press.

———. 1990. "'The Cows of Nongoloza': Youth, Crime, and Amalaita Gangs in Durban, 1900–1936." *Journal of Southern African Studies* 16, no. 1: 79–111.

———. 1992. "Drink and Cultural Innovation in Durban: The Origins of the Beerhall in South Africa, 1902–1916," in *Liquor and Labour in Southern Africa*, edited by Jonathan Crush and Charles Ambler, 101–2. Athens: Ohio University Press.

——— 1997 "Alcohol, the Ematsheni, and Popular Culture in Durban, 1902–1936.'" In *The People's City: African Life in 20th-Century Durban*, edited by Iain Edwards and Paul Maylam. Pietermaritzburg, South Africa: University of Natal Press.

Lamb, Sarah. 2018. "Being Single in India: Gendered Identities, Class Mobilities, and Personhoods in Flux." *Ethos* 46, no. 1: 49–69. https://doi.org/10.1111/etho.12193.

Landau, Loren, ed. 2011. *"Introducing the Demons" in Exorcising the Demons Within: Xenophobia, Violence, and Statecraft in Contemporary South Africa*. New York: United Nations University Press.

Langa, Malose. 2020. *Becoming Men: Black Masculinities in a South African Township*. Johannesburg: Wits University Press.

Lange, Lis. 2003. *White, Poor, and Angry: White Working Class Families in Johannesburg*. Race and Representation. Burlington, VT: Ashgate.

Lareau, Annette. 2003. *Unequal Childhoods: Race, Class, and Family Life*. Berkeley: University of California Press.

Leclerc-Madlala, Suzanne. 2003. "Transactional Sex and the Pursuit of Modernity." *Social Dynamics* 29, no. 2: 213–33. https://doi.org/10.1080/02533950308628681.

Legassick, Martin. 1974. "Legislation, Ideology, and Economy in Post-1948 South Africa." *Journal of Southern African Studies* 1, no. 1: 5–35.

Leggett, Ted. 1999. "Poverty and Sex Work in Durban, South Africa." *Society in Transition* 30, no. 2: 157–67.

———. 2001. "Drugs, Sex Work, and HIV in Three South African Cities." *Society in Transition* 32, no 1: 101–9. https://doi.org/10.1080/21528586.2001.10419034.

Leggett, Ted, and Kevin Burton. 1999. "Now Selling in the Point: Talking to Durban's Drug Syndicates." *Crime and Conflict*, no. 16: 12–16.

Li, Tania Murray. 2017. "After Development: Surplus Population and the Politics of Entitlement." *Development and Change* 48, no. 6: 1247–61. https://doi.org/10.1111/dech.12344.

Liebenberg, Alida. 1994. "Authority, Avoidances, and Marriage: An Analysis of the Position of Gcaleka Women in Qwaninga, Willowvale District, Transkei." Master's thesis, Rhodes University.

Lister, Michael. 2005. "'Marshall-ing' Social and Political Citizenship: Towards a Unified Conception of Citizenship." *Government and Opposition* 40, no. 4: 471–91. https://doi.org/10.1111/j.1477-7053.2005.00161.x.

Lister, Ruth. 1994. "'She Has Other Duties'—Women, Citizenship, and Social Security." In *Social Security and Social Change: New Challenges to the Beveridge Model*, edited by Sally Baldwin and Jane Falkingham, 31–44. London: Harvester Wheatsheaf.

———. 2003. *Citizenship: Feminist Perspectives.* 2nd ed. New York: Palgrave Macmillan.

Livingston, Julie. 2005. *Debility and the Moral Imagination in Botswana.* Bloomington: Indiana University Press.

Lloyd C. B., ed. 2005. *Growing Up Global: The Changing Transitions to Adulthood in Developing Countries.* Washington, DC: National Academies Press.

Lund, Francie Jane. 2008. *Changing Social Policy: The Child Support Grant in South Africa.* Cape Town: HSRC Press.

Maasdorp, G., and A. S. B. Humphreys. 1975. *From Shantytown to Township: An Economic Study of African Poverty and Rehousing in a South African City.* Cape Town: Juta.

Madhavan, Sangeetha, Nicholas Townsend, and Anita Garey. 2008. "'Absent Breadwinners': Father-Child Connections and Paternal Support in Rural South Africa." *Journal of Southern African Studies* 34, no. 3: 647–63. https://doi.org/10.1080/03057070802259902.

Madhavan, S., and K. J. A. Thomas. 2005. "Childbearing and Schooling: New Evidence from South Africa." *Comparative Education Review* 49, no. 4: 452–67.

Mager, Ann. 1999. *Gender and the Making of a South African Bantustan: A Social History of the Ciskei, 1945–1959.* Oxford: James Currey.

———. 2010. *Beer, Sociability, and Masculinity in South Africa.* African Systems of Thought. Bloomington: Indiana University Press.

Magubane, Zine. 2010. "Attitudes towards Feminism among Women in the ANC, 1950–1990: A Theoretical Re-interpretation." In *The Road to Democracy in South Africa: Volume 4*, edited by South African Democracy Education Trust. Cape Town: Unisa Press.

Mains, Daniel, Craig Hadley, and Fasil Tessema. 2013. "Chewing over the Future: Khat Consumption, Anxiety, Depression, and Time among Young Men in Jimma, Ethiopia." *Culture, Medicine, and Psychiatry* 37, no. 1: 111–30.

Makhulu, Anne-Maria. 2015. *Making Freedom: Apartheid, Squatter Politics, and the Struggle for Home.* Durham, NC: Duke University Press.

Malkki, Liisa H. 1996. "Speechless Emissaries: Refugees, Humanitarianism, and Dehistoricization." *Cultural Anthropology* 11, no. 3: 377–404. https://doi.org/10.1525/can.1996.11.3.02a00050.

Mamashela, Mothokoa. 2006. "Some Hurdles in the Implementation of the Maintenance Act 99 of 1988." *Obiter* 27, no. 3: 590–605.

Manicom, Linzi. 2005. "Constituting 'Women' as Citizens: Ambiguities in the Making of Gendered Political Subjects in Post-Apartheid South Africa." In *(Un)Thinking Citizenship: Feminist Debates in Contemporary South Africa*, edited by Amanda Gouws. Gender in a Global/Local World. Burlington, VT: Ashgate.

Marais, Hein. 2011. *South Africa Pushed to the Limit: The Political Economy of Change*. Illustrated ed. London: Zed Books.

Margaretten, Emily. 2011. "Standing (K)in: Street Youth and Street Relatedness in South Africa." *City and Society* 23: 45–65. https://doi.org/10.1111/j.1548-744X.2011.01055.x.

———. 2013. "Making Hairdo: Paucity and Proverbs in Durban | News | National | Mail & Guardian." *Mail and Guardian Online*, September 6, 2013. http://mg.co.za/article /2013-09-06-00-making-hairdo-paucity-and-proverbs-in-durban.

———. 2015. *Street Life under a Roof: Youth Homelessness in South Africa*. Urbana: University of Illinois Press.

Mariner, Kathryn A. 2019. *Contingent Kinship: The Flows and Futures of Adoption in the United States*. Oakland: University of California Press.

Marks, Shula. 1986. "Patriotism, Patriarchy, and Purity: Natal and the Politics of Zulu Ethnic Consciousness." Working Paper. http://wiredspace.wits.ac.za/handle/10539/9116.

———. 1991. "Patriotism, Patriarchy, and Purity: Natal and the Politics of Zulu Ethnic Consciousness." In *The Creation of Tribalism in Southern Africa*, edited by Leroy Vail, 215–41. Berkeley: University of California Press.

Marks, Shula, and Stanley Trapido, eds. 1987. *The Politics of Race, Class, and Nationalism in Twentieth-Century South Africa*. New York: Longman.

Marshall, Thomas Humphrey. 1950. *Citizenship and Social Class: And Other Essays*. Cambridge: Cambridge University Press.

Marx, Karl. 1898. *The Eighteenth Brumaire of Louis Bonaparte*. Translated by Daniel De Leon. New York: International Publishing

Marteleto L., D. Lam, and V. Ranchhod. 2008. "Sexual Behavior, Pregnancy, and Schooling among Young People in Urban South Africa." *Studies in Family Planning* 39, no. 4: 351–68.

Mase, J. 2013. "Do Households Recompose around the South African Social Pension?" PhD diss., University of Manchester.

Masquelier, Adeline. 2005. "The Scorpion's Sting: Youth, Marriage, and the Struggle for Social Maturity in Niger." *Journal of the Royal Anthropological Institute* 211, no. 1: 59–83.

———. 2013. "Teatime: Boredom and the Temporalities of Young Men in Niger." *Africa: Journal of the International African Institute* 83, no. 3: 385–402.

Matthews, Thandiwe, Candice Groenewald, and Benita Moolman. 2022. "It's a Lifeline but It's Not Enough: The COVID-19 Social Relief of Distress Grant, Basic Income Support, and Social Protection in South Africa." Mowbray, South Africa: Black Sash.

Mauss, Marcel. 2000 [1924]. *The Gift: The Form and Reason for Exchange in Archaic Societies*. Translated by W. D. Halls. New York: W. W. Norton.

Mayer, Phillip. 1961. *Townsman or Tribesman: Conservatism and the Process of Urbanization in a South African City*. Cape Town: Oxford University Press.

Mayer, P., and I. Mayer. 1972. "Report on Research on Self-Organisation by Youth among the Xhosa Speaking Peoples of the Ciskei and Transkei." Vols. 1 and 2: "The Red Xhosa." Grahamstown, South Africa: Institute of Social and Economic Research, Rhodes University.

Maylam, Paul. 1983. "The 'Black Belt': African Squatters in Durban, 1935–1950." *Canadian Journal of African Studies / Revue Canadienne des Études Africaines* 17, no. 3: 413–28. https://doi.org/10.2307/484925.

———. 1988. "Municipal Fraud: The Operation of Durban's Native Revenue Account, 1908–1953." *Journal of Natal and Zulu History* 11, no. 1.

———. 1995. "Explaining the Apartheid City: 20 Years of South African Urban Historiography." *Journal of Southern African Studies* 21, no. 1: 19–38.

Mazibuko, Nokuthula Caritus, and Ikechukwu Umejesi. 2015. "Domestic Violence as a 'Class Thing': Perspectives from a South African Township." *Gender and Behaviour* 13, no. 1: 6584–93.

Mbembe, Achille. 2001. *On the Postcolony.* Berkeley: University of California Press.

———. 2019. *Necropolitics.* Durham, NC: Duke University Press.

Mbili, Q. 2016. "This Is How Durban's Poorest People Struggle to Survive in the Streets." *Daily Vox.* April 18. Accessed January 16, 2018. www.thedailyvox.co.za/durban-homeless-beggars-hawkers-poverty.

McClintock, Anne. 1991. "'No Longer in a Future Heaven': Women and Nationalism in South Africa." *Transition*, no. 51: 104. https://doi.org/10.2307/2935081.

———. 1993. "Family Feuds: Gender, Nationalism, and the Family." *Feminist Review*, no. 44: 61. https://doi.org/10.2307/1395196.

———. 1995. *Imperial Leather: Race, Gender and Sexuality in the Colonial Context.* New York: Routledge.

McKay, Ramah. 2012. "Afterlives: Humanitarian Histories and Critical Subjects in Mozambique." *Cultural Anthropology* 27, no. 2: 286–309. https://doi.org/10.1111/j.1548-1360.2012.01144.x.

McKendrick, Brian. 1971. "The Employment, Occupational Wastage, Occupational Mobility, and Work Satisfaction of Social Workers: A Study of the European Female Social Work Graduates of the Universities of Natal and the Witwatersrand, 1955 to 1965." Master's thesis, University of Natal, Durban.

McKinnon, Susan. 1999. "Domestic Exceptions: Evans-Pritchard and the Creation of Nuer Patrilineality and Equality." *Cultural Anthropology* 15, no. 1: 35–83.

McKinnon, Susan, and Fenella Cannell, eds. 2013. *Vital Relations: Modernity and the Persistent Life of Kinship.* Santa Fe, NM: School for Advanced Research Press.

Meagher, Kate. 2010. *Identity Economics: Social Networks and the Informal Economy in Nigeria.* London: James Currey.

Meehan, Katie, and Kendra Strauss. 2015. *Precarious Worlds: Contested Geographies of Social Reproduction.* Athens: University of Georgia Press.

Meer, Fatima. 1960. "African and Indian in Durban." *Africa South in Exile* 4, no. 4: 30–41.

———. 1969. *Portrait of Indian South Africans.* Durban: Avon House.

———. 1972. "Women and the Family in the Indian Enclave in South Africa." *Feminist Studies* 1, no. 2: 33–47.

Menkiti, A. 1984. "Person and Community in African Traditional Thought." In *African Philosophy: An Introduction*, edited by Richard A. Wright, 3rd ed., 171–82. Lanham, MD: University Press of America.

Mercer, Claire, Ben Page, and Martin Evans. 2008. *Development and the African Diaspora: Place and the Politics of Home.* London: Zed Books.

Merriman, John Xavier. 1913. Report of the Select Committee on European Employment and Labour Conditions (S.C. 9–13). Cape Town: Government Printer.

Meth, Charles. 2004. "Ideology and Social Policy: 'Handouts' and the Spectre of 'Dependency.'" *Transformation* 56: 1–30.

Mezzadri, Alessandra, Susan Newman, and Sara Stevano. 2022. "Feminist Global Political Economies of Work and Social Reproduction." *Review of International Political Economy* 29, no. 6: 1783–803. https://doi.org/10.1080/09692290.2021.1957977.

Miers, Suzanne, and Igor Kopytoff, eds. 1977. *Slavery in Africa: Historical and Anthropological Perspectives*. Madison: University of Wisconsin Press.

Mills, Shereen. 2004. "Women's Poverty and the Failure of the Judicial System: Research Findings on the Maintenance System in the Johannesburg Family Court." In
What about the Children? The Silent Voices in Maintenance, edited by Debbie Budlender and Bhekinkosi Moyo. Braamfontein: Tshwaranga Legal Advocacy Center.

Minkley, Gary. 1996. "I Shall Die Married to the Beer: Gender, 'Family' and Space in the
East London Locations, c. 1923–1952." *Kronos*, no. 23: 135–57.

Mizielińska, Joanna, Jacqui Gabb, and Agata Stasińska. 2018. "Editorial Introduction
to Special Issue: Queer Kinship and Relationships." *Sexualities* 21, no. 7: 975–82.
https://doi.org/10.1177/1363460717718511.

Mngomezulu, Garth Piet. 2006. "The Role of the Masakhane Campaign in Middelburg
between 1994 and 1998: The Case of Mhluzi Township." Master's thesis, University
of the Western Cape.

Modell, Judith S. 1994. *Kinship with Strangers: Adoption and Interpretations of Kinship
in American Culture*. Berkeley: University of California Press.

Mokoena, Hlonipha. 2011. *Magema Fuze: The Making of a Kholwa Intellectual*. Scottsville: University of KwaZulu-Natal Press.

Mol, Annemarie. 2002. *The Body Multiple: Ontology in Medical Practice*. Durham, NC:
Duke University Press.

Mol A., I. Moser, and J. Pols. 2010. "Care: Putting Practice into Theory." In *Care in
Practice: On Tinkering in Clinics, Homes, and Farms*, edited by A. Mol, I. Moser, and
J. Pols, 7–20. Bielefeld, Germany: Transcript.

Molewa, Edna. 2010. Remarks by the Minister of Social Development, Mrs. Edna
Molewa on the Occasion of FoodBank South Africa Gala Dinner. Premier Hotel,
Pretoria, 2 November. Retrieved December 10, 2013, www.dsd.gov.za.

Moodie, Dunbar T., with Vivienne Ndatshe. 1994. *Going for Gold: Men, Mines, and
Migration*. Berkeley: University of California Press.

Moore, Henrietta, and Megan Vaughan. 1994. *Cutting Down Trees: Gender, Nutrition,
and Agricultural Change in the Northern Province of Zambia, 1890–1990*. London:
James Currey.

Morrell, Robert. 2001. *Changing Men in Southern Africa*. Pietermaritzburg: University
of Natal Press; London: Zed Books.

Morrell, Robert, and Georgina Hamilton. 1996. *Political Economy and Identities in
KwaZulu-Natal: Historical and Social Perspectives*. Durban: Indicator Press.

Morrell, Robert, and Linda Richter. 2004. "The Fatherhood Project: Confronting Issues
of Masculinity and Sexuality." *Agenda* 18, no. 62: 36–44.

Mosoetsa, Sarah. 2011. *Eating from One Pot: The Dynamics of Survival in Poor South*

African Households. Johannesburg: Wits University Press. https://muse.jhu.edu/pub/299/oa_monograph/book/50545.

Moultrie, Tom A., and Ian M. Timæus. 2001. "Fertility and Living Arrangements in South Africa." *Journal of Southern African Studies* 27, no. 2: 207–23. https://doi.org/10.2307/823325.

———. 2003. "The South African Fertility Decline: Evidence from Two Censuses and a Demographic and Health Survey." *Population Studies* 57, no. 3: 265–83.

Muehlebach, Andrea. 2012. *The Moral Neoliberal: Welfare and Citizenship in Italy*. Chicago Studies in Practices of Meaning. Chicago: University of Chicago Press.

Muirhead, Jennifer. 2012. "'The Children of Today Make the Nation of Tomorrow': A Social History of Child Welfare in Twentieth Century South Africa." Master's thesis, Stellenbosch University. http://scholar.sun.ac.za/handle/10019.1/20199.

Muirhead, Jennifer, and Sandra Swart. 2015. "The Whites of the Child?: Race and Class in the Politics of Child Welfare in Cape Town, c. 1900–1924." *Journal of the History of Childhood and Youth* 8, no. 2: 229–53. https://doi.org/10.1353/hcy.2015.0019.

A. L. Muller. 1968. *Minority Interests: The Political Economy of the Coloured and Indian Communities in South Africa*. Johannesburg: South African Institute of Race Relations.

Murray, Colin. 1981. *Families Divided: The Impact of Labour Migration in Lesotho*. Cambridge: Cambridge University Press.

Narayan, Uma. 1997. *Dislocating Cultures: Identities, Traditions, and Third-World Feminism*. New York: Routledge.

Nattrass, Nicoli, and Jeremy Seekings. 2010. "The Economy and Poverty in the Twentieth Century in South Africa." Working Paper. Center for Social Science Research: University of Cape Town. https://open.uct.ac.za/handle/11427/20222.

Neves, David, and Andries Du Toit. 2012. "Money and Sociality in South Africa's Informal Economy." *Africa* 82, no. 1: 131–49.

Neves, David, Michael Samson, Ingrid van Niekerk, Sandile Hlatshways, and Andries Du Toit. 2009. *The Use and Effectiveness of Social Grants in South Africa*. Cape Town: Institute for Poverty, Land, and Agrarian Studies (PLAAS), University of Western Cape; Economic Policy Research Institute (EPRI), University of Cape Town.

Ngubane, H. 1981. "Marriage, Affinity, and the Ancestral Realm." In *Essays on African Marriage in Southern Africa*, edited by E. J. Krije and John L. Comaroff, 84–95. Cape Town: Juta.

Niehaus, Isak. 2012. "Gendered Endings: Narratives of Male and Female Suicides in the South African Lowveld." *Culture, Medicine and Psychiatry* 36, no. 2: 327–47. https://doi.org/10.1007/s11013-012-9258-y.

Norling, Johannes. 2019. "Family Planning and Fertility in South Africa under Apartheid." *European Review of Economic History* 23, no. 3: 365–95. https://doi.org/10.1093/ereh/hey016.

Nowbath, Ranji. 1978. *Durban Indian Child Welfare Society, 1927–1977*. Publication in commemoration of the fiftieth anniversary of the society. Durban: Lithotone.

Nussbaum, Martha. 2000. *Women and Human Development: The Capabilities Approach*. Cambridge: Cambridge University Press.

———. 2003. "Capabilities as Fundamental Entitlements: Sen and Social Justice." *Feminist Economics* 9, no. 2–3: 33–59.

———. 2011. *Creating Capabilities: The Human Development Approach.* Cambridge, MA: Harvard University Press.

Nuttall, Timothy Andrew. 1993. "Class, Race, and Nation: African Politics in Durban, 1929–1949." PhD diss., University of Oxford.

Nyamnjoh, Francis B. 2002. "'A Child Is One Person Only in the Womb': Domestication, Agency, and Subjectivity in the Cameroonian Grassfields." In *Postcolonial Subjectivities in Africa,* edited by Richard Werbner. London: Zed Books.

———. 2007. "From Bounded to Flexible Citizenship: Lessons from Africa." *Citizenship Studies* 11, no. 1: 73–82. https://doi.org/10.1080/13621020601099880.

———. 2018. "Citizenship." In *Critical Terms for the Study of Africa,* edited by Gaurav Desai and Adeline Masquelier, 56–68. Chicago: University of Chicago Press.

Ochonu, Moses. 2013. "African Colonial Economies: State Control, Peasant Maneuvers, and Unintended Outcomes." *History Compass* 11, no. 1: 1–13. https://doi.org/10.1111/hic3.12024.

O'Connor, J. S. 1996. "Understanding Women in Welfare States." *Current Sociology* 44, no. 2: 1–12.

O'Connor, J. S., Ann Shola Orloff, and S. Shaver. 1999. *States, Markets, Families: Gender, Liberalism, and Social Policy in Australia, Canada, Great Britain, and the United States.* Cambridge: Cambridge University Press.

Offe, Claus, and Guy Standing. 2011. "The Precariat: The New Dangerous Class." *Archives Européennes de Sociologie* 52, no. 3: 466.

O'Meara, Dan. 1983. *Volkskapitalisme: Class, Capitalism and Ideology in the Development of Afrikaner Nationalism, 1934–1948.* Johannesburg: Ravan Press.

———. 1996. *Forty Lost Years: The Apartheid State and the Politics of the National Party, 1948–1994.* Johannesburg: Ravan Press.

Ong, Aihwa. 1999. *Flexible Citizenship: The Cultural Logics of Transnationality.* Durham, NC: Duke University Press.

O'Reilly, Andrea. 2006. *Rocking the Cradle: Thoughts on Feminism, Motherhood, and the Possibility of Empowered Motherhood.* Toronto: Demeter.

O'Reilly, Andrea, ed. 2004. *From Motherhood to Mothering: The Legacy of Adrienne Rich's "Of Woman Born."* New York: State University of New York Press.

Orloff, Ann Shola. 1993. "Gender and the Social Rights of Citizenship: The Comparative Analysis of Gender Relations and Welfare States." *American Sociological Review* 58, no. 3: 303–28. https://doi.org/10.2307/2095903.

———. 2009. "Gendering the Comparative Analysis of Welfare States: An Unfinished Agenda." *Sociological Theory* 27, no. 3: 317–43. https://doi.org/10.1111/j.1467-9558.2009.01350.x.

Oyewumi, Oyeronke. 2000. "Family Bonds/Conceptual Binds: African Notes on Feminist Epistemologies." *Signs: Journal of Women in Culture and Society* 25, no. 4: 1093–98. https://doi.org/10.1086/495526.

Padayachee, Vishnu. 1999. "Struggle, Collaboration, and Democracy: The 'Indian Community' in South Africa, 1860–1999." *Economic and Political Weekly,* February 13, 1999.

Parnell, S. 1992. "Slums, Segregation, and Poor Whites in Johannesburg, 1920–1934." In *White but Poor: Essays on the History of Poor Whites in Southern Africa, 1880–1940*, edited by R. Morrell. Pretoria: University of South Africa.

Parry, J., and M. Bloch. 1989. "Introduction: Money and the Morality of Exchange." In *Money and the Morality of Exchange*, edited by J. Parry and M. Bloch. Cambridge: Cambridge University Press.

Patel, L. 2011. "Race, Inequality, and Social Welfare: South Africa's Imperial Legacy." In *Colonialism and Welfare: Social Policy and the British Imperial Legacy*, edited by J. Midgley. Cheltenham: Edward Elgar.

Patel, L., T. Hochfeld, J. Moodley, and R. Mutwali. 2012. "The Gender Dynamics and Impact of the Child Support Grant in Doornkop, Soweto." CSDA Research Report. Johannesburg: Centre for Social Development in Africa, University of Johannesburg. www.childwatch.uio.no/publications/research-reports/gender%20dynamics%20and%20child%20support.pdf.

Patel, Leila, Trudie Knijn, and Frits Van Wel. 2015. "Child Support Grants in South Africa: A Pathway to Women's Empowerment and Child Well-Being?" *Journal of Social Policy* 44, no. 2: 377–97. https://doi.org/10.1017/S0047279414000919.

Pateman, Carol. 1988. *The Sexual Contract*. Cambridge, MA: Polity Press.

Patterson, Ann. 1953. *Colour and Culture in South Africa: A Study of the Status of the Cape Coloured People within the Social Structure of the Union of South Africa*. Volume 6. New York: Grove Press.

Pauli, Julia. 2019. *The Decline of Marriage in Namibia: Kinship and Social Class in a Rural Community*. Bielefeld, Germany: Transcript.

Peterson, Bhekizizwe. 2003. "Kwaito, 'dawgs,' and the Antimonies of Hustling." *African Identities* 1, no. 2: 197–213. https://doi.org/10.1080/1472584032000175650.

Petryna, A. 2002. *Life Exposed: Biological Citizens after Chernobyl*. Princeton, NJ: Princeton University Press.

Petryna, Adriana, and Karolina Follis. 2015. "Risks of Citizenship and Fault Lines of Survival." *Annual Review of Anthropology* 44: 401–17.

Pettifor, Audrey, Catherine MacPhail, Althea Anderson, and Suzanne Maman. 2012. "'If I Buy the Kellogg's [sic] Then He Should [Buy] the Milk': Young Women's Perspectives on Relationship Dynamics, Gender Power, and HIV Risk in Johannesburg, South Africa." *Culture, Health, and Sexuality* 14, no. 5: 477–90.

Phillips, Anne. 1993. *Democracy and Difference*. Cambridge: Polity Press.

Pinto, Sarah. 2011. "Rational Love, Relational Medicine: Psychiatry and the Accumulation of Precarious Kinship." *Culture, Medicine, and Psychiatry* 35, no. 3: 376–95.

Polanyi, Karl. 2001 [1944]. *The Great Transformation: The Political and Economic Origins of Our Time*. Boston: Beacon Press.

Posel, Deborah. 1992. *The Making of Apartheid, 1948–1961: Conflict and Compromise*. Oxford: Clarendon Press.

———. 2005. "The Case for a Welfare State: Poverty and the Politics of the Urban African Family in the 1930s and 1940s." In *South Africa's 1940s: Worlds of Possibilities*, edited by Saul Dubow and Alan Jeeves, 64–86. Cape Town: Double Storey.

———. 2006. "Marriage at the Drop of a Hat: Housing and Partnership in South Africa's Urban African Townships, 1920s–1960s." *History Workshop Journal* 61: 57–76.

Posel, Dorrit, and Daniela Casale. 2013. "The Relationship between Sex Ratios and Marriage Rates in South Africa." *Applied Economics* 45, no. 5: 663–76.

Posel, Dorrit, and S. Rudwick. 2014. "Ukukipita (Cohabiting): Socio-Cultural Constraints in Urban Zulu Society." *Journal of Asian and African Studies* 49, no. 3: 282–97.

Posel, Dorrit, Stephanie Rudwick, and Daniela Casale. 2011. "Is Marriage a Dying Institution in South Africa? Exploring Changes in Marriage in the Context of Ilobolo Payments." *Agenda* 25, no. 1: 102–11. https://doi.org/10.1080/10130950.2011.575589.

Povinelli, Elizabeth A. 2006. *The Empire of Love: Toward a Theory of Intimacy, Genealogy, and Carnality.* Durham, NC: Duke University Press.

Preston-Whyte, Eleanor 1974. "Kinship and Marriage." In *The Bantu-Speaking Peoples of Southern Africa*, edited by W. D. Hammond-Tooke and Isaac Schapera. London: Routledge and K. Paul.

———. 1978. "Families without Marriage: A Zulu Case Study." In *Social System and Tradition in Southern Africa*, edited by W. J. Argyle and Eleanor Preston-Whyte. Cape Town: Oxford University Press.

———. 1993. "Women Who Are Not Married: Fertility, 'Illegitimacy,' and the Nature of Households and Domestic Groups among Single African Women in Durban." *South African Journal of Sociology* 24, no. 3: 63–71.

Preston-Whyte, E., and M. Zondi. 1992. "Assessing Illegitimacy in South Africa." In *Questionable Issue: Illegitimacy in South Africa*, edited by S. Burman and E. Preston-Whyte. Cape Town: Oxford University Press.

Prince, Ruth. 2006. "Popular Music and Luo Youth in Western Kenya: Ambiguities of Modernity, Morality, and Gender Relations in the Era of AIDS." In *Navigating Youth, Generating Adulthood: Social Becoming in an African Context*, edited by Catrine Christiansen, Mats Utas, and Henrik E. Vigh. Uppsala, Sweden: Nordiska Afrikainstitutet.

Rabe, Marlize. 2017. "Family Policy for All South African Families." *International Social Work* 60, no. 5: 1189–200.

Ratele, Kopano, Tamara Shefer, and Lindsay Clowes. 2012. "Talking South African Fathers: A Critical Examination of Men's Constructions and Experiences of Fatherhood and Fatherlessness." *South African Journal of Psychology* 42, no. 4: 553–63.

Redding, Sean. 1992. "Beer Brewing in Umtata: Women, Migrant Labor, and Social Control in a Rural Town." In *Liquor and Labor in Southern Africa*, edited by Jonathan Crush and Charles Ambler, 235–51. Athens: Ohio University Press.

Redfield, Peter. 2013. *Life in Crisis: The Ethical Journey of Doctors without Borders.* Berkeley: University of California Press.

Republic of South Africa. 1996. *Constitution of the Republic of South Africa.* www.gov.za/documents/constitution/constitution-republic-south-africa-1996-1.

Republic of South Africa (RSA). 2015. *Budget Highlights Card.* Retrieved July 16, 2015, www.treasury.gov.za.

Reynolds, Lindsey. 2016. "Deciphering the 'Duty of Support': Caring for Young People in KwaZulu-Natal, South Africa." *Social Dynamics* 42, no. 2: 253–72. https://doi.org/10.1080/02533952.2016.1218141.

Rheinalt-Jones, J. D. 1949. "Social Welfare." In *Handbook of Race Relations in South Africa*, edited by E. Hellman. London: Oxford.

Rice, Kathleen. 2017. "Rights and Responsibilities in Rural South Africa: Implications for Gender, Generation, and Personhood." *Journal of the Royal Anthropological Institute* 23no. 1: 28–41. https://doi.org/10.1111/1467-9655.12542.

———. 2023. *Rights and Responsibilities in Rural South Africa: Gender, Personhood, and the Crisis of Meaning.* Bloomington: Indiana University Press.

Rich, Adrienne. 1986 [1976]. *Of Woman Born: Motherhood as Experience and Institution.* London: Virago.

Riesman, Paul. 1986. "The Person and the Life Cycle in African Social Life and Thought." *African Studies Review* 29, no. 2: 71–138.

Robbins, Jessica C. 2020. *Aging Nationally in Contemporary Poland: Memory, Kinship, and Personhood.* New Brunswick, NJ: Rutgers University Press.

Roberts, Dorothy E.1993. "Racism and Patriarchy in the Meaning of Motherhood." *Faculty Scholarship.* Paper 595. http://scholarship.law.upenn.edu/faculty_scholarship/595.

Robeyns, Ingrid. 2003. "Sen's Capability Approach and Gender Inequality: Selecting Relevant Capabilities." *Feminist Economics* 9, no. 2–3: 61–92. https://doi.org/10.1080/1354570022000078024.

Rogerson, C. M. 1992. "'In Their Right Place': Beer Halls in Johannesburg, 1938–1962." *African Studies* 51, no. 1: 95–122. https://doi.org/10.1080/00020189208707751.

Rondganger, L. 2015. "Housing Time Bomb for Poor." *Daily News,* October 12.

Roos, Neil. 2015. "Alcohol Panic, Social Engineering, and Some Reflections on the Management of Whites in Early Apartheid Society, 1948–1960." *Historical Journal* 58, no. 4: 1167–89.

Roth, C. 2008. "'Shameful!' The Inverted Intergenerational Contract in Bobo-Dioulasso, Burkina Faso." In *Generations in Africa: Connections and Conflicts,* edited by Erdmute Alber, Sjaak Van Der Geest, and Susan Reynolds Whyte. Berlin: Lit.

Ruddick, Sara. 1995. *Maternal Thinking: Toward a Politics of Peace.* Boston: Beacon Press.

Ruddick, Sue. 2008. "At the Horizons of the Subject: Neo-Liberalism, Neo-Conservatism, and the Rights of the Child, Part Two: Parent, Caregiver, State." *Gender, Place, and Culture* 14, no. 6: 627–40.

Rudwick, Stephanie, and Dorrit Posel. 2014. "Contemporary Functions of Ilobolo (Bridewealth) in Urban South African Zulu Society." *Journal of Contemporary African Studies* 32, no. 1: 118–36. https://doi.org/10.1080/02589001.2014.900310.

———. 2015. "Zulu Bridewealth (Ilobolo) and Womanhood in South Africa." *Social Dynamics,* July, 1–18. https://doi.org/10.1080/02533952.2015.1060683.

Rugunanan, Pragna, and Ria Smit. 2011. "Seeking Refuge in South Africa: Challenges Facing a Group of Congolese and Burundian Refugees." *Development Southern Africa* 28, no. 5: 705–18.

Sadler, Katherine D. 2002. "'Trouble Was Brewing': South African Women, Gender Identity, and Beer Hall Protests, 1929 and 1959." PhD diss., University of California, Los Angeles.

Sagner, A. 2000. "Ageing and Social Policy in South Africa: Historical Perspectives with Particular Reference to the Eastern Cape." *Journal of Southern African Studies* 26: 523–53.

Sainsbury, Diane. 1996. *Gender, Equality, and Welfare States*. Cambridge: Cambridge University Press.

Sambureni, N. T. 1996. "State Labour Control Policies and African Workers of Durban, South Africa, 1960–1985." *South African Historical Journal* 34, no. 1: 77–105.

———. 1997. "The Apartheid City and Its Labouring Class: African Workers and the Independent Trade Union Movement in Durban, 1959–1985." PhD diss., University of South Africa.

Sandwell, Rachel. 2022. "Fantasy States: Nationalism, Intimacy, and Transgression in South African Women's Political Memoirs." *Signs: Journal of Women in Culture and Society* 47, no. 3: 765–87. https://doi.org/10.1086/717734.

Schapera, Isaac. 1940. *Married Life in and African Tribe*. London: Faber and Faber.

Schatzberg, Michael G. 2001. *Political Legitimacy in Middle Africa: Father, Family, Food*. Bloomington: Indiana University Press.

Scheper-Hughes, Nancy. 1993. *Death without Weeping: The Violence of Everyday Life in Brazil*. Berkeley: University of California Press.

Schumaker, Lynette. 1996. "A Tent with a View: Colonial Officers, Anthropologists, and the Making of the Field in Northern Rhodesia, 1937–1960." *Osiris* 11 (January): 237–58. https://doi.org/10.1086/368762.

Schuster, Caroline E. 2015. *Social Collateral: Women and Microfinance in Paraguay's Smuggling Economy*. Berkeley: University of California Press.

Seekings, Jeremy. 2000. "The Origins of Social Citizenship in Pre-Apartheid South Africa." *South African Journal of Philosophy* 19, no. 4: 386–404. https://doi.org/10.1080/02580136.2000.11644285.

———. 2007. " 'Not a Single White Person Should Be Allowed to Go Under': Swartgevaar and the Origins of South Africa's Welfare State, 1924–1929." *Journal of African History* 48, no. 3: 375–94.

———. 2008. "The Carnegie Commission and the Backlash against Welfare State-Building in South Africa, 1931–1937." *Journal of Southern African Studies* 34 no. 3: 515–37. https://doi.org/10.1080/03057070802259688.

———. 2016. "State-Building, Market Regulation and Citizenship in South Africa." *European Journal of Social Theory* 19 no. 2: 191–209. https://doi.org/10.1177/13684310 15600021.

Seekings, Jeremy, and Nicoli Nattrass. 2005. *Class, Race, and Inequality in South Africa*. New Haven, CT: Yale University Press.

Semley, Lorelle. 2010. *Mother Is Gold, Father Is Glass: Gender and Colonialism in a Yoruba Town*. Bloomington: Indiana University Press.

———. 2012. "Public Motherhood in West Africa as Theory and Practice." *Gender and History* 24 no. 3: 600–616. https://doi.org/10.1111/j.1468-0424.2012.01698.x.

Sen, Amartya. 1990. "Gender and Cooperative Conflicts." In *Persistent Inequality*, edited by I. Tinker. New York: Oxford University Press.

———. 1999. *Development as Freedom*. Oxford: Oxford University Press.

Sennott, C., G. Reniers, F. X. Gómez-Olivé, and J. Menken. 2016. "Premarital Births and Union Formation in Rural South Africa." *International Perspectives on Sexual and Reproductive Health* 42, no. 4: 187–96.

Sevenhuijsen, Selma, Vivienne Bozalek, Amanda Gouws, and Marie Minnaar-

McDonald. 2003. "South African Social Welfare Policy: An Analysis Using the Ethic of Care." *Critical Social Policy* 23, no. 3: 299–321. https://doi.org/10.1177/026101 83030233001.

Shipton, Parker. 2007. *The Nature of Entrustment: Intimacy, Exchange, and the Sacred in Africa.* Yale Agrarian Studies. New Haven, CT: Yale University Press.

Shope, J. H. 2006. "'Lobola Is Here to Stay': Rural Black Women and the Contradictory Meanings of Lobolo in Post-Apartheid South Africa." *Agenda* 68: 64–72.

Silva, E. 1996. *Good Enough Mothering?: Feminist Perspectives on Lone Motherhood.* London: Routledge.

Silverstein, Michael, and Greg Urban, eds. 1996. *Natural Histories of Discourse.* Chicago: University of Chicago Press.

Simons, H. J., and Ray E. Simons. 1969. *Class and Colour in South Africa, 1850–1950.* Harmondsworth: Penguin.

Simons, Harold Jack. 1968. *African Women: Their Legal Status in South Africa.* Evanston, IL: Northwestern University Press.

Singh, D., K. Naidoo, and L. Mokolobate. 2004. "Coming to Court for Child Support—the Policy, the Practice and Reality: A Case Study of Black Women in the Maintenance System at the Johannesburg Family Court [2002–2004]." *Acta Criminologica* 17, no. 2: 143.

Sirijit, Sunanta. 2013. "Gendered Nation and Classed Modernity: Perceptions of Mia Farang (Foreigners' Wives) in Thai Society." In *Cleavage, Connection, and Conflict in Rural, Urban, and Contemporary Asia*, edited by Tim Bunnell, D. Parthasarathy, and Eric C. Thompson, 183–99. Dordrecht: Springer.

Sirijit, Sunanta, and Leonora C. Angeles. 2013. "From Rural Life to Transnational Wife: Agrarian Transition, Gender Mobility, and Intimate Globalization in Transnational Marriages in Northeast Thailand." *Gender, Place, and Culture* 20, no. 6: 699–17.

Smith, Daniel Jordan. 2003. "Patronage, Per Diems and 'The Workshop Mentality': The Practice of Family Planning Programs in Southeastern Nigeria." *World Development* 31, no. 4: 703–15.

———. 2004. "Contradictions in Nigeria's Fertility Transition: The Burdens and Benefits of Having People." *Population and Development Review* 30, no. 2: 221–38.

Sodergren, Marie-Claire, Vipasana Karkee, and Steven Kapsos. 2023. "Assessing the Current State of the Global Labour Market: Implications for Achieving the Global Goals." International Labour Organization. *ILOSTAT* (blog). March 13, 2023. https://ilostat.ilo.org/assessing-the-current-state-of-the-global-labour-market-implications-for-achieving-the-global-goals/.

Soga, John Henderson. 1932. *The Ama-Xosa: Life and Customs.* Lovedale, South Africa: Lovedale Press.

Soske, Jon. 2017. *Internal Frontiers: African Nationalism and the Indian Diaspora in Twentieth-Century South Africa.* Athens,: Ohio University Press.

South African Congress Alliance. 1955. "Freedom Charter." United Nations Center against Apartheid.

South African Law Commission (SALC). 1997. *Project 100: Review of the Maintenance System.* Issue paper 5. www.justice.gov.za.

———. 2014. *Project 100: Review of the Maintenance System. Issue paper 28.* www.justice
.gov.za.

Southall, Roger. 2016. *The New Black Middle Class in South Africa.* Johannesburg:
Jacana.

Stack, Carol B. 1974. *All Our Kin: Strategies for Survival in a Black Community.* New
York: Harper and Row.

Stack, Carol B., and Linda M. Burton. 1993. "Kinscripts." *Journal of Comparative Family
Studies* 24, no. 2: 157–70.

STATSSA. 2012. *Documented Immigrants in South Africa, 2011* (D0351-D). Statistics
South Africa. Pretoria: Stats SA.

———. 2014. "Quarterly Labour Force Survey: Quarter 2 (April to June), 2014 Press
Statement." Statistical Release P0211. Pretoria: Stats SA. Accessed from www.statssa
.gov.za/?p=2951 on November 14, 2015.

———. 2015. "General Household Survey 2014." Statistical Release P0318. Statistics
South Africa. www.statssa.gov.za/publications/P0318/P0318.2014.pdf.

———. 2020. "General Household Survey 2018." Statistical Release P0318. Pretoria,
South Africa: Statistics South Africa. www.statssa.gov.za/publications/P0318/P0318
2018.pdf.

Stephens, Rhiannon. 2013. *A History of African Motherhood.* Cambridge: Cambridge
University Press.

Stevenson, Lisa. 2014. *Life Beside Itself: Imagining Care in the Canadian Arctic.* Oakland: University of California Press.

Stoler, Ann Laura. 2001. "Tense and Tender Ties: The Politics of Comparison in North
American History and (Post) Colonial Studies." *Journal of American History* 88, no.
3: 829. https://doi.org/10.2307/2700385.

———. 2002. *Carnal Knowledge and Imperial Power: Race and the Intimate in Colonial
Rule.* Berkeley: University of California Press.

Stout, Noelle. 2015. "When a Yuma Meets Mama: Commodified Kin and the Affective
Economies of Queer Tourism in Cuba." *Anthropological Quarterly* 88, no. 3: 665–91.
https://doi.org/10.1353/anq.2015.0040.

Strathern, Marilyn. 1988. *The Gender of the Gift: Problems with Women and Problems
with Society in Melanesia.* Studies in Melanesian Anthropology 6. Berkeley: University of California Press.

———. 1992. *Reproducing the Future: Essays on Anthropology, Kinship, and the New
Reproductive Technologies.* Manchester: Manchester University Press.

Strebel, Anna, Tamara Shefer, Cheryl Potgieter, Claire Wagner, and Shabalala Nokuthula. 2013. "'She's a Slut . . . and It's Wrong': Youth Constructions of Taxi Queens
in the Western Cape." *South African Journal of Psychology* 43, no. 1: 71–80.

Swanson, M. W. 1976. "'The Durban System': Roots of Urban Apartheid in Colonial
Natal." *African Studies*, 35.

———. 1977. "The Sanitation Syndrome: Bubonic Plague and Urban Native Policy in the
Cape Colony, 1900–1909." *Journal of African History* 18, no. 3: 387–410.

———. 1983. "'The Asiatic Menace': Creating Segregation in Durban, 1870–1900." *International Journal of African Historical Studies* 16, no. 3: 401. https://doi.org/10.2307/
218743.

Swidler, Ann, and Susan Cotts Watkins. 2007. "Ties of Dependence: AIDS and Trans-actional Sex in Rural Malawi." *Studies in Family Planning* 38, no. 3: 147–62.

Tafira, Kenneth Matesanwa. 2010. "Black Racism in Alexandra: Cross-Border Love Relationships and Negotiation of Difference in Post-Aapartheid South African So-ciety." Master's thesis, University of the Witwatersrand.

TallBear, Kim. 2019. "Caretaking Relations, Not American Dreaming." *Kalfou* 6, no. 1. https://doi.org/10.15367/kf.v6i1.228.

Tallie, T. J. 2019. *Queering Colonial Natal: Indigeneity and the Violence of Belonging in Southern Africa*. Minneapolis: University of Minnesota Press.

Taylor, C. 1994. "The Politics of Recognition." In *Multiculturalism: Examining the Poli-tics of Recognition*, edited by Amy Gutman. Princeton, NJ: Princeton University Press.

Taylor, V. 2002. "Committee of Inquiry into a Comprehensive System of Social Security for South Africa 2002." Transforming the Present, Protecting the Future: Consoli-dated Report of the Committee of Inquiry into a Comprehensive System of Social Security for South Africa. Pretoria: Government Printer.

Teppo, Annika Bjornsdotter. 2004. *The Making of a Good White: A Historical Ethnog-raphy of the Rehabilitation of Poor Whites in a Suburb of Cape Town*. Research Series in Anthropology. Helsinki: Helsinki University Press.

The Economist. 2021. "Unpicking Inequality in South Africa." September 23, 2021. www.economist.com/middle-east-and-africa/2021/09/23/unpicking-inequality-in-south-africa.

Thelen, Tatjana, and Erdmute Alber, eds. 2017. *Reconnecting State and Kinship*. Phila-delphia: University of Pennsylvania Press.

Thelen, Tatjana, and Cati Coe. 2019. "Political Belonging through Elderly Care: Tempo-ralities, Representations, and Mutuality." *Anthropological Theory* 19, no. 2: 279–99. https://doi.org/10.1177/1463499617742833.

Thiara, Ravi K. 1999. "The African-Indian Antithesis? The 1949 Durban 'Riots' in South Africa." In *Thinking Identities*, edited by Avtar Brah, Mary J. Hickman, and Máirtín Mac An Ghaill, 161–84. London: Palgrave Macmillan. https://doi.org/10.1057/9780230375963_8.

Thieme, Tatiana. 2013. "The 'Hustle' amongst Youth Entrepreneurs in Mathare's Infor-mal Waste Economy." *Journal of Eastern African Studies* 7, no. 3: 389–412.

Thomas, Lynn M. 2003. *Politics of the Womb: Women, Reproduction, and the State in Kenya*. Berkeley: University of California Press.

———. 2006. "The Modern Girl and Racial Respectability in 1930s South Africa." *Jour-nal of African History* 47, no. 3: 461–90.

———. 2019. "Consumer Culture and 'Black Is Beautiful' in Apartheid South Africa and Early Postcolonial Kenya." *African Studies* 78, no. 1: 6–32. https://doi.org/10.1080/00020184.2018.1540530.

Thomas, Lynn M., and Jennifer Cole. 2009. "Introduction: Thinking through Love in Africa." In *Love in Africa*, edited by Jennifer Cole and Lynn M. Thomas. Chicago: University of Chicago Press.

Tibandebage, Paula, and Maureen MacIntosh. 2005. "The Market Shaping of Charges,

Trust, and Abuse: Health Care Transactions in Tanzania." *Social Science and Medicine* 61, no. 7: 1385–95.

Ticktin, Miriam I. 2011. *Casualties of Care: Immigration and the Politics of Humanitarianism in France.* Berkeley: University of California Press.

Tilly, Charles. 2008. *Contentious Performances.* Cambridge: Cambridge University Press.

Time. 1960. "South Africa: The Sharpeville Massacre." April 4, 1960. https://content. time.com/time/subscriber/article/0,33009,869441,00.html.

Transvaal Government. 1908. *Report of the Transvaal Indigency Commission, 1906–1908* (T.G. 13–08). Pretoria, South Africa: Government Publishing and Stationery Office.

Transvaal Provincial Administration (TPA). 1922. Report of the Local Government Commission. T.P. 21, Pretoria.

Tronto J. 1993. *Moral Boundaries: A Political Argument for an Ethic of Care.* London: Routledge.

Trotter, Henry. 2007. "The Women of Durban's Dockside Sex Industry." In *Undressing Durban,* edited by Rob Pattman and Sultan Kahn, 441–52. Durban: Madiba Publications.

———. 2009. "Soliciting Sailors: The Temporal Dynamics of Dockside Prostitution in Durban and Cape Town." *Journal of Southern African Studies* 35, no. 3: 699–713. https://doi.org/10.1080/03057070903101904.

Ungerson C. 1990. "The Language of Care: Crossing the Boundaries." In *Gender and Caring: Work and Welfare in Britain and Scandinavia,* edited by C. Ungerson, 8–33. London: Harvester Wheatsheaf.

United Nations, Department of Economic and Social Affairs (UNDESA). 2015. Trends in International Migrant Stock: Migrants by Destination and Origin (United Nations database, POP/DB/MIG/Stock/Rev.2015).

United Nations, Department of Economic and Social Affairs (UNDESA), and Gapminder. 2019. "Total Fertility Rate in South Africa from 1925 to 2020." Chart. Statista. August 31, 2019. www.statista.com/statistics/1069710/fertility-rate-south-africa -historical/.

United Nations High Commissioner for Refugees (UNHCR). 2012. Global Trends 2012—Displacement: The New 20th Century Challenge. Geneva: United Nations High Commissioner for Refugees.

University of Durban–Westville. 1985. "Aspects of Family Life in the South African Indian Community, Proceedings of a Conference." Institute for Social and Economic Research. March 25–26, University of Durban–Westville.

University of Natal. 1952. *The Durban Housing Survey.* Pietermaritzburg: University of Natal Press.

———. 1959a. "A Survey of Bantu Income and Expenditure in Durban (Interim Report)." Durban: Department of Economics, University of Natal. Killie-Campbell archive, Bourquin papers KCM 99/42/30/4.

———. 1959b. Rent-Paying Capacity and the Cost of Living of Urban African Families in Durban. Durban: Department of Economics, University of Natal.

Vahed, Goolam. 1997. "The Making of 'Indianess': Indian Politics in South Africa during the 1930s and 1940s." *Journal of Natal and Zulu History* 17, no. 1: 1–36. https://doi.org/10.1080/02590123.1997.11964094.

Van Allen, Judith. 2009. "Radical Citizenship: Powerful Mothers and Equal Rights." In *Power, Gender, and Social Change in Africa*, edited by Muna Ndulo and Margaret Grieco. Newcastle upon Tyne: Cambridge Scholars.

Van der Berg, Servaas. 1997. "South African Social Security under Apartheid and Beyond." *Development Southern Africa* 14, no. 4: 481–503.

Van der Berg, Servaas, Leila Patel, and Grace Bridgman. 2022. "Food Insecurity in South Africa: Evidence from NIDS-CRAM Wave 5." *Development Southern Africa* 39, no. 5: 722–37. https://doi.org/10.1080/0376835X.2022.2062299.

Van der Merwe, T. 1997. "Events, Views, and Ideologies Which Shaped Social Security in South Africa." *South African Journal of Economic History* 12: 76–90.

Van Gennep, Arnold. 1960 [1909]. *The Rites of Passage: A Classic Study of Cultural Celebrations*. Translated by Monika B. Vizedom and Gabrielle L. Caffee. Chicago: University of Chicago Press.

Van Onselen, Charles. 1982. *Studies in the Social and Economic History of the Witwatersrand, 1886–1914*. Volume 1. Johannesburg: Ravan Press.

Van Schalwijk, L. 1950. "Report of the Departmental Committee of Enquiry into the Training and Employment of Social Workers." Pretoria: Department of Social Welfare.

Vansina, Jan. 1990. *Paths in the Rainforests: Toward a History of Political Tradition in Equatorial Africa*. Madison: University of Wisconsin Press.

Vasconcelos, Joana. 2010. "The Double Marginalisation: Reflections on Young Women and the Youth Crisis in Sub-Saharan Africa." In *7º Congresso Ibérico de Estudos Africanos, 9, Lisboa, 2010—50 Anos Das Independências Africanas: Desafios Para a Modernidade: Actas*.

Venkatesh, Sudhir. 2002. "'Doin' the hustle': Constructing the Ethnographer in the American Ghetto." *Ethnography* 3, no. 1: 91–111.

Verheijen, Janneke. 2013. *Balancing Men, Morals, and Money: Women's Agency between HIV and Security in a Malawi Village*. Leiden: African Studies Centre, University of Amsterdam.

Vigh, Henrik E. 2006. "Social Death and Violent Life Chances." In *Navigating Youth, Generating Adulthood: Social Becoming in an African Context*, edited by Catrine Christiansen, Mats Utas, and Henrik E. Vigh. Uppsala, Sweden: Nordiska Afrikainstitutet.

Vincent, L. 1999. "The Power behind the Scenes: The Afrikaner Nationalist Women's Parties, 1915 to 1931." *South African Historical Journal* 40, no. 1: 51–73.

———. 2000. 'Bread and Honour: White Working Class Women and Afrikaner Nationalism in the 1930s." *Journal of Southern African Studies* 26, no. 1:61–78.

Vogel, Ursula. 1991. "Is Citizenship Gender Specific?" In *The Frontiers of Citizenship*, edited by U. Vogel and M. Moran. Basingstoke: Macmillan.

Von Schnitzler, Antina. 2014. "Performing Dignity: Human Rights, Citizenship, and the Techno-Politics of Law in South Africa." *American Ethnologist* 41, no. 2: 336–50. https://doi.org/10.1111/amet.12079.

———. 2016. *Democracy's Infrastructure: Techno-Politics and Protest after Apartheid*. Princeton, NJ: Princeton University Press.

Vorster, J., and L. De Waal. 2008. "Beneficiaries of the Child Support Grant: Findings from a National Survey." *Social Work Practitioner-Researcher* 20, no. 2: 233–48.

Wacquant, Loïc J. D. 1997. "Three Pernicious Premises in the Study of the American Ghetto." *International Journal of Urban and Regional Research* 21, no. 2: 341–53.

Walby, Sylvia. 1994. "Is Citizenship Gendered?" *Sociology* 28, no. 2: 379–95.

Walker, C. 1992. "Attitudes to Lobola: Findings from Students' Research Projects." *Agenda* 13, no. 13: 57–58.

Walker, Cherryl. 1991. *Women and Resistance in South Africa*. 2nd rev. ed. Cape Town: David Phillips Publishers.

———. 1995. "Conceptualising Motherhood in Twentieth Century South Africa." *Journal of Southern African Studies* 21, no. 3: 417–37.

———. 2013. "Uneasy Relations: Women, Gender Equality, and Tradition." *Thesis Eleven* 115, no. 1: 77–94, https://doi.org/10.1177/0725513613512493.

Walker, Liz. 2005a. "Men Behaving Differently: South African Men since 1994." *Culture, Health, and Sexuality* 7: 225–38.

———. 2005b. "Negotiating the Boundaries of Masculinity in Post-Apartheid South Africa." In *Men Behaving Differently: South African Men since 1994*, edited by Graeme Reid and Liz Walker. Cape Town: Double Storey Books.

Walton, Sarah-Jane. 2021. "Motherhood, Morality, and Materiality: How Material Changes to Wartime Cape Town Affected Discourses around Women, Racial Health, and the City, 1914–1919." *Urban History* 48, no. 1: 54–70. https://doi.org/10.1017/S0963926820000279.

Wamhoff, Steve, and Sandra Burman. 2002. "Parental Maintenance for Children: How the Private Maintenance System Might Be Improved." *Social Dynamics* 28, no. 2: 146–76.

Warren, Scott. 2015. "A New Apartheid: South Africa's Struggle with Immigration." *Huffington Post*, September 1, 2015. www.huffingtonpost.com/scott-warren/south-africa-immigrationapartheid_b_8068132.html.

Wassermann, Johan, and Brian Kearney. 2002. *A Warrior's Gateway: Durban and the Anglo-Boer War, 1899–1902*. Pretoria: Protea Book House.

Watts, H. L., and N. K. Lamond. 1966. "A Study of the Social Circumstances and Characteristics of the Bantu in the Durban Region Report No. 2: The Social Circumstances of the Bantu." Durban: Institute for Social Research, University of Natal.

Webb, Christopher, and Natasha Vally. 2020. "South Africa Has Raised Social Grants: Why This Shouldn't Be a Stop-Gap Measure." *The Conversation*, May 7 2020. https://theconversation.com/south-africa-has-raised-social-grants-why-this-shouldnt-be-a-stop-gap-measure-138023.

Webster, Edward, and Karl von Holdt, eds. 2005. "Work Restructuring and the Crisis of Reproduction: A Southern Perspective." In *Beyond the Apartheid Workplace: Studies in Transition*, 3–40. Scottsville, South Africa: University of KwaZulu-Natal Press.

Weeks, Kathi. 2011. *The Problem with Work: Feminism, Marxism, Antiwork Politics,*

and Postwork Imaginaries. Durham, NC: Duke University Press. https://doi.org/10
.1215/9780822394723.

Weinreb, Alexander A. 2001. "First Politics, Then Culture: Accounting for Ethnic Differences in Demographic Behavior in Kenya." *Population and Development Review* 27, no. 3: 437–67.

Weiss, Brad, ed. 2004. *Producing African Futures: Ritual and Reproduction in a Neoliberal Age.* Leiden: Brill.

Wells, Julia C. 1993. *We Now Demand! The History of Women's Resistance to Pass Laws in South Africa.* Johannesburg: Witwatersrand University Press.

———. 1998. "Maternal Politics in Organizing Black South African Women: The Historical Lesson." In *Sisterhood, Feminisms, and Power: From Africa to the Diaspora,* edited by Obioma Nnaemeka, 251–62. Trenton: Africa World Press.

Weston, Kath. 1997. *Families We Choose: Lesbians, Gays, Kinship.* Rev. ed. New York: Columbia University Press.

White, Hylton. 2004. "Ritual Haunts: The Timing of Estrangement in a Post-Apartheid Countryside." In *Producing African Futures: Ritual and Reproduction in a Neoliberal Age,* edited by Brad Weiss, 141–66. Netherlands: Brill.

White, Louise 1990. *The Comforts of Home: Prostitution in Colonial Nairobi.* Chicago: University of Chicago Press.

Whooley, P. 1975. "Marriage in Africa: A Study of the Ciskei." In *Church and Marriage in Modern Africa,* edited by T. D. Verryn. Pretoria: Ecumenical Research Unit.

Witbooi, Vanessa. 2002. *For Our Children: Thirteen Women Tell Their Stories.* Cape Town: Human Rights Media Center.

Wojcicki, J. M. 2002. "Commercial Sex Work or *Ukuphanda*? Sex-for-Money Exchange in Soweto and Hammanskraal Area." *South Africa: Culture, Medicine, and Psychiatry* 26: 339–70.

Wolpe, Harold 1972. "Capitalism and Cheap Labour-Power in South Africa: From Segregation to Apartheid." *Economy and Society* 1, no. 4: 425–56. https://doi.org/10
.1080/03085147200000023.

"Women's Charter." 1954. South African History Online. 1954. www.sahistory.org.za/
article/womens-charter.

Woolard, I. and M. Leibbrandt. 2010. "The Evolution and Impact of Unconditional Cash Transfers in South Africa." Southern Africa Labour and Development Research Unit, Working Paper 51. Cape Town: SALDRU.

Woolard I., R. Metz, G. Inchauste, N. Lustig, M. Maboshe, and C. Pureld. 2015. "How Much Is Inequality Reduced by Progressive Taxation and Government Spending?" Econ3x3. Viewed January 18, 2018, www.econ3x3.org/article/how-much-inequality
-reduced-progressive-taxation-and-government-spending.

World Bank. 2014. South Africa Economic Update: Fiscal Policy and Redistribution in an Unequal Society. Washington, DC: World Bank.

———. 2016 GINI index (World Bank estimate). https://data.worldbank.org/indicator/
SI.POV.GINI?most_recent_value_desc=true&view=map&year=2016. Accessed October 21, 2016.

Wylie, Diana. 2001. *Starving on a Full Stomach: Hunger and the Triumph of Cultural Racism in Modern South Africa.* Charlottesville: University Press of Virginia.

Xolo, Nomfundo. 2021. "Are We Meant to Struggle until We Die?" *New Frame*, July 14, 2021, sec. COVID-19.

Yanagisako, Sylvia. 2002. *Producing Culture and Capital*. Princeton, NJ: Princeton University Press. https://press.princeton.edu/books/paperback/9780691095103/producing-culture-and-capital.

Yanagisako, Sylvia, and Jane Collier, eds. 1987. *Gender and Kinship: Essays toward a Unified Analysis*. Palo Alto, CA: Stanford University Press.

Yarbrough, Michael W. 2017. "Very Long Engagements: The Persistent Authority of Bridewealth in a Post-Apartheid South African Community." *Law and Social Inquiry* 3, no. 3: 647–77.

———. 2018. "Something Old, Something New: Historicizing Same-Sex Marriage within Ongoing Struggles over African Marriage in South Africa." *Sexualities* 21, no. 7: 1092–108. https://doi.org/10.1177/1363460717718507.

Yarris, Kristin E. 2017. *Care across Generations: Solidarity and Sacrifice in Transnational Families*. Stanford, CA: Stanford University Press.

Yuval-Davis, Nira. 1997a. *Gender and Nation*. London: Sage Publications.

———. 1997b. "Women, Citizenship, and Difference." *Feminist Review Citizenship: Pushing the Boundaries* 57: 4–27.

———. 1999. "The 'Multi-Layered Citizen.'" *International Feminist Journal of Politics* 1, no. 1: 119–36. https://doi.org/10.1080/146167499360068.

——— 2007. "Intersectionality, Citizenship, and Contemporary Politics of Belonging." *Critical Review of International Social and Political Philosophy* 10, no.: 561–74. https://doi.org/10.1080/13698230701660220.

Yuval-Davis, Nira, and Floya Anthias. 1989. *Woman, Nation, State*. Basingstoke: Macmillan.

Zelizer, Viviana. 1995. *The Social Meaning of Money*. New York: Basic Books.

———. 2005. *The Purchase of Intimacy*. Princeton, NJ: Princeton University Press.

INDEX

Note: Page numbers in italic type indicate illustrations.